BRITAIN'S
WILDERNESS FRONTIER

BRITAIN'S
WILDERNESS FRONTIER

JOHN OLIPHANT

For Pippa, who knows that it's about time

First published 2025

Amberley Publishing
The Hill, Stroud
Gloucestershire, GL5 4EP

www.amberley-books.com

Copyright © John Oliphant, 2025

The right of John Oliphant to be identified as the Author of this work has been asserted in accordance with the Copyright, Designs and Patents Act 1988.

ISBN 978 1 3981 2117 1 (hardback)
ISBN 978 1 3981 2118 8 (ebook)

All rights reserved. No part of this book may be reprinted or reproduced or utilised in any form or by any electronic, mechanical or other means, now known or hereafter invented, including photocopying and recording, or in any information storage or retrieval system, without the permission in writing from the Publishers.

British Library Cataloguing in Publication Data.
A catalogue record for this book is available from the British Library.

1 2 3 4 5 6 7 8 9 10

Typesetting by SJmagic DESIGN SERVICES, India.
Printed in the UK.

Appointed GPSR EU Representative: Easy Access System Europe Oü, 16879218
Address: Mustamäe tee 50, 10621, Tallinn, Estonia
Contact Details: gpsr.requests@easproject.com, +358 40 500 3575

CONTENTS

Acknowledgements 7

1 Borderlands 9
2 Lord Halifax Has a Vision 21
3 The Fall of a Half-King 30
4 The Breaking of the Covenant Chain 43
5 Cherokees 52
6 Direct Intervention 61
7 Failed Offensive 65
8 Wars in the Forests 75
9 Pitt, Recovery and Conquest 83
10 The Forbes Expedition and the Treaty of Easton 91
11 Southern Crisis 102
12 The Anglo-Cherokee War 106
13 Lord Egremont Draws a Line 121
14 Wyoming Tragedy 130
15 Pontiac's War of Independence 135

16	Plans and Boundaries	147
17	John Stuart's Empire	155
18	Speculation, Fraud, Murder and Revolt	166
19	The Road to Fort Stanwix	174
20	Lord Hillsborough Stands His Ground	180
21	The Path to Lochaber	186
22	Dunmore's Little War	189
23	Lord Dartmouth's Intolerable Act	198
24	Collapse	208

Appendix 1	213
Appendix 2	221
Maps	230
Notes	242
Bibliography	252
Index	282

ACKNOWLEDGEMENTS

I wish to record my appreciation of the all the librarians, archivists and curators who made this book possible.

The Stafford County Record Office squeezed me in for an afternoon in the midst of building work and when every chair and hour was at a premium. Staff manning the British Library's Humanities and Manuscript Reading Rooms were very helpful, as were staff at The National Archives at Kew (not to mention the cheerful lady downstairs who served me innumerable coffees). The Wisconsin Historical Society allowed me remote use of Shelburne's papers. James Ito at the Washington Lee University went out of his way to ensure that we could use the 1772 Peale portrait of George Washington.

My editors at Amberley, Shaun Barrington and Alex Bennett, were encouraging, patient and helpful.

I

BORDERLANDS

The Peace of Aix-la-Chapelle in 1748 deserved a celebration. After all, it had ended the eight-year War of the Austrian Succession in which Britain and its allies had been driven from the Austrian Netherlands (modern Belgium). The United Kingdom itself had been riven by a dangerous uprising at the same time, yet invasion had been averted, the Jacobite rising had been crushed, British fleets were at last successful, and Louisbourg in Canada had been captured from the French and exchanged for Madras in India. There were some worrying portents: its ally Austria had failed to regain Silesia from Prussia and was already courting France as a more useful continental partner. In North America, British and Bourbon (French) colonies were competing for spheres of influence, and for the allegiances of Native Americans determined to remain independent of both. Frontier violence, which had been a feature of the war, continued unofficially. For the moment, however, the survival of the Hanoverian regime was an occasion for rejoicing.

George II insisted on a spectacular fireworks display. An elaborate wooden structure was painstakingly built in Green Park, its centre a mock Doric temple 100 feet tall with wings on either flank, each ending in a pavilion. The whole was lavishly decorated, including a bas-relief showing the king delivering peace to Britannia. George Freidrich Handel, who was engaged to compose an overture, wanted violins, but the king – whose musical tastes were emphatically martial – insisted that there must be no 'fiddles' and lots of wind and percussion. To be truly spectacular the display would require elaborate illuminations and backlit transparencies, not to mention established skill in staging outdoor events. Because much of the required expertise (and £750 worth of borrowed equipment) was provided by Jonathan Tyers, the proprietor of Spring Gardens at Vauxhall, it was agreed that the music should be first performed there. It would be an elaborate and triumphant demonstration of the strength and competence of a regime which barely three years earlier had almost been toppled by a rebellious Scots army.[1]

Colonial reform too was a necessity. Far away to the west, fourteen British colonies lined the 3,000-mile Atlantic seaboard of North America, with a total population of about 1.2 million whites compared with 390,00 in 1720. This startingly rapid growth, most marked on the South Carolina frontier, was driven more by natural increase than by immigration. There were also roughly 400,000 blacks (as opposed to 68,000 three decades earlier), about half of whom were concentrated in the slave-based plantation economies of the south. They are more or less invisible in the paper records of frontier life and military campaigns, but most of the many packhorse men, drivers, herdsmen and servants must have been black. The total of 1.6 million and rising (as compared to 11 million in the whole of the British Isles), combined with what appeared to be limitless land to the west, helps to explain why the colonial frontier was constantly expanding – at the expense of perhaps 48,000 woodland Indians.[2]

The consensus regarding the nature of the American frontier was previously dominated by the nineteenth-century American historian Frederick J. Turner, and his influence lingers on at a popular cultural level. Turner interpreted a frontier as an advancing line dividing civilisation from savagery, the process transforming the society from which it sprang. For him, there were three 'waves' of development: first the 'pioneer', who with his family survives and prospers through hunting and a little horticulture, then the systematic farmers, and finally the 'men of capital and enterprise'. Because these first pioneers were free of the usual constraints of civilisation, and also because by the mid-eighteenth century many were not British, they became 'Americanised' and created a truly democratic and exceptional culture. For Turner, the east – Britain before 1783, and the eastern seaboard cities thereafter – was a drag on the liberating process of ever-westward movement. The whole process flowed from the abundance of 'vacant' land, supposedly there for the taking.[3]

Of course, the land was not empty. We can no longer ignore the displacement and dispossession of Native Americans, and the civilisation/savagery dichotomy now has uncomfortably racist connotations. For some historians, Turner's perspective – which excludes the viewpoints of the various Indian peoples, women and blacks – so distorts serious study that they reject the term 'frontier' altogether. 'Borderlands' is a term favoured by some for its relative lack of racist associations, but also because it exchanges the idea of a simple line for the notion of a zone of cultural, economic, diplomatic and military interaction. Far more appropriate to American conditions, where wilderness frontiers were ragged and fractured, it nonetheless has its own deficiencies, not least that areas of cultural interaction can be so vast that the term loses all real meaning. For instance, the whole vast region from the Allegheny Mountains to the Mississippi River could be classed as a frontier by this approach.

One reasonable response has been to differentiate between a more or less fixed 'boundary', and a moving 'frontier', though we might not accept the same author's contention that in eighteenth-century minds a 'frontier' existed only in times of defence against aggression, even if contemporaries used the word in that way. Nor might we agree that frontiers 'were not areas of active expansion, exploration and economic opportunity'.[4] It might be better to use 'frontier' to refer to inland zones of cultural encounter where there were clearly disputes over what was Indian land and what was not, accepting at the same time that the commercial, cultural, military and jurisdictional encounters occurred over a much wider territorial band.

The idea of a zone of equal interaction between Amerindian and European cultures was given prominence by Richard White in *The Middle Ground* (1991) and has been a staple of historical analysis ever since. Here language, diet, dress, ideas, social and diplomatic behaviour and even methods of warfare could mingle freely. The concept works well when applied to the *pays d'en haut*, the region around the upper Great Lakes, where French-licensed Canadian traders and government agents conducted trade and diplomacy. However, there was always some kind of cultural meeting ground and accommodation on all the North American frontiers. Matthew Ward has recently reminded us that stereotyping all frontier settlers as violent racists ignores the complexity of borderland relationships. Even men famed as enemy combatants by the Indians, like Daniel Boone, deeply admired them as friends, foes and neighbours. Both of Boone's sons suffered grisly deaths at the hands of Indians, yet he disliked talking about killing them and admitted to slaying only one, and in his old age he was visited by relatives of Shawnees who had once held him captive.

But even Boone, like most frontiersmen, saw no incongruity between maintaining friendly relations and seeking to acquire Native lands, and some did commit atrocities. As we shall see, these were usually carried out not by individuals but by groups, mostly unofficial militias whose members believed they were acting in defence of their communities.[5] In any case, we must not lose sight of the fact that embedded hostility and violence towards Indians became an increasingly strident feature of frontier life.

Vastly different socially and economically, the thirteen colonies were to various degrees self-governing. The New England provinces – New Hampshire, Massachusetts, Rhode Island and Connecticut – were governed under their own charters; Maryland and Pennsylvania were proprietary colonies, owned by the Calvert and Penn families respectively; and only the royal colonies – New York, New Jersey, Virginia, the Carolinas and recently founded Georgia – were directly under the Crown. But even each of these royal provinces had its elected assembly, with formidable fiscal and legislative powers, representing local interests. The most recent attempt to unite a group of colonies under tighter metropolitan control – James II's Dominion of New England – had been brought down by the Glorious Revolution in 1688–89, when the king was deposed in favour of the Protestants William and Mary. Since then, the provinces had been left pretty much to their own devices in what has been called a period of 'salutary neglect'.

Each province governed its own frontier with the Indians of the great forest that ran from the sea to the Mississippi, to say nothing of the great arc of French and Spanish territory around them. Canada – or New France as it was known – was centred on the St Lawrence Valley and, in terms of trade and alliance, to the region around the Great Lakes. Louisiana in theory embraced the whole of the Mississippi River system. Settlements here were sparse, apart from grain-producing farms in Illinois country and the port of New Orleans at the river's mouth. To the east of New Orleans lay Spanish Florida and its disputed border with Georgia, so completing the enclosing arc.

What they lacked in population, Canada and Louisiana made up for in deep commercial and diplomatic links with Native Americans. Unlike those in the expanding and largely agricultural British provinces, French traders, soldiers and officials did not threaten to dispossess the Indians they encountered, and they in turn were dependent upon French trade for desirable European goods. This created a formidable barrier to the British colonies' westward expansion and even to their survival. The key to a successful frontier policy was therefore a sound and uniform Indian policy. To fully understand that it is vital to examine Native cultures and traditions and their environment.

◆

In the beginning was the forest. It spread over the eastern half of the North American continent, from Hudson Bay to the steamy margins of the Gulf of Mexico, from the Atlantic Ocean to the Mississippi River and even beyond. Threaded with rivers and pocked with huge flooded valleys, the forest stretched from the sea to blanket the parallel ridges of the Blue Ridge Mountains and the Appalachians. From there the rivers flowed south and west towards the Ohio and Mississippi. Long before Europeans arrived this area was home to Native Americans, misnamed 'Indians'. Woodland Natives lived by a mixture of hunting and horticulture, producing maize, beans and squash, and inhabited towns with houses built in a variety of traditional styles. The Iroquoian longhouse, for example, provided rooms for several families, and the sugarloaf Cherokee town houses were particularly distinctive.

Native populations were shrinking rapidly, partly because of imported European diseases such as smallpox but also because their hunting grounds were being steadily eroded by farmers who cleared land, by white hunters who competed for game, and by white men's livestock which damaged the forest and so reduced the availability of game. Warfare was another factor, and it did not always involve whites. There were intertribal rivalries aplenty, and in the late seventeenth century the 'Beaver Wars' of the Iroquois cleared vast areas of the north-east – Hurons, Delawares, Shawnees and Chickasaws all suffered. Catawbas, Cherokees and Creeks exchanged raids with them throughout the period covered by this book. Nor did the Iroquois escape the demographic consequences of their own aggression, migration and disease: from an estimated 11,835 people across five 'nations' in 1630, their numbers had fallen to 4,780 by 1750. Though all nations (of which there were now six) were affected, the decline was most marked among the Mohawks, who mustered no more than 480 souls.[6]

Native Americans tended to avoid commitment to the French, Spanish or British, but they could not do without them. After over a century of inter-communal trade, European goods had become necessities. Guns, knives, hatchets, cloth and clothing, fishing hooks, pots, pans and strong drink had all become part of Amerindian culture. To purchase these items, Natives turned from mere subsistence hunting to hunting for the market, particularly beaver pelts and the hides of white-tailed deer, which were the currency of wilderness trade. As far as preference, the French posed little territorial threat but their trade goods were less desirable and more expensive than those offered by British traders. Natives therefore had to weigh the cost of necessities against the danger of white encroachment – and choice was often dictated by geographical proximity.

In turn, Europeans had to come to terms with Indian ways of commerce, war and diplomacy. At treaty conferences presents were expected by both sides as pledges of sincerity, and public discussions often featured long speeches and colourful oratory, as well as the exchange of wampum belts and strings of beads. Most of the real negotiations, however, took place out of sight, 'in the bushes'. Again, the French were usually the better players on what Richard White called the 'Middle Ground' where cultures met.[7]

If Natives were increasingly dependent upon European weapons, they used them to great effect in their own style of woodland warfare. Stealthy raids were aimed at taking scalps and prisoners, either as revenge ('mourning war') or to replace their own losses from warfare and European diseases. Maximum impact with minimal loss was key, and the forest lent itself to ambush and surprise: those lying in wait would adopt a semi-circular formation adapted to a sudden stroke followed by a rapid retreat with scalps and captives.

In the north, from Hudson's Bay to the Great Lakes, the St Lawrence and beyond, the Algonquian language group was spoken by a kaleidoscope of nations sharing a great deal of culture but very little political sympathy, if any. Mahicans could still be found in the upper Hudson Valley and on the eastern slopes of the Green Mountains facing Lake Champlain. The Western Abenakis, who inhabited the Green Mountains between Lake Champlain and the New England settlements, fought successfully to restrain New England's expansion, raiding settlements and attacking forts almost at will. In 1752, after a brief interlude of passable peace, a British attempt to form a settlement at Cowas on the headwaters of the Connecticut River provoked a warning: no settler was to come beyond Fort No. 4, a good 75 miles downstream. The warning was repeated in 1753, and the following year a war party attacked Deerfield, a settlement to the south of the fort and the target of destructive raids since the seventeenth century. Further east in Nova Scotia, Abenakis and Mi'qmacs had managed to keep the British presence confined to a handful of military enclaves on the Bay of Fundy.[8]

To the west of Lake Champlain and the Hudson lay the lands of the Iroquois Confederation, the Haudenosaunee, or the 'people of the longhouse'. Originally formed in the sixteenth century to end inter-tribal conflicts, the original five nations – from east to west the Mohawks, Oneidas, Onondagas, Cayugas and Senecas – were joined after 1722 by the refugee Tuscaroras fleeing from South Carolinian aggression. The Mohawks, on the doorstep of New York and dependent upon that colony for trade, saw themselves as the diplomatic and commercial gatekeepers of Iroquoia. At the other extreme, the Senecas were closer to New France and tended to favour the French.

The Iroquois claimed to have defeated and subjugated other peoples, and staked claim to lands they did not occupy. Through the Covenant Chain, a system of alliances channelled through New York, they tried to control British relations with those peoples they considered subordinate. These included the Delawares and Shawnees of the Susquehanna and Ohio valleys, whose lands they were inclined to cede to the advancing British colonies. They were also not above defrauding their supposed vassals; one such incident had occurred in 1737, in a dispute between the Delawares (Lenape) and Pennsylvania over a land deed, probably forged, which went back to 1686. Fake or not, the whites of Pennsylvania put a very generous interpretation on its scope and the Delawares agreed to cede as much land as a man could walk around in a day and a half. The whites then produced a team of three vigorous men who covered 55 miles in that time. When the defrauded Delawares appealed to the Iroquois for help they were curtly refused, and, not having the means to resist on their own, had to yield more than a million acres in what became known as the Walking Purchase. Marking the Penn family's departure from the benign policies of the colony's founder, this episode rankled for many years, engendering dangerous anti-British hostility on that part of the frontier. It certainly explains much of the behaviour of Teedyuscung, self-styled king of the Eastern Delawares from this time until his murder in 1763, of whom more later. It was not to be the last deal of its kind.[9]

Tensions were high on the southern frontiers, where Bourbons and British competed for the trade and alliances of Cherokees, Creeks, Catawbas and Choctaws. The Creeks, though suspicious of British intentions, and occasionally inciting the Cherokees to violence, were content to play the Louisiana French, the Florida

Spanish and the British province of Georgia off against each other. Strong enough to confront Florida with annihilation, they did not feel directly threatened. The Choctaws, though sometimes tempted by British goods and prices, were much closer to Louisiana and inevitably tied to the French. The Catawba nation was now a tiny congeries of refugees almost encircled by North Carolina, and could usually be considered a British ally. It was the powerful Cherokees who teetered on the brink between French and British friendship.

There were therefore a number of challenges to be faced by the British government. Though far more populous than French Canada or Florida, the individual colonies were disinclined to co-operate in self-defence, or indeed in aggression. There was also a real danger that they might break away from British control altogether, gravely weakening the home country in relation to its Bourbon rivals. Finally, Native Americans treated badly or dispossessed by encroaching settlements would be dangerous enemies in a forest war, especially if they allied with the French. To deal with all these threats, a dedicated team in London would need reliable agents on the ground, working to common rules yet able to respond creatively in emergencies: after all, it could take up to six weeks for a dispatch to cross the Atlantic and months to pen a reply. The whole structure of the British Empire needed to be overhauled.

The Earl of Halifax, recently appointed president of the Board of Trade, wanted to do just that. He had a vision of a metrocentric empire controlled from London, working to a common constitution and set of laws. If this goal was not immediately achievable in the thirteen self-governing provinces, it was possible to extend London's control at the northern and southern extremes of British North America in Nova Scotia and Georgia, as both could be regarded as outposts against French and Spanish attacks respectively. In the long term it might be possible to create a single legal system for the whole mainland empire, eroding the powers of elected provincial assemblies and appointing reliable governors and other officials instead. Most importantly, frontier policy would have to be taken into imperial hands: settler expansion must be carefully controlled, the trade with the Natives must come under a single set of regulations and diplomatic relations must be conducted on a uniform pattern. Such policies would doubtless provoke dangerous resistance, perhaps even revolution; but if they could not be implemented, the British Empire in America would inevitably collapse. How successful could such a gamble be?

Let us return to Handel and the royal fireworks.

◆

On 21 April 1749, up to 12,000 people of all classes flocked to Vauxhall to hear Handel's music rehearsed, creating gridlock on London Bridge and mingling promiscuously once there. Spring Gardens, on the south bank of the River Thames, was a popular place to see and be seen. One could dine in its little supper boxes, drink copiously, stroll in the leafy avenues, and marvel at sights such as a waterfall made of metal and a beautifully illuminated mock-ancient ruin. Tyers, the aforementioned proprietor of the pleasure grounds, had once placed his musicians in a pit so that their music appeared to becoming from the bushes, but the damp had not been good for the instruments. Now Spring Gardens boasted a raised pavilion upon which an orchestra delighted their public; and it was in this relaxed, gaudy and slightly sleazy atmosphere that the *Music for the Royal Fireworks* – without pomp or pyrotechnics – was revealed to a vast and appreciative audience. In the event, the rehearsal was to prove more successful than the final offering.

Six days later, another crowd, this time with enclosures provided for aristocracy and gentry, gathered in Green Park for the music and fireworks proper, but the weather was a distinct hindrance.

It was a hot, humid, drizzly evening, and, although the Handel went down well, many of the fireworks refused to fire, or just fizzed and faded. There were long pauses when nothing happened. The crowd grew restless, and bored workmen in the wings grew careless. One wing caught fire, and the blaze quickly spread to the rest of the structure: a woman's dress caught alight and three soldiers were injured. The magnificent building was consumed by roaring flames and burned to the ground. A splendid and necessary scheme had been wrecked by ill fortune, self-interest, incompetence and indifference. Satirists thrived upon its humiliating failure, and the unused fireworks were sold to the Duke of Richmond for his own, far more successful display some weeks later.[10] There was, as far as we can tell, no deliberate sabotage; nevertheless, one may imagine Lord Halifax feeling a sharp chill as he considered his own plans for the survival of the British Empire.

2

LORD HALIFAX HAS A VISION

George Montagu, 2nd Earl of Halifax, was shrewd, ambitious and adept at pursuing his own political, financial, social and sexual goals. For example, at twenty-four he proposed to marry sixteen-year-old Ann Dunk, heiress to a Kentish estate. Her late father, who had changed his name from Richards to Dunk to secure an inheritance, had insisted that her suitor should take that name and also establish a connection with the business world. He met the first condition by signing all his subsequent correspondence 'Dunk Halifax', and the second by obtaining the freedom of the City of London. In that way he secured his young bride, her six-figure dowry and the friendship of the banking and business community. Politically, he attached himself to two rivals in the governing Whig elite, the dukes of Newcastle and Bedford (with whom he shared an enthusiasm for cricket). Yet he was also intellectually brilliant, hard-working, and driven by a vision of a reformed metrocentric empire. The allegation that his patriotism never took precedence over his personal interests is at best misleading.[1]

Halifax's first opportunity to press his political ideas and ambition came in February 1748, when Prime Minister (officially First Lord of the Treasury) Henry Pelham-Holles reshuffled his cabinet. Pelham's brother Thomas, Duke of Newcastle, was replaced as Secretary of State for the Southern Department (responsible for relations with southern Europe and the colonies) by John Russell, Duke of Bedford, and moved to become Secretary of State for the Northern Department. For too long regarded as an incompetent patronage monger, Newcastle had built up a considerable knowledge of colonial and foreign affairs, and was well aware of the need to check French expansion in America – if that could be done without precipitating a European war. Bedford, meanwhile, was a colonial expansionist whose unfulfilled wartime plan for an attack on Canada indicated his ambition. With the support of these two stalwarts, when the death of Lord Monson created a suitable vacancy, Halifax became president of the Lords Commissioners of Trade and Plantations – known more succinctly as the Board of Trade.[2]

First formed in 1696, the Board of Trade (hereafter the Board) had functioned as an embryonic colonial office, but since 1722 it had lost its oversight of colonial affairs (including its right to appoint to governorships) to the Secretary of State for the Southern Department (hereafter Southern Secretary). Halifax was determined to win back the lost ground, work for a more centralised empire and in the process gain a seat in the Cabinet. He and his patron Newcastle failed to persuade George II to make the Board a formal colonial department – apparently because Bedford lobbied against it – but by 1751 there was a new Southern Secretary, the Earl of Holderness. In 1752 the Board was given back its right to appoint colonial governors, and in 1757 Halifax was allowed to sit at the Cabinet table. That did not mean that Halifax could have it all his own way in the selection of colonial governors, nor that all his choices were happy ones. Yet the arrangement was undoubtedly an acknowledgement of Halifax's ability and expertise as tensions in North America threatened to precipitate a general war.[3]

The sheer volume of colonial legislation, all of which should ideally have been reviewed and approved or rejected by the

Board, was overwhelming, and too often efficient administration was frustrated by differences between the colonies' different legal systems. Halifax envisaged replacing all this with a generic code applicable to every part of the empire, a measure which would undermine provincial assemblies, empower local executives and centralise authority in London. And as one scholar has pointed out, the Board's very obscurity gave Halifax a powerful tool to shape in his own image.[4]

The Board had only eight members: while an expanded Great Board could include both secretaries of state, the Chancellor of the Exchequer, the Lord Chancellor and the First Lord of the Admiralty, it met only once in Halifax's time, in 1749. The exclusion of the most powerful ministers meant that a president who so wished could dominate the Board and see to it that the Cabinet received advice which suited his own agenda. And Halifax did so wish. Using the Board's resources and exploiting ministers' fears of a new war, he was able to press for fundamental reform.

Halifax inherited a competent staff, among them chief clerk Martin Bladen and secretary John Pownall, with both of whom Halifax developed close working relationships and friendships. He was able to harness his whole staff's collective loyalty and expertise in return for considerate and respectful stewardship, good salaries, free use of the Post Office, and job security. A junior clerk's pay and perquisites could amount to £300 a year and there were chances for promotion. Such conditions attracted good men whom Halifax personally selected.[5]

Halifax did not rely on the office staff alone, nor on reports from colonial governors and other active officials: experienced men who had returned from America to Britain were a key source of ideas. James Abercromby, a Scots vice-admiralty officer with fourteen years of American experience, circulated to ministers 'An Examination of the Acts of Parliament Relative to the Trade and Commerce of Our American Colonies'. Abercromby argued that the problems of governance facing the British American empire were unique, being as it was a commercial empire with a very loose and diverse political connection. Henry McCulloh, a revenue collector newly returned from North Carolina, agreed that a more effective and uniform system of imperial government must be implemented if the empire were to survive French encroachment and avert colonial independence. From 1750 Halifax was courted by Edmond Atkin, a South Carolina trader and council member who had developed a very wide knowledge of the southern nations and wrote a comprehensive plan for management of relations with them at Halifax's behest. Atkin's plan and report, delivered in May 1755, were to have a significant effect upon frontier policy during and immediately after the Seven Years War (1756–63).[6]

Halifax also cultivated clients of his own, men who had direct business or other experience of America, among them the Irish MP Arthur Dobbs. MP for Carrickfergus, a serial office holder and an intellectual polymath, Dobbs had been applying his Irish experience to systematic thinking about the nature of empires. To him empires could be founded upon either dominance and exploitation or commerce. In terms of frontier policy, he was clear that the dispossession of Natives would produce a violent, perhaps fatal backlash, until and unless they could be absorbed into the colonial population. His somewhat optimistic solution was the conversion of both slaves and Natives to Anglicanism. Sensitivity to indigenous dispossession did not prevent Dobbs from acquiring 400,000 North Carolinian acres and encouraging his Scots-Irish tenants to settle there. Furthermore, he was a close associate of the Quaker tobacco merchant John Hanbury, and together they drew up a petition on behalf of the speculative Virginian venture called the Ohio Company – of which more later.[7]

Finally, Halifax tapped into the enthusiasm of John Mitchell, a Virginian gentleman botanist, part-qualified physician and self-taught cartographer who had returned to Britain for health reasons. It used to be thought that Mitchell, worried that ministers paid too little attention to colonial matters, sought Halifax's attention with his first attempt at a map in 1750. In fact, it was Halifax who approached him: from 1750 Mitchell was producing draft maps of North America, which Halifax circulated among his fellow ministers, and in 1755 he completed a final eight-sheet version putting forward an expansionist view of Britain's claims in North America. To achieve this Mitchell oversimplified the confusion of charters to show the more northerly colonies stretching sea to sea, right across French Louisiana, while he showed the southerly ones extending to the Mississippi. He also exaggerated the reach of Iroquois domination so that they could be shown to have (or have the right to cede) lands extending west to the Mississippi and north beyond the Great Lakes. This gave Halifax a powerful weapon with which to convince ministers like the Lord Chancellor, the Earl of Hardwicke, and to beat down the arguments of sceptics like Sir Thomas Robinson. The Mitchell map became the standard geographical reference for ministers dealing with North America and international conferences as late as 1782.[8]

Halifax's first project requiring the consent of senior ministers was to secure the vulnerable province of Nova Scotia as a model colony. He was aided by the widespread assumption that renewed war was likely and that New England needed to reassured about the return of Louisbourg through the establishment of a British base at Chebucto Sound on the Atlantic coast. At the Peace of Utrecht in 1713, France had technically ceded the whole of Acadia, which the British correctly interpreted as including not only the peninsula but all region between the St Lawrence and the Penobscot on the northern edge of Massachusetts. The French not only disputed this wider claim but since 1713 had been quietly extending their settlements down to the Bay of Fundy. While the Peace of Aix-la-Chapelle provided for a joint commission to resolve American boundary disputes, in 1749 the governor of New France ordered the construction of a fort on the St John's River, the only ice-free outlet from Quebec to the sea in winter. It was time to act.[9]

Moreover, the settlement of Protestants – for which he enlisted the support of the Society for the Propagation of the Gospel in Foreign Parts – could neutralise the insurgent Catholic Acadians and their Native allies. To Halifax, who favoured full religious toleration, this would lead not to sectarian strife but to confessional integration. Lord Sandwich, the newly appointed First Lord of the Admiralty, and his fellow cricketing enthusiast Bedford were already sympathetic – indeed, during the War of the Austrian Succession they had both advocated increased expenditure in that region; Lord Chancellor Lord Hardwicke and First Lord of the Treasury Henry Pelham, meanwhile, were convinced by Halifax's arguments. The expedition, led by Colonel Edward Cornwallis, sailed in 1749.[10]

Unfortunately, the settlement at Chebucto Sound – appropriately named Halifax – violated a tacit agreement between the British and the Mi'kmaq that had been in place since 1734. The immediate result was a Mi'kmaq–Acadian uprising led by a Jesuit missionary priest, Father Le Loutre. Not all Acadians chose revolt, but those who did were encouraged by the French, who in 1750 built Fort Beauséjour on the Chignecto isthmus, which the British – finding it too strong to take at once – immediately countered with a fortification of their own, Fort Lawrence. The war of skirmishes spluttered on for years, disrupting Halifax's settlement plans, and serving to highlight the colony's vulnerability and the importance of keeping it under direct royal control. Even the wholesale expulsion of the Acadians in 1755 did not end the war with the Mi'kmaq.[11]

Suspicions of French activities also informed decisions respecting two other flashpoints: the Hudson–Lake Champlain corridor connecting New York to New France, and the Ohio country.

From 1749 the governors of New France sent a series of military expeditions to clear Pennsylvanian traders from the Ohio, to win over or intimidate the Natives living there, and to deter Virginian plans for settlement. By 1753 they had begun to build a chain of forts from Lake Eire to the headwaters of the Ohio.

That same year, the newly formed Ohio Company of Virginia petitioned for a grant of 200,000 acres, rising to 500,000 if it managed to settle a hundred families there. Its agent was John Hanbury of Tower Street, an eminent (though not particularly strict) Quaker merchant. Hanbury's business imported tobacco from Virginia (where he dealt with gentlemen planters) and Maryland (where his clients were independent local merchants) and was friendly with Sir William Gooch, lieutenant governor of Virginia, and with Lord Fairfax, the proprietor of Maryland. He was well liked and consulted on American affairs by Henry Pelham and the Duke of Newcastle, and probably by Halifax too. He and his cousin and business partner Osgood were political supporters of Newcastle's interest in Bristol, and he was influential in securing desirable colonial appointments for his friends. Whatever Hanbury had to say about the Ohio project would be taken seriously.[12]

Hanbury's petition – which he had composed with Dobbs' assistance – pressed all the right buttons. He stressed the improved security a settlement would provide against French expansion, coupled with the friendship of Indians who had already asked for British goods. From those benefits would follow others: access to the inland fur trade and expansion of the market for British manufactures. Halifax certainly saw settlement in the region as a natural way to secure the frontier against French incursions. Nevertheless, the ministry did not rush to judgement but carefully considered the implications.

Instead, the Board wrote to Gooch asking him for clarification. Why had he not made the grant on his own authority? What was the grant to be used for and where was it to be located? Gooch might have replied that a majority of his executive councillors were rivals of the narrow clique from which the Ohio investors were drawn. Instead, he answered that he had not wanted to imperil the Aix-la-Chapelle negotiations, that the grantees wanted four years in which to complete their surveys, and that the grant would lie beyond the mountains. His answers were passed to the Privy Council, which asked the Board to examine likely benefits for both Great Britain and Virginia. Not until December 1748 was the application approved, subject to the Ohio Company building a fort at its own expense. The danger of depopulating existing settlements (and of hurting the colonial government's revenue) was met by a ban on the recruitment of settlers already paying quit rents. Security was thus the key issue. There was no question of Hanbury getting automatic approval for his friends' business enterprise.[13]

By 1754 the situation in America was fast deteriorating. Newcastle had long seen French actions in Europe and America as two parts of an overarching policy of expansion. He also feared that a France freed of European distractions could outbuild the Royal Navy, seize control of the Atlantic and threaten the whole British Empire. He agreed with Halifax that firm action should be taken in America, as long as the risk of it developing into a general war was low. In this he was perhaps more perceptive even than Halifax, who tended – naturally enough – to focus his mind upon the colonies and therefore at times lacked Newcastle's caution. Newcastle continued this circumspect approach after his brother's death in 1754, when he became First Lord of the Treasury.

French fort-building on the American frontier seemed to prove their ambition, yet no one colony was capable of resisting them. In late 1753 a Virginian mission to warn off the French failed miserably. Nor would the colonies act together as a whole: a Virginian military expedition attracted only the loan of an independent company of regulars from North Carolina.

Pennsylvania, having not even its own militia, contributed nothing. At the same time it was painfully evident that relations with Native Americans were in crisis, not just on the Ohio but along the whole Appalachian frontier.

Drastic measures were needed. In the autumn of 1753 the Board of Trade, for the first time in its history, ordered all the mainland colonies to attend a conference with the Natives at Albany. In April 1754 Halifax suggested matching the French encroachments fort by fort. There should be six such fortifications: on the Nova Scotian isthmus, on the St John's River, on the Kennebec River in Massachusetts, at Crown Point to confront Fort St. Frédéric, on the Ohio, in the Cherokee country, and on the Mobile River.

By the summer of 1754 Newcastle was contemplating the appointment of a commander-in-chief whose authority would override that of individual governors. He put the idea forward in alliance with the king's younger son, the Duke of Cumberland, Captain General of the Army and an apostle of military solutions. Halifax liked the idea, partly because he had long advocated a strong frontier policy but also because it would be a step towards the metrocentric imperial system he saw as necessary to the survival of the empire.

Then came the news of military disaster.

3

THE FALL OF A HALF-KING

The Ohio country began where the southward-flowing Allegheny and the northward-flowing Monongahela met to form the Ohio. That river then ran broadly south-west from the Forks, fed by major tributaries: the Beaver, Muskingum, Great Kanawha, Scioto, Great Miami, and Kentucky Rivers, until it met the Mississippi. It was a vast, forested, mountainous region of water-borne communications, interrupted only by the Falls of the Ohio, a series of barely navigable rapids below the Kentucky. And between the innumerable creeks and streams was a complex system of old Native trails and portages.

This region, having been emptied of most of its inhabitants by the late seventeenth-century 'beaver wars', was now claimed and used as a vast hunting ground by the victorious Iroquois. Since the 1720s Shawnees and Delawares, pushed westward by the spread of Pennsylvanian settlement, had been filtering back into the region. Delaware migrants, led by the brothers Shingas, Pisquetomen, Nenatcheehunt and Tamaqua, formed a town at Kittanning on the Allegheny. At Logstown, about 15 miles below the Forks, a Shawnee settlement grew into a substantial multi-ethnic community. Other Shawnees settled at Lower Shawneetown at the mouth of the Scioto. Miamis moved from around Lake

Michigan to the Scioto and to the Great Miami where they founded Pickawillany. Some Iroquois, mainly Senecas and known locally as Mingos, were pushed westward by thinning game and encroaching settlement.¹

This migration, and growing signs of Shawnee, Delaware and even Mingo independence, caused the Onondaga council to employ Tanaghrisson, a Catawba who had been captured as a child and adopted by the Senecas. By 1747 he had emerged as leader capable of representing Mingo and other Ohio groups both to Onondaga and to the British. His title of Half-King (one which he shared with the Ohio Shawnee leader Scarouady) may have been an Iroquois designation or a British invention, but for a time Six Nations influence was strong enough for his role to be taken seriously. From the beginning, however, it was threatened by the growing autonomy of the other Ohio nations and by weak British support.²

French strategists saw the region as a barrier to dangerous British expansion through traders and land speculators from Virginia, Pennsylvania and Maryland. As early as the Treaty of Lancaster in 1744, representatives of these three colonies had persuaded the Iroquois to allow settlement within the boundaries of Virginia: while the Iroquois thought they had drawn a line at the foot of the Allegheny plateau, the colonists interpreted it to mean at least the whole Ohio country, if not the ocean-to-ocean bounds prescribed in the original Virginian charter. Should Pennsylvanians seduce the Ohio nations with goods better, cheaper and more abundant than their own traders could provide, settlements and British control would follow, threatening the French waterborne communications between New France and Louisiana.

Already an Irish Pennsylvanian called George Croghan was established on the southern shore of Lake Erie, attracting Natives from across the lake with his plentiful and cheap trade goods. In 1749 he established a major post at Pickawillany on the Great

Miami River, where a chief called Memeskia (later 'Old Briton' to the British) sent out invitations to Native nations far and wide. Hundreds of families responded and Croghan extended his activities by boat and packhorse far down the Ohio. Should this continue, the French would find their traditional allies deserting them for the British, not only in the Ohio basin but even in the *pays d'en haut* itself. No wonder they put a price on Croghan's scalp.[3]

There could be no halting the Pennsylvanians without a firm demonstration of French power. In June 1749 the governor general of New France, La Galissoniére, despatched about 200 Canadian militia accompanied by perhaps thirty Natives led by a veteran officer, Pierre-Joseph Céleron de Blainville. Blainville's men crossed Lake Erie and made their way overland to the Allegheny River and so to the Ohio, nailing up copper representations of the royal French arms and burying lead plates declaring French possession at intervals along the way. At Logstown, at Lower Shawneetown, at Pickawillany on the Great Miami, and at encounters with pack trains the road he ordered British traders to depart – with increasingly little effect. His hectoring tone and the burying of the plates aroused the suspicions of the Ohio peoples, and even some of his accompanying Iroquois went home went home in disgust.[4]

An even worse threat was on its way. As early as 1745, the Virginia assembly had granted a third of a million acres of Ohio land to a syndicate of about twenty wealthy Virginians, who in 1748 formed the Ohio Company of Virginia. The principal investors included Thomas Lee, lieutenant governor and head of the colony's executive council, whose contribution was taken up after his death in 1752 by newly arrived governor Robert Dinwiddie. Another prominent stakeholder was Lawrence Washington, whose younger half-brother George later acted as the company's clerk. Their plan was to sell land near the Forks to incoming German and Scots-Irish settlers already moving into the Susquehanna Valley and beyond. The following year they obtained a royal grant of

The Fall of a Half-King

300,000 acres, rising to 500,000 once thirty families were settled. A rival enterprise led by one Joshua Fry, the Loyal Company, was given an even better deal: their grant of 800,000 Kentucky acres was conditional upon survey, not on physical settlement.

Meanwhile the Ohio Company sent Christopher Gist, a Maryland trader now settled in the region, to survey the upper Ohio for suitable land. Gist posed as a royal emissary, promised the Natives a vast quantity of British goods (which he claimed was already on its way) and tried – unsuccessfully – to minimise Native suspicions by keeping his compass out of sight. Within two years he had amassed enough knowledge of the Ohio and its resources to support a purchase negotiation. In 1752 three Virginian commissioners met the delegates of the Mingo, Shawnee, Delaware (Lenape) and Wyandot nations at Logstown, where the Half-King – representing what was left of Iroquois authority – presided.

The composition of the Virginian mission was significant. The commissioners were Joshua Fry of the Loyal Company, Lumsford Lomax of the Ohio Company and James Patton, who had been granted 200,000 acres in the Ohio region as early as 1745. In other words, they were business rivals, united by their common desire to make good their respective Ohio land grants. They were supported by Gist (now openly representing the Ohio Company) and Croghan (posing as a delegate of Pennsylvania) and their interpreter was Andrew Montour. Of the twelve others, William Preston and John Tayloe were Ohio Company founders, as was Thomas Cresap who was in charge of supplying diplomatic presents, while William Crawford was an Ohio Company surveyor. William Trent, Michael Teaffe and Thomas McKee were frontier traders connected to Croghan and useful because of their relations with the Indians.[5]

It quickly became apparent that the sides were at cross-purposes. Citing the Treaty of Lancaster, Gist announced the planned British settlement, assuring them that it would bring down the prices of trade goods and provide protection for the Natives. The Natives, who had believed that the Virginians simply wanted to build a fortified trading house, refused and Tanaghrisson declared that the cession had never been intended to extend further than the base of the Allegheny ridge. When Gist replied that the settlement would be necessary to provision the fort, he answered that they would see to its supplies themselves and reminded the Virginians that any agreement would have to be confirmed by the Onondaga council. Pitching for support from the Delawares – the only Ohio group more numerous than the Mingos – he ceremonially recognised Shingas as their 'king'.[6] On the face of it the Ohio Company's gambit had failed.

But in a private meeting Tanaghrisson and four fellow *sachems* (paramount chiefs) gave way on almost every point. Perhaps viewing the conference as an opportunity to shore up Iroquois authority, probably calculating that only cession of the settlement would commit Virginia to action against the French, and perhaps tempted by presents, they agreed to 'a Settlements or Settlements' on the south-eastern side of the Ohio, and that these settlements would not be 'molested' by any of the Ohio Natives. Everything would now depend upon Virginian ability and willingness to protect the Ohio nations against the French, and in particular how quickly and effectively they could build their fort.

The inevitable violent French response was already in progress. On 21 June, thirty French soldiers and 200 Chippewas and Ottawas attacked and burned Pickawillany. They killed one trader and captured five, and then ritually slaughtered, cooked and ate Memeskia. The message was clear: Pennsylvanian traders and those who did business with them could expect a grisly end. The traders understood and fled, while the Miamis sent to Pennsylvania and Virginia for succour. Their appeals were in vain: Pennsylvania still had a large pacifist Quaker element in its assembly and did not even possess a militia, while Virginia saw no reason to support so distant a people. Worse, the Ohio Company was in no hurry to build the promised fort and by the autumn nothing had been done. Tanaghrisson's prestige was damaged, possibly already beyond repair, while the French had secured a firm hold on the Ohio.

Next spring, following orders from Paris and the arrival of a determined new governor general, the Marquis de Duquesne, New France set out to consolidate its advantage. Fort Presque Isle was built on the southern shore of Lake Erie, to cover the head of the portage leading to French Creek, where Fort Le Boeuf was constructed. At Venango, where the Creek joined the Allegheny River, they made a third fortification, Fort Machault. The next building site on Duquesne's list was at the Forks, exactly where the Ohio Company planned to construct its own trading post. Governor Dinwiddie was in no position to meet force with force, so instead he sent a messenger with a warning. Twenty-one-year-old George Washington was instructed to go straight to Logstown and there to confer with Tanaghrisson and 'other *sachems* of the Six Nations', who were to be persuaded to give him 'a sufficient Number of their Warriors to be your Safeguard' before approaching the French.[7]

Washington was the scion of socially ambitious colonial gentry. At sixteen he had joined a surveying expedition that crossed the Blue Ridge, and by the time he was twenty he had travelled with several other western expeditions, qualified as a surveyor, invested his profits into over 2,000 Shenandoah acres and become a member of the Ohio Company. His older half-brother Lawrence, a founding investor, became company president in 1751 and in 1752 George inherited Lawrence's stake as well as his share of the family estates. Now the owner of 4,291 acres, and with the prospect of acquiring more in the Ohio, young Washington counted as a middling member of the planter elite.[8]

Only then did he turn to military activities, for reasons of social and political prestige rather than from dreams of soldierly glory.

He was commissioned into the provincial militia and appointed – despite his own total lack of experience – to be adjutant in the Southern District of Virginia. In 1753, this absurdly young major with no linguistic skills, anxious to make his mark as a soldier-ambassador and keen to visit the lands where the Ohio Company would make its fortune, volunteered to be the governor's messenger to the French.[9] Whatever he later became, Washington was at bottom a uniformed provincial expansionist, with almost no knowledge of Native diplomacy.

En route from Williamsburg, Washington picked up a Dutch settler with passable French, and at Wills Creek he was joined by five frontiersmen led by Christopher Gist. Along the way he learned of French determination and, alarmingly, of Native reluctance to assist the British. A conference at Logstown failed to produce an escort to take him to Fort Machault: only Tanaghrisson and four other Mingos accompanied him and they for their own reasons. At Machault the commanding officer politely referred them to his superior at Fort Le Boeuf. Rain, snow and swollen creeks soaked and bedraggled the travellers: it was a less than impressive little band that arrived at the fort on 11 December 1753. Certainly it was not one able to deliver convincing demands or threats.

Nevertheless, Washington handed over Dinwiddie's letter stating that the French must desist and depart. The French commandant, Captain Jacques Legardeur de St Pierre, was hospitable but kept him waiting for his reply. When it came it was uncompromising: the Ohio was French and his men would descend the river in force in the spring to clear out all trespassers. It was not a bluff: Washington saw over a hundred French troops there already, and his men observed over 200 finished canoes and more in preparation. Worse, probably more than Washington knew, were Legardeur's attempts to seduce Tanaghrisson. The Virginian withdrew with what little dignity he could muster and made a difficult winter return journey to Williamsburg. Conspicuous

British weakness and tardiness had alienated the Ohio nations and driven the Half-King to despair.

By now Dinwiddie had in his hands the Board's circular instruction to governors to resist force with force, as well as Lord Holderness's specific order to defend Virginia. As we have seen, the Board and Secretary of State, by their own independent judgement, understood those limits to include the upper Ohio Valley.

Washington's report convinced Dinwiddie that the French had committed an armed hostile act – or at least gave him a plausible excuse for thinking so – and with the council's consent he ordered the creation of a Virginia Regiment of volunteers led by none other than Joshua Fry. He commissioned the Ohio Company's servants near the Forks as officers of a company in the same regiment, and sent them tools and carpenters to immediately begin the planned fort at the Forks. Washington – now suddenly a lieutenant colonel and second-in-command of the regiment – was to raise 200 men to reinforce them as early as possible. Only then did the governor approach the House of Burgesses – the Virginian elected assembly – for funds, well aware that, given that body's suspicion of any measure likely to push up taxes or strengthen the executive, he was in for a fight.

True to form, the House authorised only the raising of £10,000 – far too little as it turned out, and even then only on condition that it should scrutinise all expenditure. Pay was miserable – for privates a fraction of a workman's daily wage. Washington was unable to recruit more than 160 men, despite his personal promise that all ranks would receive land grants upon the Ohio. Clothing and equipment were in depressingly short supply and only backwoods vagrants were prepared to enlist. Virginia was committed to a war which it was in no condition to fight.

Meanwhile at the Forks on 7 February 1754 the building of a fort had begun. The Half-King, still hoping that the arrival of tools and workmen heralded a more forceful Virginian approach, laid the first log, but even among the Mingos his authority was almost gone. The local Delawares refused to hunt to provision the fort builders, forcing Captain Trent, their commander, to travel east for supplies, leaving Ensign Ward in charge. On 17 April, with the fort barely finished, some 500 waterborne French troops appeared on the Allegheny. When they landed with eighteen field guns and formed up before the flimsy stockade their commander, Captain Claude-Pierre Pécaudy de Contrecoeur, offered a choice between honourable terms and an assault. Ward, with barely forty men, did the sensible thing and surrendered. Tanaghrisson raged as the Virginians marched away the following day, but his cause was lost. He decamped with about eighty followers, of whom only twelve or so were warriors, to a place near Great Meadows, some 60 miles to the south-east. Meanwhile, Contrecoeur began to build a bigger and stronger fort of log-faced earth-infill with bastions, a protective outwork, a ditch, an internal well and mounting – initially – eight guns. He names it Fort Duquesne.[10]

Washington was in near-ignorance of the vastly superior force he was ordered to drive away. The reinforcements supposed to be coming from other British colonies, and from the Cherokees and Catawbas, failed to appear. Worse, a novice commander eager to cut a heroic military figure, he advanced some 90 miles from Wills Creek towards a fortified trading post at Red Stone Creek, only 40 miles short of the Forks. The advance through dense woods was painfully slow and vulnerable to ambush. On 24 May the column halted to build a flimsy fort at Great Meadows, a location attractive for its running water supply and grass but overlooked by higher wooded ground.

Contrecoeur could have eliminated the Virginia Regiment with ease. Instead, conscious of his orders to avoid unnecessary provocation, he sent a patrol to warn it off. If Dinwiddie and Washington were reckless enough to risk all-out war, the French were not.[11]

The Fall of a Half-King

On 26 May, the French detachment of thirty-five soldiers led by Ensign Joseph Coulon de Villiers de Jumonville passed Christopher Gist's trading post 12 miles north of Great Meadows. Gist set off to warn Washington and next day saw tracks less than 5 miles from Washington's force. Washington, assuming that Jumonville had travelled up the Monongahela by canoe, sent half his force off in that direction. But at nightfall Tanaghrisson appeared to report the real French position: 7 miles to the north-east behind the height called Laurel Ridge. Seizing what he knew to be his last chance to commit Virginia to strong action, the Half-King persuaded Washington to help him surprise Jumonville in camp.

What happened next is unclear. Washington later claimed that volleys were exchanged, killing Jumonville and nine of his men. The French, so his account went, then surrendered and twenty-one were taken prisoner. Unfortunately, as Professor Anderson has shown, that does not square with the accounts of a Frenchman who escaped, a Virginian soldier who later talked to men who were there, and a Mingo sent, probably deliberately by the Half-King, to Fort Duquesne.

It seems that when the Virginians first opened fire the French at once surrendered, and a wounded Jumonville handed Washington his message from Contrecoeur. Washington retired to read it, raising the possibility that the incident would stop short of an irrevocable act of war – something that Tanaghrisson could not permit. The Mingos blocking the Frenchmen's only line of escape opened fire, and in the confusion the Half-King loomed over the wounded Jumonville. Exclaiming, 'You are not yet dead, my father', he buried his hatchet in the ensign's skull, scooped his brains out and rubbed them between his hands. The Half-King had formally broken with the French king, his 'father', and had committed Virginia to a war which it could not win alone, and which could not restore Tanaghrisson's fortunes. Washington and his men returned to Great Meadows.

Even now, Washington could have saved himself by a prompt withdrawal. Instead, he hurried the completion of the Great Meadows stockade, misleadingly called Fort Necessity, and prepared to meet the expected French assault. As at the Forks, there was neither the time nor the manpower to create a formidable fortification: it was circular, so the defenders could not concentrate their fire, and at only 50 feet across it was too tiny to contain the whole of the Virginian force. It was supplemented by hurriedly dug external trenches, too shallow to give meaningful protection and wide open to the elements. Tanaghrisson tried to explain the fatal weaknesses of 'that little thing upon the Meadow', only to be stonewalled by the arrogant self-confidence of the amateur commander. But worse still was Washington's decision to advance upon Fort Duquesne.

Washington really believed in the intercolonial reinforcements and supplies supposed to be coming to his aid. What appeared to be proof came in the guise of 200 more Virginians with nine 2-pounder swivel guns and an independent company of regulars from South Carolina. He even convinced himself that he could still rally the Ohio nations to the British cause. On 16 June, leaving the regulars at Fort Necessity, he led the way towards the Forks. After two exhausting weeks he had only reached Gist's trading post, where he spent three days trying to persuade a meeting of Shawnees, Delawares and Mingos to join him. To the Natives that was a truly uninviting prospect: war would force their families into would exile, defeat would mean expulsion by the French, and victory would open the region to swarms of British settlers. Indeed, observing the state of Washington's meagre force, they might well be better off joining the French. The last vestige of the Half-King's authority was gone: Tanaghrisson quietly gathered his family and a handful of followers and set out for a Pennsylvanian exile.[12]

Unknown to Washington, Contrecoeur had received about 1,000 reinforcements and was being pressed by Jumonville's brother,

The Fall of a Half-King

Captain Louis Coulon de Villiers, to seek revenge. Towards the end of June, Villiers led 600 Canadian troops and perhaps 100 Natives to intercept the exhausted Virginians. Not until 28 June did Washington learn of his approach and begin to retreat. When on 1 July they reached Fort Necessity, his men were too tired and hungry to go any further. After a night's rest they struggled to strengthen their defences. Then it began to rain.[13]

By the morning of Thursday 3 July a quarter of the men were unfit for duty. When the French attack began, Washington marched the remainder out for a fight in the open but Coulon de Villiers kept his men on the high ground in the shelter of the trees. The Virginians fell back – most to shelter in waterlogged trenches only 2 or 3 feet deep – while the French and Indians continued to pepper them from cover. Within hours most of the drenched British muskets were out of action and by nightfall a third of the men were dead or wounded. Others broke into the rum store inside the stockade and before long most of the soldiers were drunk.[14]

They were saved by Villiers' orders to avoid an irreconcilable conflict while Britain and France were officially at peace. Having avenged his brother and his men, Villiers was prepared to let Washington's shrivelled force depart on honourable terms: in return they must evacuate the Ohio country, undertake not to return within a year, release their prisoners, and leave two officers behind as hostages. Like Ward at the Forks, Washington had no option but to sign the proffered document. Given the wet, the dark and his execrable French, the Virginian commander did not see that he was also signing his confession to Jumonville's murder.

Tanaghrisson died miserably on 4 October at Aughwick in Pennsylvania, complaining of Washington's powerful will and refusal to be advised about frontier warfare. Meanwhile the French had burned pitiful Fort Necessity, Gist's trading post and the Redstone Creek fortification. Duquesne set about conciliating the Ohio Indians by reducing his own garrisons, ordering them to remain on the defensive, and by providing cheap subsidised trade goods. In October, shortly after the Half-King's demise, an Iroquois delegation appeared at Quebec. The French had finally secured the Ohio country and probably had no further aggressive ambitions, but that was not how it looked from the British side.

Desertion was fast destroying what was left of the Virginia Regiment at Wills Creek, and the burgesses in Williamsburg refused to raise more money and men. Virginia alone could not defend itself, let alone drive the French from the Ohio. In London the disaster confirmed the need for the imperial intervention, which Halifax and his allies had already set in motion.

4

THE BREAKING OF THE COVENANT CHAIN

By 1748, the relationship between the Mohawks and New York was at breaking point. The colony extended up the Hudson River to the city of Albany, at the mouth of its Mohawk tributary. The Mohawk Valley was a major and long-established trading route between the Hudson and Lake Ontario by way of Wood Creek, which flowed into Lake Oneida. However, the Mohawks' role as intermediaries between Albany and the nations of the *pays d'en haut* had been seriously weakened by the establishment of Fort Oswego on Lake Ontario in the 1720s. While traders travelling that way had to pass through one of the Mohawks' 'castles', they were no longer the commercial middlemen. Moreover New York's Indian agents, the Albany Commissioners, increasingly did business directly with the Catholic Mohawks from Kahnawake, one of three French-created reserves on the St Lawrence opposite Montreal. The Kahnawake people did not even have to follow the Mohawk River: they could travel via the Richelieu River, Lake Champlain and the Hudson.

Worse, the New York Mohawks' numbers had never recovered from a mix of warfare, disease and northward migration in the late seventeenth century. By 1740 there were only two towns on the Mohawk: Tiononderoge (the 'Lower Castle'), about 30 miles upstream from Albany, and Canajoharie ('Upper Castle'), about another 30 miles further on. Both were pressed upon by the claims of speculators and German and Scots-Irish settlers; and while Tiononderoge was home to an Anglican mission established in the reign of Queen Anne, it looked out upon a visible symbol of British intrusion and plague-bringing in the form of New York's Fort Hunter. Though Tiononderoge's acculturated elite grew rich, living in two-storied houses furnished in the English manner, the poorer folk of Canajoharie developed a reputation for quarrelsome and even violent resentment, suspicious trade and land fraud.

Land indeed was the crux of the problem. New York interests claimed that three seventeenth-century patents, dubious deeds of sale, entitled them to huge swathes of remaining Mohawk lands. The city of Albany's claim included the very site of Tiononderoge, while that of the Livingston family would have deprived Canajoharie of its fertile riverside territory. Both towns were particularly incensed by the Kayaderosseras patent, which threatened to take 800,000 acres of mountainous hunting ground between the west bank of the Hudson and the northern side of the Mohawk.

However, the Mohawks were in a stronger position than the Ohio nations. They spoke for themselves diplomatically and the governor of New York had recently sidelined the Albany Commissioners, who had handled Indian affairs in peacetime, in favour of face-to-face councils. These occasions, usually at Albany, sometimes became intercolonial conferences as well, attended by delegates from New England and even Pennsylvania. Their object was the 'brightening' of the Covenant Chain, the understanding which recognised the Iroquois as the channel for New York's Native diplomacy and accepted Iroquois sovereignty over vast areas they claimed by right of conquest but did not occupy. Because Natives as a rule did not recognise treaty arrangements as permanent fixtures, the Chain had to be periodically refreshed with new arrangements and gifts. This custom provided New York with its best form on inland defence and could not be ignored; whereas most of the Iroquois had remained neutral during the War of the Austrian Succession, the Mohawks had gone faithfully to war against the French and their Native allies, and suffered heavy losses in the process. By 1748, however, all of that was in crisis.

In that year, Governor George Clinton announced that since peace had been made in Europe the Mohawks too should put down the hatchet. It would be most inconvenient if continuing Iroquois raids should spark a fresh conflict, he said. The Mohawks were infuriated that they were denied both revenge through 'mourning war' and the enrichment of condolence gifts. Not for the first time, British convenience trumped Iroquois need. The most prominent spokesman on the Six Nations side was the Mohawk leader Theyanoguin (Hendrick to the British), and he was angry.

Hendrick worked in conjunction with a colourful Irishman, William Johnson, who had arrived in America in 1738 to manage a Mohawk Valley estate acquired by his naval officer uncle, Peter Warren. Johnson, who had no intention of remaining in another man's employ, bought his own piece of land between the two villages on the on the north bank of the river. From there he was able to tap into the fur trade, cutting out the Albany middlemen and making a fortune before setting himself up as a sort of squire. In 1748 he acquired a neighbouring patch of land and began to build a fortified stone mansion he called Johnson Hall.

Johnson was generous and hospitable – in one year he spent £3,500 on presents, compared with the Albany Commissioners' average of £175 – in the manner of a self-consciously benevolent landlord, and to some extent he identified with Mohawk culture. They in turn saw him as the powerful British friend they needed: as early as 1742 they adopted him as a *sachem* with the name of Warraghiyagey, which meant 'Man Who Does Much Business' but according to Johnson was better translated as 'Man Who Does Great Things'. In 1746 he had led a party of warriors into an Albany conference dressed and painted as an Indian headman, so impressing Clinton that he made the Irishman New York's sole agent for Indian affairs and a provincial colonel commanding those Iroquois who chose to fight with the British.

In general, the Iroquois trusted Johnson because he took their part against the colonial authorities and Indians like the Ohio nations, whom they claimed to have subjugated by conquest. But he was not particularly scrupulous. The kettles, knives, hatchets, guns, gunpower, clothing and other items he supplied as agent (and claimed as expenses) all came from his own business, and he was not above exploiting Indian customs to acquire more land. The story goes that a *sachem* once told him that he had dreamed of being given an expensive coat Johnson was wearing. Knowing that custom required it, he removed the coat and handed it over before announcing he had dreamed of being given a large tract of land. He was, however, the Iroquois' only hope of reversing the neglect they felt so acutely.

Between them, Hendrick and Johnson were operating on the intercultural middle ground. Hendrick appeared at councils wearing a red coat, lace ruffs and a tricorn hat: the image of him brandishing a tomahawk in these clothes captures the essence of his role. Johnson, who from 1750 was a member of Clinton's executive council, was inclined to underline his dual role by appearing in Mohawk dress.

The tensions came to a head in 1751, when the New York assembly's refusal to pay for Johnson's services led him to resign. As he had calculated (and probably planned), all six Iroquois nations sent delegates to New York City to demand Johnson's reinstatement and presence at a forthcoming Albany conference. He arrived triumphantly, the hero of the Iroquois and an embarrassment to Clinton, who left the conference suddenly

The Breaking of the Covenant Chain

without the customary farewells. That unceremonious departure was bad enough, but a few months later he sacked Johnson, who wanted a royal commission with a salary attached, in favour of the reinstated Albany Commissioners.

Two years later, in June 1753, New York seemed about to give in to the partners pushing the Kayaderosseras patent. This infuriated Hendrick but it also gave him a means to assert Mohawk independence. He travelled down to New York City, confronted the governor, and declared the Covenant Chain broken. In effect, acting on his own authority, Hendrick had broken off diplomatic relations. He told Clinton, 'You are not to expect to hear from me any more, and Brother we desire to hear no more from you.' There was now a real danger that the Mohawks, the guardians of New York's northern frontier, would side with the French, and that others of the Six Nations would join them.

This was the crisis that moved Halifax's Board of Trade to order an intercolonial conference at Albany to restore relations with the Iroquois. Opening on 4 July 1754, the very day of Washington's surrender, it turned out to be the largest such congress ever, though significantly no colony south of Pennsylvania chose to take part. New York was there, of course, and so were representatives of Maryland, Massachusetts, Pennsylvania, Rhode Island and New Hampshire. Connecticut delegates came because eyes there were fixed on land claimed by the Iroquois (but inhabited by Delawares) in the Susquehanna Valley. Partly to counter the Connecticut claim, a Pennsylvanian team led by Benjamin Franklin was also present. Confronting them were 150–200 Iroquois from across the Six Nations, led by Hendrick and in no mood to tolerate New York's one-sided demands for alliance. Of 103 recorded names, forty-nine have between identified as Mohawks and seventeen as Oneidas or Tuscaroras, while the western nations sent even fewer: seven Senecas, five Cayugas and four Onondagas. These surprisingly low numbers for such an important congress probably reflected deep dissatisfaction with the British among the Six Nations. Certainly, Hendrick's oratory indicated as much.[1]

James Delancey, the acting governor of New York, tried to use the Board's instructions to seek one general treaty with the Iroquois which would guarantee his colony's domination of northern Indian affairs. The Pennsylvanians and New Englanders, however, wanted to pursue their own interests – land and frontier defence – by establishing direct diplomacy with the Iroquois, a process assisted by the custom of separate negotiations and by the Mohawks own desire to achieve greater freedom of action. And Johnson, who attended as a New York councillor, wanted to promote his conception of British imperial interests and to become a salaried imperial official.

Delancey's opening speech asked the Iroquois to renew the Covenant Chain and to stand firm with the British to resist encroachments by the French but did not address the grievances raised by Hendrick the previous year. Over the next two days some Natives, probably Iroquois, met him privately to seek assurances about those issues, but whatever they were told was not good enough. When the public meeting resumed, Hendrick admonished the lieutenant governor for ignoring the Iroquois and tolerating the Albany traders who did business with the enemy and effectively armed the French against the Six Nations and British. If New Yorkers were weak and defenceless, he offered, it was their own fault. Then Hendrick's brother Abraham demanded that the Albany Commissioners be sacked and Johnson reinstated. Otherwise, there could be no alliance. 'The fire,' he said directly to the Albany Commissioners, 'has burnt out.'

There it was: no Johnson, no Covenant Chain. New York had been suitably embarrassed and the Iroquois' grievances would now be carried far and wide. Delancey responded the following day but offered little, and Hendrick's next speech seemed to accept the situation. Superficially, relations were repaired and the Iroquois confederacy as a whole was committed to neutrality. But New York did not commit itself either to addressing the Kayaderosseras question or to immediately reinstating Johnson. In reality, the Covenant Chain remained broken on the ground.

Unfortunately, Pennsylvanians and the Connecticut men were more intent on their rival land claims in the 25-mile Wyoming Valley and along the northern branch of the Susquehanna River. It was claimed by the Iroquois by right of conquest, and by the Penn proprietorship as already ceded to Pennsylvania. Both parties ignored the Eastern Delaware inhabitants: probably to forestall the Albany talks, Eastern Delaware leader Teedyuscung and about eighty of his followers had just moved to the town of Wyoming. The Pennsylvanian negotiator, Conrad Weiser, had already begun talks with the Tuscaroras and Oneidas, so if the Mohawks were to assert their role as gatekeepers they must intervene. Hendrick tried to argue that the Pennsylvanians should have less than they asked for, but Weiser answered that it must be the whole claim or nothing. Hendrick gave in: the Iroquois yielded all previously unceded land in Pennsylvania to proprietor Thomas Penn. There were two very specific exceptions – sacred Shamokin and the Wyoming Valley – and the Iroquois later insisted that they had meant to give up only the already settled regions. The Pennsylvanians, however, chose to interpret it as yielding the whole of their claim and later behaved accordingly. Yet Hendrick had re-established the Mohawks' right to lead such negotiations, inserted them into the Pennsylvanian Chain of Friendship and extracted a high price in cash and presents.[2]

John Henry Lydius conducted more covert and even less scrupulous discussions, liberally lubricated with drink. A trader on the Upper Hudson, Lydius had a long history of fraudulently acquiring Indian lands in New France and New York (where he was believed to be a Catholic mole) and in both places was strongly suspected of spying. He was the perfect choice to represent the

Susquehanna Company, one of three such associations driven by a growing land shortage in western Connecticut. Formed as recently as the July 1753, and shakily basing its claims on the sea-to-sea limits prescribed in its 1662 charter, it was quite unlike the tight-knit, elite Virginian groups: it now had 800 members and its shares, which were transferrable, had risen in value from two Spanish dollars to almost nine. Most importantly, they had already voted to send an exploratory 'Journeying Committee' to survey suitable Wyoming sites.[3]

Lydius knew that Hendrick and others had pledged never to sell Wyoming, so he entertained headmen individually at his Albany house, serving drink until they were inebriated enough to add their marks to the deed he produced. This deed claimed that the seventeen signatories were the owners of land between 41 and 43° N and had sold it to the Susquehanna Company for £2,000 in New York currency. Liberally funded by the company, Lydius bribed a large party of Oneidas and continued to collect signatures from Onondagas, Cayugas and Senecas until the following March. It did not trouble Lydius or the Connecticut men that Iroquois lands were held in common and the vendors had no right to sell, nor that the deed created a long-term conflict with Pennsylvania. But the fraud was not one-way. Not only had the Iroquois cheerfully sold other people's lands but they had sold some of them twice (to Pennsylvania and Lydius) in return for thirty wagonloads of presents, including 400 good guns. Now they were properly armed for whatever the coming conflict might bring – whether they remained neutral or not – at no cost to themselves.[4]

Franklin dismissed all this as 'nothing of much importance', partly because he regarded his plan of colonial union, to which the white delegates had agreed, as the most important achievement of the conference. In the end, his scheme came to nothing: not one of the colonial assemblies ratified it, and, being quite unlike the metrocentric empire Halifax had in mind, it would not have been approved in London. It has been put forward, unconvincingly, as a prototype of the Constitution of the United States which emerged more than three decades later. Of much greater significance, however, was the conference's failure to deliver a workable intercolonial military alliance: combined with the military disaster in the Ohio country, it forced the imperial government to further centralise power in London. It was decided that a vice-regal commander-in-chief for the whole of North America would have to be appointed.

5

CHEROKEES

To understand the Cherokees, it is helpful to consider their creation myth.

At first the whole world was water, say the Cherokees, and all the animals were in the space above the stone arch of the sky vault; but it was very crowded and they wanted more room. They wondered what was below the water, and at last the little Water Beetle offered to go to find out. He darted in every direction over the surface of the water but could find no place to rest. Then he dived down to the bottom and came up with some soft mud which began to grow and spread on every side until it became the island we call the earth. It was afterwards fastened to the sky with four cords, but no one remembers who did this.

At first the earth was flat and very soft and wet. The animals were anxious to get down and sent out various birds to see if it was yet dry, but they could find no place to land. At last they sent out the Great Buzzard. He flew all over the earth, low down near the ground, and it was still soft. When he reached the Cherokee country he was very tired, and his flapping wings began to strike the ground, and wherever they struck the ground there was a valley, and where they turned up again there was a mountain. When the animals saw this, they were afraid that the whole world would be mountains, and they called him back, but the Cherokee country remains full of mountains to this day.[1]

In sum, the Cherokees were mountaineers who knew very well how their world had been created. Their home lay within the Great Smoky and Unicoi Mountains at the southern tip of the great Appalachian chain. The mountains sustained them, protected them and, as their creation story demonstrates, defined them. This highland fastness, perhaps 100 miles long and 50 wide, protected their sixty or so little towns against the advancing white settlements to the east.

The mountains even protected against the worst ravages of alien pathogens. Even early in the eighteenth century there were more Cherokees in the mountains than whites in the whole colony of South Carolina. By 1750 there were between 9,000 and 11,000 Cherokees, able to field 3,000 warriors against 25,000 white colonists who also had to beware of potential rebellion among their 39,000 black slaves. North Carolina had a far larger white population but also many more slaves, and at this time had limited contact with the Cherokees. Georgia had only 4,200 whites and faced possible annihilation by the Creeks. Numerically, the Cherokee nation punched above its weight.

Internally, however, division weakened them. The mountains split them into four or five regions. The main Smoky ridges and the Unicoi peaks to the south separated the Overhill settlements nearest the Mississippi from the Middle Towns on the Little Tennessee River and the Valley Towns on the Hiwassee and Valley Rivers to the south. Each region had a central council and could and went its own way when circumstances dictated. Even within regions the towns were essentially self-governing: the regional 'beloved' towns – Keowee in the Lower Towns, Hiwassee in the Valley Towns, Chota among the Overhills – had virtually no coercive power so their decisions could not be made binding.

From their highlands they looked down upon the white settlements creeping across the eastern Tidewater and Piedmont lowlands, and upon the river traffic and sparse French settlements. In the east, Carolinian settlers had reached Long Canes Creek, a tributary of the Savannah River fed by a stream called the New River. Should the Cherokees align themselves with South Carolina, the nearest, most reliable and least expensive source of trade goods, and reach an accommodation respecting the boundary of settlement? Or should they look for more distant, less threatening but less reliable alternatives in Virginia or Georgia or the Louisiana French? Among the Overhills the towns of Tellico and Settico tended to favour the French, while the 'mother town' of Chota, home to the spiritual leader, or *uku*, was less certain.

For their part, the British had long wished to find a recognisable central government with which they could do business. In 1730, when a completely unrepresentative embassy visited London, Moitoi of Tellico had been recognised as 'emperor'. In effect the Board of Trade recognised a Hiwassee–Tellico alliance over the traditional spiritual authority of the *uku*. This fiction was tolerated as a way of managing relations with the British, and because the alliance was powerful enough to impose some discipline upon wayward Overhill towns and warriors, but it was very far from being an effective government. From about 1743 Moitoi's successor, Amouskositte, was undermined by Chota's overtures to the French and by repeated South Carolina trade embargoes, which left the Cherokees unable to repel Creek raids. In 1753 Amouskositte was displaced by the *uku* of Chota, Connecorte (Old Hop to the British), who built up a more centralised but still limited 'priestly' state. His ally, Attakullakulla or Little Carpenter, became the nation's chief diplomatic emissary, an achievement that was due not only to his skill but also to the prestige deriving from his participation in the London embassy of 1730, when he was about fifteen.

Oconostota, the 'Great Warrior' of Chota, in the meantime became the war leader of all the Cherokees, with a theoretical right to manage all war parties. An enlarged Chota town council became something akin to a national government.

The Cherokees' options were further complicated by a long-running war with their southern neighbours, the Creeks. Hostilities went far back, even beyond the Yamasee War of 1715, in which the Cherokees had allied with South Carolina and the Creeks with the Yamasees. Labelled the Cherokee–Creek War, much of the conflict took place in sporadic small-scale raids. However, it was complicated by the Iroquois, who frequently raided the Creek towns and expected Cherokees to supply them with food and shelter. If the Cherokees refused, the Iroquois would visit violence upon them; if they abetted the northern marauders, however, fierce Creek attacks would result. Worse still for the Cherokees, occasional violence against dishonest South Carolina traders would be met with arms embargoes which gave the upper hand to the Creeks.

Then came a ferocious intensification. About 1750, the Upper Towns offered to help South Carolina against the Creeks but encountered resistance from the Lower Towns. When the Lower Town of Tugaloo received a Creek peace delegation, Upper Cherokee warriors, desperate to disrupt negotiations, slaughtered the Creek emissaries in the Tugaloo townhouse. The Creeks had to avenge this atrocity and began to launch massive assaults: most of the Lower Towns were soon destroyed or abandoned.

Into the resulting power vacuum stepped the Overhills. They sheltered Lower Towns refugees, sought help through their connections with northern Indians and made counter-attacks on the Creeks. By 1753 Chota had risen to prominence and the Settico–Tellico alliance was eclipsed. It was the Chota council that had to deal with the population explosion on the South Carolia frontier – and with that province's imperialistic governor.

Governor James Glen was an ambitious Scot who fancied himself an expert on Indian affairs, and Cherokee affairs in particular. From his perspective there was a double danger: the Creek–Cherokee conflict hampered trade, but it also might attract Bourbon support for one side or the other. As early as 1746, alarmed by reports of French offers of peace and a protective military post, Glen offered Amouskositte a British fort in return for driving out the French. The offer came to nothing – neither man was able to keep his promises.

Glen also sought to erode Cherokee independence by exploiting settler pressure on their hunting grounds. The advance of hunters into the woods closest to the Lower Cherokees was steadily thinning out game, while settlers' land clearances and intrusive livestock further degraded them. The hunter–settler advance was followed by pressure from would-be speculators – trivial by Virginian standards but still a force to be reckoned with. In 1747 Glen was able to negotiate the cession of the whole of the left bank of Long Canes Creek, which at least until 1763 the Cherokees held as their fixed frontier.

For Glen and his successor William Henry Lyttelton, however, it was only a temporary expedient. By 1751 one John Hamilton had obtained a 200,000-acre grant around an area called Ninety Six, part of which stretched across Long Canes Creek. Hamilton's investment brought slow returns from sales but by the mid-1750s settler numbers were growing fast. Over 300 families from Pennsylvania arrived in 1755, and by 1756 official surveys were encouraging people to filter into the fertile bottoms along the Little River. These violations were thinly disguised by representing the river as the north-west fork of Long Canes Creek.

In September 1749 Glen brokered a peace treaty between Creeks and Cherokees, a major diplomatic achievement which almost immediately broke down when the Cherokees continued to harbour northern Indians. Two years later, however, developments on the Ohio and a Cherokee war scare in South Carolina raised the fort issue once again. Chota abandoned its French connection in order to bid for the fort's location, and Glen was astute enough to see that in the long term Chota would be a better choice than Tellico. The South Carolina assembly was more intent on acquiring frontier lands: it voted £3,000 for a fort but in the Lower Towns – not among the Overhills – and on condition that the Cherokees yielded most of the land between Ninety Six and Keowee. This would have rendered the Lower Cherokees permanently dependent upon South Carolina – not quite what Glen aspired to, but a beginning.

In fact, the Lower Towns yielded only the use – not the ownership – of enough land for a fort at Keowee, and a strip 200 feet wide to join it to Ninety Six. The frontier remained where it had been since 1747, at Long Canes Creek. Glen, however, told the Board that the Cherokees had ceded of all the land up to Keowee. The fort itself, named Prince George, was overlooked by hills and woods well within rifle range, and largely dependent upon the Cherokees for food. Far from restraining the Indians, its garrison would be their hostages. Cherokee sovereignty was hardly compromised.

Glen's next extravagant scheme was to send a Cherokee delegation to London to make a formal submission to the Crown in return for a protective Overhill fort. With Cherokee support and at least one regiment of British regulars, he would then push west to where the Ohio emptied into the Mississippi and so sever Louisiana from New France. The scheme chimed with Halifax's plan for a chain of forts along the whole frontier, and Sir Thomas Robinson, the Southern Secretary, sent £10,000 to pay for its construction. Unfortunately, he sent the money via Dinwiddie in Virginia, who had his own eyes on the Ohio and confiscated most of the money for his own colony's use. Moreover, Robinson firmly vetoed the idea of a new Cherokee embassy. Worse still, the Cherokees saw straight through Glen's expansionist intentions.

When Glen invited the Fire King to Charleston to make a formal submission, that wily old man declined, saying that the journey would be too long for a cripple. Instead, he sent Attakullakulla and Oconostota to invite Glen to meet him halfway, at Saluda Old Town on the river of the same name. In short, they would meet as equals or not at all. The conference finally assembled at Saluda towards the end of June.

Glen tried to confine the discussions to sovereignty and land cessions, whereas the Cherokees tried to confine the talks to trade. The treaty concluded on 2 July 1755 gave the Cherokees more licensed traders, better trade prices and a ban on rum. In return the Cherokees agreed to an Overhill fort (at an unspecified location), and Attakullakulla laid a bag of earth at Glen's feet. Glen (and for some time historians too) interpreted the gesture as the Cherokees knowingly yielding sovereignty over their lands to George II. More recent scholarship, giving due weight to Cherokee culture, has pointed out that the bag of earth represented not submission but alliance. Even though the Cherokees gave way to Glen's insistence on paying for what he believed were the acquired lands, they did so only out of courtesy. The land was not for sale.

Moreover, rival colonies and imperial officials were unimpressed. Edmond Atkin, who in 1756 became the first southern Superintendent of Indian Affairs, conducted himself as an ambassador to a foreign power rather than a resident authority imposed from outside. The governors of Virginia and North Carolina, and even Croghan, feared that Glen's apparent greed for territory would lead other nations to cling to the French. Halifax, finding Glen disturbingly erratic, agreed – not even Bedford could defend him. Glen was sacked for general incompetence.

As for the Cherokees, the long delay in building the Overhill fort left their towns dangerously exposed to Creek and northern raids. The trade promises also failed to materialise. Overhunting was reducing the supply of deer hides and exacerbated competition between traders, fundamental problems only superficially addressed by South Carolina now licensing traders for particular towns. Traders were caught between the need to extend credit to their Cherokee clients and the need to pay their Charleston suppliers. More and more traders resorted to fraud, often through false weights and measures, and a few became notorious. The worst was John Elliott, licensed to trade at Chota.

Thus, some Cherokees advocated finding other sources of vital trade goods. In December 1755, Ostenaco of Tomotly explored strengthening relations with Virginia. He suggested a Virginian attack on the Shawnee town on the Great Sandy River, but was disappointed by the Virginians' performance and the expedition was abandoned without meeting the Shawnee. Again at his prompting, at Broad River in March 1756, Dinwiddie then offered an Overhill fort himself in return for 400 Cherokee warriors to serve on the Virginian frontier. This treaty not only broke South Carolina's near monopoly of the Cherokee trade but was followed by action: on 29 June 1756, Major Andrew Lewis arrived with a party to begin construction of the promised fort.

In April, Ostenaco followed up his diplomatic success with a visit to Williamsburg in search of compensation for the Great Sandy warriors. Though unsuccessful, he was treated like a king. En route and on his return he stayed with the Jefferson family, and in Williamsburg the governor's own carriage was at his disposal. At home his prestige was boosted by the appearance of Major Lewis with his team of fort builders. While axes rang, trees fell and logs were hauled into position, the Cherokees kept their part of the bargain: hundreds of warriors went north to stem the onslaught against Virginia and Pennsylvania. Even though neither side quite trusted the other, it seemed that a close friendly relationship was in the offing. It was not to be. The Virginian fort never received a garrison.

When it became clear that Lewis would not leave anyone behind, the Cherokees gave him a message requesting Dinwiddie send 100 men. He made a show of finding 150 but refused to send them until the 400 Cherokees arrived in Virginia, and then found other transparent excuses – there was no money, no one would volunteer for so distant a service, the men were needed elsewhere. The fort remained empty and soon fell into ruin. Yet in 1757 and 1758 Cherokee warriors again streamed north, hoping that their services would at last secure ample presents and trade goods. It was a triumph of hope – or rather necessity – over experience.[2]

6

DIRECT INTERVENTION

William Augustus, Duke of Cumberland, Captain-General of the British Army, owed his position entirely to family influence. The favourite son of George II, at nineteen he had entered the army as a colonel and was promoted to major-general at twenty-two. At Dettingen in 1743 he displayed great physical courage and suffered a grapeshot wound which prevented him from walking comfortably thereafter (and indirectly led to the rapid weight gain which would ultimately shorten his life). Two years later he was given the command of the 'Pragmatic Army', the allied forces in the Austrian Netherlands, where at Fontenoy his inexperience – notably his preference for front-line bravery over careful control of his whole army – led to defeat and the consequent loss of the Netherlands. Nevertheless, the lessons he learned about firepower were put to good use when he defeated the Jacobite army at Culloden in 1746. He returned in 1747 to the Low Countries, where his tactical uncertainty contributed to defeat by Saxe's much larger French army, but he remained his father's favourite and could look forward to a long career of high command.

Cumberland was one of Bedford's enemies and bitterly opposed to the Pelhams, so when the Duke of Newcastle approached him in September 1754 about appointing a commander-in-chief for

America and sending British regulars there, it was a clear sign of the depth of the crisis.

Newcastle's initial plan was for at least one Highland regiment to be sent to march on Fort Duquesne and secure the Ohio country. Cumberland was much more ambitious and convinced that only wide-ranging hammer blows would deter the French from encroaching further. The plan was thus amended to a three-stage offensive to be led by a commander-in-chief for the whole of North America, Major General Edward Braddock. First Braddock should secure the Ohio, then move north to secure New York by removing the French from Fort St Frédéric at Crown Point on Lake Champlain, and finally shore up the Nova Scotian isthmus by taking Fort Beauséjour. Newcastle went along with this expanded strategy, hoping that the strict secrecy required would prevent France from reinforcing Canada in time. French weakness in America and the necessary delays between the planned British operations would then provide openings for a negotiated settlement before any general war could break out. The plan also appealed to Halifax, who had long argued for decisive action, and satisfied his vision of imperial centralisation: Braddock would supersede the colonial governors in military matters, be empowered to conduct an overall strategy and have the fiscal support of a common defence fund – another of the earl's cherished ideas. In effect, the commander-in-chief would be something akin to a viceroy on the Spanish model.

Unfortunately, Cumberland and his ally Henry Fox, the Secretary at War, were far from satisfied and knew that the king would back them. Cumberland still probably believed that secrecy was essential, but not so Fox. When he used a newspaper advertisement to order the colonels intended for America to report to their posts, the French were alerted. The king was easily persuaded to accept a much more ambitious scheme, and Newcastle was obliged to acquiesce. Within weeks Braddock was formally instructed to launch no fewer than four near-simultaneous assaults, leaving no intervals for negotiations. Moreover, the list of targets now included Fort Niagara, which gave the fundamentally defensive scheme a provocatively offensive edge. Braddock's military powers were expanded: two regular provincial regiments disbanded after the last war were to be recreated.

Newcastle still feared that this ambitious scheme would trigger a general war in Europe, where Britain's diplomatic position was crumbling. He already had his suspicions – soon to be confirmed – that the Austrian alliance he was seeking was a mirage: Vienna was instead courting Russia, with the ultimate aim of defeating Prussia and reclaiming Silesia. If that happened, and the Dutch Republic insisted on neutrality, the Austrian Netherlands would once again become a potential base for a French invasion of the British Isles. For European allies to divert the French, and to secure strategically and politically important Hanover, he would have to fall back upon Prussia and Russia.

Halifax was more sanguine about Europe, but he, who knew more than anyone about American frontier conditions, saw that the American plan was deeply flawed. The wooded and mountainous approaches to Fort Duquesne, followed by the unfortunate Washington and recommended to the ministry by Dinwiddie, were too hazardous compared with the routes to Niagara and Crown Point, and even taking those two objectives would require a much greater concentration of force than Cumberland's plan allowed. However, he saw that taking Niagara first would weaken French influence among the Ohio nations and check the flow of reinforcements to Fort Duquesne so he counselled leaving the Ohio alone for the moment, making Crown Point a secondary but achievable objective and concentrating efforts against Niagara.[1]

When the Cabinet rejected both arguments, Halifax seems then to have thrown in his lot with the Cumberland faction by publishing John Mitchell's final map, apparently proving that

Britain had a prior claim not only to the disputed borderlands but to the whole of North America east of the Mississippi River. By inflaming public opinion, the map's publication arguably made any reduction of the Cumberland plan politically impossible. Newcastle was helpless.[2]

Now all depended upon Braddock achieving rapid and dramatic success – and that in turn depended upon naval interception of the French reinforcements soon to embark for America. Because the British had ice-free American ports, Braddock could sail almost at once and the French not until the St Lawrence began to thaw in the spring.[3] But Braddock would still need time to muster his provincials, find supplies and wagons to transport them, and move on his objectives. If the French convoy could not be stopped, the target forts would be reinforced with seasoned regulars long before they could be attacked.

The surest way to intercept the French ships would be as they sailed from their home port, but – as the French ambassador made clear – a peacetime clash in home waters was bound to spark a European conflict. In April, Vice-Admiral Boscawen was dispatched with eleven ships of the line to intercept the French in the Gulf of St Lawrence – a peacetime clash in European waters would be sure to provoke a European conflict – but before he could make contact the French convoy was dispersed by fog off Newfoundland. Only three ships were found and engaged, and of those only two were taken after hard actions. Most of the French reinforcements were now loose in America, and soon they would surface at one or more of the British army's targets. Everything now must turn on time and speed, and Major-General Braddock had neither.

7

FAILED OFFENSIVE

Edward Braddock has been caricatured as a Colonel Blimp, already turned sixty, full of fuss and noise but hopelessly incompetent in an unfamiliar environment, contemptuous of both provincials and Indians, and lacking experience of independent command. As his biographer puts it, he was supposed to be 'ignorant of every point of parade, except the merits of as bottle and the looks of a woman, brave as a bulldog, savage, lustful, prodigal, generous, gentle in soft moods, easy of love and laughter, dull of wit, utterly unread, believing his country the first in the world and he as good a gentleman as any in it, and why not?'[1] There is also the view that he attended to the minutiae of every detail of his expedition except 'the one that mattered most: Indian affairs'.[2]

The much-cited story goes that when Johnson summoned the Ohio Indians to meet Braddock at Fort Cumberland, Scarouady, Shingas and four others took up the invitation. They were still suspicious of the British but just as anxious to clear the French out of their country, so they were open to an alliance that might guarantee their independence. To prove his sincerity, Shingas even produced a detailed plan of Fort Duquesne, drawn by a British prisoner there and smuggled out by the Oneida Half-King himself. Braddock, so the tale goes, misunderstood the significance of their mission. When Shingas asked what he would do with the land once the French were expelled, the general replied that 'the English should Inhabit and Inherit the Land'. Shingas then asked whether Indians friendly to the British, who had nowhere else to go, might not be allowed to remain there, Braddock replied that 'No Savage Should Inherit the Land'. Next day, so it is said, Shingas tried again and got the same answer. While colourful, this yarn of a British general's arrogant obtuseness is based upon a remark reported second-hand years later, and ignores the fact as late as August Scarouady was still hoping for British support. In short, if not quite the stuff of legend, it is extremely dubious and its survival may be explained by later colonial efforts to display the British general as a bumbling, uncomprehending and unimaginative outsider.

Braddock neither despised Indians nor underrated their usefulness to his army. Other accounts of their meeting record the general's respectful attitude and promises that the Indians would keep their lands. He certainly lost most of the forty or fifty Mingo warriors brought by Johnson – Tanaghrisson's former followers from Aughwick – by insisting that their families should leave the camp, but that was more a misguided move to instil camp discipline than a judgement on Indians as allies. Indeed, he quizzed Dinwiddie about the Indians who were with the French and those friendly to the British and how many he could expect to join his army. Impressed by the governor's insistence that he should try to win back the friendship of the Iroquois, he asked Governor Sharpe of Pennsylvania to recruit friendly Indians for the expedition and appointed Johnson as Superintendent of Indian Affairs. Braddock was concerned when the 120 Catawbas and 400 Cherokees promised by Dinwiddie failed to appear; he could not be expected to know that Cherokees and Catawbas could not work with Iroquois, let alone leave their towns open to northerners' attacks. Nor could he have bargained for the interference of James Glen of South Carolina, who imagined himself supreme manager of southern Indian affairs. It is telling that even George Croghan, who was placed as leader of the scouts, thought that Braddock did all he could to cultivate the trust of those Indians who appeared to join him.[3]

Nor did he dismiss importunate provincial expertise or aspirations on principle. He certainly sent some hopeful gentry on their way – including a son of Thomas Lee, founder of the Ohio Company – but those with knowledge or experience were welcomed. Washington, for example, came begging for a place as a volunteer, at the same time refusing to accept a commission on the grounds that it would entail deferring to more junior professionals. This posturing from a failed and still raw ex-colonel must have grated, but what the young Virginian knew about the road to Fort Duquesne, and possibly about Indians, could be very useful indeed. Braddock therefore employed him as a volunteer – an *aide-de-camp* without rank – and unofficial advisor. If Washington is to be believed, he influenced Braddock's decision to take his old route (which of course would suit the Ohio Company) and was allowed to debate the details of the campaign. Then there was Benjamin Franklin, pretending to have come as Pennsylvanian post-master general to ensure the army had efficient communications. Finding that Sir John St Clair, Braddock's eccentric quartermaster general, had failed to procure enough wagons, horses and supplies, Franklin shrewdly offered to use his own business contacts to fill the void. Braddock very sensibly accepted, although he must have known that the Pennsylvanian was really angling for his province's advantage once the Ohio was conquered.[4]

Provincial rank and file were another matter: those of the reconstituted and new Virginia regiments were no better than the sorry misfits led by Washington in 1754. Skinny, sallow-faced, often shirtless or shoeless, they were untrained men who were unable to make a living elsewhere. Both provincial units were woefully understrength and the two Irish regiments had to make up their own numbers – from Virginia, Maryland and Pennsylvania – with the same material. Luckily the redcoats had a hard core of disciplined and well-drilled troops, something the Virginians did not possess.[5]

Nor can it be said that Braddock failed to adapt his men's tactics, equipment and dress to the environment. Useless belts and equipment were left behind and the soldiers were encouraged to travel light. He was preparing them for their final obstacle: more than 100 miles of mountainous woodland, far more than he had been led to expect. At the same time, he studiously sought out tactical and logistical information to ease his safe passage through the forest.

Unfortunately, Braddock was not the man to unilaterally adapt his superiors' strategy to the conditions he found on the ground. As Halifax had foreseen, the sheer number of simultaneous operations would stretch the available resources to breaking point and induce competition between the commanders for supplies, transport, Indian scouts and recruits. But Braddock was a man of supreme confidence and determination who felt himself utterly bound to carry out his exact orders. He was deterred neither by the challenge of hauling siege artillery across so much mountain and forest, nor by the fact that he retained only eight Mingo scouts. Far from switching the main effort towards Niagara, then, Fort Duquesne remained his principal objective. On 29 May he set out from Fort Cumberland.

As his army toiled its way to the Monongahela, Indian raiders slipped around its flanks to hit settlements and convoys in its unprotected rear. Shawnees, Delawares and Great Lakes warriors struck settlements behind Fort Cumberland, killing or capturing hundreds of people and spreading panic in the back settlements of Pennsylvania and Maryland. Resistance was minimal: Pennsylvania had no formal militia and in Virginia many men either refused to turn out or fled eastwards; others mustered with few or no arms or declined to march outside their own county. Those who did engage were easily evaded by the raiders, while fleeing settlers choked the roads and those who remained refused to supply the army without armed escorts. It was not only the cutting of a road for the artillery and wagons that slowed the British advance to a crawl.[6]

A week into his march and only 35 miles from Fort Cumberland, Braddock realised that his progress was indeed too slow. Leaving his massive mortars, heavy 12-pounders and most of the lumbering baggage train behind with the bulk of the of the troops, he pushed forward with a hand-picked column. This consisted of Croghan and his eight Mingos, the well-trained redcoats who had come from Ireland, a company of New Yorkers and about 100 Virginians, labourers and axemen to clear the road, light artillery, a number of wagons, women and livestock. Though not exactly designed for reckless speed, this flying column made such relatively good progress – between 3 and 7 miles a day – that by early July the main body was some 60 miles behind.

This forward detachment toiled its way right up to and along Monongahela without incident thanks to Braddock's insistence upon adequate flank guards. Time and again these parties deflected French-allied Indians trying to reconnoitre the column, and on 6 July they prevented an actual attack. Braddock was careful to pass round places favourable for ambush; to avoid a defile known as Turtle Creek Valley he crossed the Monongahela twice. After that second crossing on 9 July, he was only 10 miles from Fort Duquesne.

Contrecoeur, monitoring the advance through his scouts, knew that he must take the offensive. The fort could hold barely half of his 1,600 regulars, militia and Indians – some from the Ohio nations but most from the north – and once Braddock had broken ground there and begun a formal siege, the Indians would vanish. He therefore sent about half of his men forward, hoping that the flying column could be ambushed as it recrossed the river. They were too late: the British were already fording the Monongahela for the second time.

Now all the systematic caution that had brought them this far was thrown to the winds. Lieutenant Colonel Thomas Gage, commanding the advance party, made two fatal mistakes. He apparently failed to restore the flank guards after crossing the river – something Braddock himself should have ensured – and neglected to occupy a rise commanding the path on the right. This was open woodland – hunting country where Indians regularly burned the undergrowth – so they were not constrained by dense forest. Perhaps, with the Monongahela crossed and Fort Duquesne only a few miles away, both men became overconfident just when they should have been especially cautious. At this moment the French-led column appeared ahead, and Gage's soldiers instantly deployed into line.

Three crashing volleys shattered the French regulars and militia, killing their commander. For a moment even the Indians were about to turn tail and flee. Then – perhaps rallied by a militia officer, perhaps just reacting instinctively – they poured down the flanking ravines and fired into the troops exposed on the path. The redcoats replied by turning to fire into the woods, but their enemies were almost invisible, no more than four or five in sight at once as they darted from tree to tree. Within minutes, fourteen of Gage's eighteen officers were down. Workmen fleeing to the rear collided with the troops moving forward to support the vanguard and confusion grew. Braddock rode forward to take personal command of the fight and for three hours the British regulars bravely held their ground in a battle in which their very training told against them. They huddled together, vainly trying to form front to an enemy whose war-whoops sounded all round them. All Braddock could do was hope that desperate courage and iron discipline would at last overwhelm the enemy irregulars.

It could not last. When Braddock took a musket ball in the chest and fell, word spread quickly. Without a specific order the men began to retreat, still huddled together, until they reached the river. The Indians, sensing victory, surged forward and the retreat became a headlong rout. The enemy did not pursue beyond the ford, turning back to scalp the dead and wounded, and to secure prisoners they had tied to trees. But that did not halt the flight of the terrified troops: those who could ran for two days more before meeting Dunbar's rear echelon. Dunbar could have stood his ground: even had the French and Indians pursued the fugitives, his column would have been strong enough to defend itself. Instead, he had the artillery and stores destroyed before ordering a general retreat to Fort Cumberland. Braddock and the other wounded were evacuated on wagons but the general did not survive the journey. He died and was buried on 14 July in the middle of the road his men had made in an attempt to hide his grave from the Indians still supposedly close behind.

The one clear-cut success of 1755 came in Nova Scotia. Because the Crown had promised to pay the troops for this expedition, the New England assemblies raised no objections and many enlisted in the hope of being rewarded with Acadian lands. Furthermore, the approaches to that province being by sea, there was no time-wasting need to recruit wagons and wagoners. By mid-June they had broken ground before Fort Beauséjour and on the 17th, after a British shell exploded inside one of the casemates, the French surrendered. That was followed by the expulsion of nearly all the French Acadians – about 7,000 were deported to other British colonies, perhaps 10,000 escaped to French territory – after they had been challenged to pledge unqualified loyalty to George II instead of the neutrality demanded of them in 1713. At one level this ethnic cleansing was the result of decades of resistance, and particularly of Father Le Loutre's War, which had been sparked by the founding of Halifax and Edward Cornwallis's efforts to import Protestant settlers from Germany and elsewhere. At another it may have been the real and principal goal of Braddock's successor as North American Commander-in-Chief, William Shirley, to clear the land for New Englanders; it is certainly true that between 1760 and 1763 some 5,000 settlers moved north. But resettlement signally failed to end Indian resistance. As late as 1757, when the army of Shirley's successor Lord Loudoun arrived in Halifax, foragers disappeared without trace and boats were fired upon from the woods.

On 23 June, Jean-Armand de Dieskau and his newly arrived regulars, along with the Marquis de Vaudreuil, the new governor general, reached Quebec. Dieskau's first instinct was to reinforce Fort Niagara: if that fell, Canada would be cut off from its western posts and from Louisiana. Instead, news of Johnson's advance sent him towards Lake Champlain and ill-maintained Fort St Frédéric.

Shirley's advance was delayed even longer than Braddock's, largely because his Albany base was shared with Johnson's, producing wasteful competition for recruits, wagons, stores and Indian scouts. While Shirley took away some of Johnson's troops, the superintendent saw to it that he didn't get Mohawk scouts. Provincial and commercial rivalries also played a part: Shirley and Governor Morris of Pennsylvania used their own contacts in Boston, Philadelphia and New York to find provisions for the Niagara expedition. James Delancey, New York's lieutenant governor, whose family had been cut out of the military contracts, obstructed the Massachusetts governor as much as he could, even to the extent of denying him artillery which would otherwise remain unused. It was August before Shirley was able to travel up the Mohawk to the portage called the Oneida Carry where he received the news of Braddock's defeat. He pressed on to Wood Creek which flowed down to Lake Oneida, crossed the lake and descended the Onondaga River to Lake Ontario. There he found Fort Oswego – intended to be the base for the final waterborne push against Niagara – vulnerable and hopelessly decayed. He cut his losses by refortifying Oswego and garrisoning it with his two provincial regiments, and leaving a small stockade, Fort Bull, to guard the head of the Carry. With luck, he hoped, he would be able to resume the offensive in the spring.[7]

Johnson's thrust towards Lake Champlain was even later, delayed by rivalry for manpower and supplies, efforts to have Shirley removed from overall command, and the need to build hundreds of rivercraft to carry the expedition up the Hudson. At the Great Carrying Place a secure base, Fort Edward, had to be built and 17 miles of road cut through the woods to Lac St Sacrement. It was September before his troops reached the southern shore of the lake, which Johnson symbolically renamed Lake George, and only then did the Mohawks led by Hendrick appear. By then it was known that Braddock's campaign plans had been among the papers captured on the Monongahela, so Johnson expected that Dieskau would have reinforced Fort St Frédéric and probably brought northern Indians to scour the woods. All too aware of his amateur military status, he knew he must advance with caution.

He was right: Dieskau had brought 3,000 regulars, militia and Indians down to Crown Point, whence he sent out patrols to reconnoitre Johnson's position. Their reports encouraged him to mount a swift raid, rather like the one sent against Braddock, which might destroy Fort Edward before it could be built and burn the expedition's boats and supplies. At worst, Johnson would then be stuck on the southern shore; at best he would retire, leaving Albany itself exposed. Upon receiving their reports, Dieskau decided to leave his regulars at Crown Point and advance with a mixed force of 1,500 Canadian militia and Indian allies. Perhaps, as some historians have argued, he was more aware of the capacities of irregular troops than British officers like Braddock.

By 7 December, Dieskau's force had paddled from Lake Champlain to the southern shore of Lake George and, circumventing Johnson's camp, reached the road 3 miles from Fort Edward. Here his Indians announced that they would not attack a fort, so the expedition turned back to assail the British camp.

Already they had been detected by Johnson's Mohawks, and while the camp was prepared for defence 1,000 provincials and 200 Mohawks led by Hendrick were sent out to engage the enemy. In turn Dieskau detected their advance and laid an ambush, his regulars blocking the road, the militia and Indians hidden on both sides. The first volleys killed Hendrick, thirty other Mohawks and about fifty provincials. The remaining Mohawks and perhaps 100 provincials made a fighting retreat while the rest fled pell-mell. Dieskau pursued closely towards a camp now fully alert and with four guns facing the road from behind the improvised breastworks.

The French militia and Indians refused to attack, so Dieskau ordered them to fire from the woods and formed his two grenadier companies into an assault column of six abreast. The regulars charged bravely but were shredded by grapeshot. After five hours of firing from the surrounding woods the French began to retire, carrying the dying Dieskau. When about 400 attempted to rally further down the road, they were surprised and shot up by 200 provincials from Fort Edward. The battle petered out and the British could plausibly claim a victory.

Of course, the victory was an illusion. The Mohawks plundered the dead and left with their prisoners for home, and without them nothing more could be done. Supplies were running short and the provincials were sickening. Before long reconnaissance showed that the French were building a fort on the narrows between Lake George and Lake Champlain, a place the French called Carillon and the British Ticonderoga. Johnson, now wounded in the buttock, had been decisively stopped far from his objective and Crown Point was further out of reach than ever. Instead, they began to build Fort William Henry to secure the lakeside end of the portage. The last of the four British offensives had failed. The enemy could now switch to a devastating counter-attack, a European war was all but certain, and London would have to commit even more resources to America.

8

WARS IN THE FORESTS

The frontier raids now redoubled and intensified. Yet, even after Braddock's defeat, the leading Ohio Delawares and Mingos held back from joining the French, and – Virginia now being a visibly broken straw – made a last appeal to Pennsylvania. In August, Half-King Scarouady, Shingas and Captain Jacobs, the most prominent Delaware warrior, went personally to Philadelphia to plead for arms. For a week they negotiated, but Governor Morris and his council would not spare the weapons and as yet had no militia. Lamely they told the Native emissaries to appeal to Onondaga, a useless recommendation as the Iroquois had already promised neutrality. The three headmen returned despondently to the Ohio, knowing that they had run out of options. They chose the Shawnees, the French and their Wyandot and Ottawa allies and by the autumn they were leading Franco-Indian war parties against the back settlements of Virginia and Pennsylvania.

Montcalm, the new French commander, sought to defend New France from such superior British numbers by going vigorously onto the offensive. Concentrating his regulars to protect the St Lawrence and to threaten New England and New York, he relied on Indian raids to paralyse the Virginian, Maryland and Pennsylvanian frontiers. While the French chose the regions for large combined operations, the Indians selected the precise targets; and the Ohio Indians, the Susquehanna Delawares and the Great Lakes nations needed no urging to go marauding on their own. Though reliant upon an increasingly unsure supply of French arms and goods, they possessed a superiority in forest warfare that colonial militias, provincials and British regulars could not yet match.

During the winter of 1755–56, Virginia, Pennsylvania and Maryland built chains of forts to cover their frontiers, a few of them quite substantial and well sited. Most, however, were simple blockhouses or little stockades enclosing settlers' houses. Intended to be linked by patrolling soldiers, they were in reality 18–20 miles apart and easily bypassed. In any case, most were so undermanned that extensive external patrolling was out of the question. They therefore presented tempting targets for raiders who thought they could carry them quickly by surprise, stratagem or fire.

Virginia's assembly had reacted to Braddock's defeat by voting a new 1,200-strong Virginia Regiment but it says something about the province's military capacity that the most experienced commander they could find was the twice-defeated George Washington. While Washington took his job seriously, finding suitable recruits, equipment, arms and carriage was a nightmare.

In October the Eastern Delawares joined with the Ohio Indians, sacking settlements along the Susquehanna and pressing deeper into Pennsylvania. The province's only retaliatory operation was a miserable affair. A raid against Lower Shawneetown, it was plagued by a poorly chosen route, inadequate supplies, thick forest and streams swollen by melting snow. When at last they reached the Great Sandy River and launched canoes, Virginian mishandling resulted in the capsizing of two of the craft and the loss of essential weapons and powder. The 130 accompanying Cherokees led by Ostenaco left in disgust, their hopes of cultivating Virginia as an alternative to South Carolina sadly bruised.

Fort Cumberland, once perched on the fringe of settlement, was now far beyond the frontier and dangerously exposed. The Marylanders who usually provided its garrison had evacuated and withdrawn all their troops far to the east. Washington too would have abandoned the fort but he had to bow to the demands of Dinwiddie and Shirley, who wanted it as a base for future offensive operations. As a result, Virginian troops provided a new Fort Cumberland garrison just when they were desperately needed elsewhere. By the end of the year the Indians had taken 500 scalps and hundreds of prisoners to Fort Duquesne.

While Virginia's military system proved miserably inadequate, Pennsylvania's assembly spent the month debating the merits of forming the province's first militia and first provincial regiment. When the assembly and the proprietors reached an agreement over funding and the militarisation went ahead, most of the Quakers abandoned politics for pacifism. The new forces, however, did little to halt the raids. In August, 300 Pennsylvanians led by a Colonel John Armstrong struck back against Shingas's base at Upper Kittanning on the Allegheny. At dawn on 8 August they surprised the town but met with heavy resistance. Firing from his cabin window, Captain Jacobs picked off soldier after soldier while his wife reloaded his guns. Eventually the attackers torched the building and the gunpowder inside blew up, killing his whole family. As the soldiers retreated from the burning town with eleven rescued captives and a dozen scalps they split into several parties and were ambushed, losing seventeen dead, thirteen wounded and nineteen captured. Hardly even a Pyrrhic victory, the brutal destruction of Kittanning only provoked the Indians to intensify their raids. Even winter, the Indians' hunting season, brought only limited relief. Shingas was especially active, and in spring the defences of both provinces were overrun.[1]

On 30 July, Delawares and French struck Fort Granville on the Juniata River in Pennsylvania. Its position, perched on the brink of a ravine, provided the assailants with safe dead ground, and here they packed in cut undergrowth and fired it, setting the poles of the palisade ablaze and forcing the garrison to surrender. Once Granville was gone, Fort Shirley, further west at Aughwick, had to be evacuated. The frontier was now rolled back to within about 100 miles of Philadelphia and raiders were striking closer still.[2]

Further north, where Shirley had been planning attacks upon Crown Point and Fort Frontenac, combined French and Indian raids wrought havoc. In March 1756, 200 French soldiers and 100 Iroquois and Hurons attacked Fort Bull at Wood Creek, wiping out the garrison and firing the palisade and buildings. The consequent explosion of thousands of pounds weight of gunpowder was enormous. The raiders vanished back into the woods before the British could react. The crucial Oneida Carry now had no protection at all, and the whole Mohawk Valley was open to attack.[3]

Shirley soon built a new storehouse on the site and set eighty labourers to work to clear Wood Creek of obstacles; but there was still no security for Fort Oswego's bateau-borne supplies until Colonel John Bradstreet, a regular officer with a penchant for woodland warfare, raised and trained Rangers to escort them. By the summer the British could afford to be more optimistic: supplies reached Oswego, and the garrison tried to improve the fortifications. When newly arrived Lord Loudoun took over Shirley's command, he sent Major General Webb up with the regular 44th regiment, but when Webb reached German Flats on the upper Mohawk he heard reports of a major French attack. Whether that attack was imminent or had already happened, and whether the fort had held out or was taken, was unclear. Webb proposed to be intelligence led, edging forward to the Oneida Carry before deciding whether relief or recapture was possible. Loudoun approved but it was now 23 August, and, unknown to Loudoun, the fort had fallen ten days earlier.[4]

Fort was an optimistic name for the Oswego post. It consisted of three separate fortifications, each frighteningly vulnerable and unable to support the other two. The original trading post was in the western angle of the river and lake, with only a horn-work battery to protect its landward side, and overlooked by two hills well within artillery range. On these hills Shirley had built two forts, Ontario to the east and new Oswego to the west, but they too were rudimentary and unfit to withstand bombardment. The new Oswego was so flimsy that the officers and men called it Fort Rascal. Moreover, the 1,135 defenders were far too few to cope with the organised attack that began on 10 August 1756.

That afternoon, the finding of a scalped soldier's body was followed by a scouting schooner's discovery of Montcalm's camp. By evening, Indians were firing into the fort from the treetops. The simple wooden palisade and four rudimentary bastions of Fort Ontario were the first target. The digging of an entrenchment was followed by the construction of batteries, and on 12 August their guns began to batter in the stockade from close range. The garrison was withdrawn next day, which enabled the French to place twelve guns on the hilltop, able to fire directly down into the original post. Caught with his own cannon facing the wrong way, Colonel James Mercer ordered them turned round, but without earthworks to protect them the crews were hideously exposed. While this one-sided duel went on the French were seen crossing the river from east to west, out of range and too numerous to be checked by sortie, so the fort to the west had to be abandoned. At that point Mercer was beheaded by a round shot and his successor surrendered. Despite Montcalm's unenforceable promise to the contrary, his Indians now took their reward: thirty to a hundred soldiers' scalps, countless prisoners from their families, and huge quantities of rum and other loot. Montcalm had to pay out 8,000 to 10,000 livres to ransom even some of the captives.

Webb was at the Oneida Carry when he heard the news, together with a story that 6,000 enemies were even now bearing down on him. Should he stay and try to hold the portage against possibly overwhelming numbers? Or should he retreat to preserve his command? Whether out of panic or simple prudence, Webb opted for retreat, burning reconstructed Fort Bull and filling Wood Creek with felled trees to obstruct navigation. The Carry was thus left unfortified and the Mohawk settlements open to attack.[5]

In 1757 matters went from bad to worse. Orders from Britain forced Loudoun to abandon his planned offensive towards Crown Point, which would at least have had the merit of covering that part of the New York frontier. Instead he was to move all his available regulars by sea to Halifax, where he would meet reinforcements from Britain; then the whole force would proceed by sea to capture Louisbourg before pressing up the St Lawrence to Quebec. The seaborne movements were extremely hazardous in themselves – the Royal Navy was yet to fully establish its supremacy in European waters, let alone off North America – and completely ignored the threat of Franco-Amerindian thrusts like that against Oswego. The army and its reinforcements safely reached Halifax, but even there the forest war followed them. Foraging parties went into the surrounding woods and did not return; a boat was fired upon from the shore. Subsequent reconnaissance revealed that three French squadrons had crossed the Atlantic to concentrate at Louisbourg. An assault by sea was now too hazardous to be contemplated and Loudoun took his men back to New York by sea. On arrival he received unwelcome news: in his absence Montcalm had taken Fort William Henry.

Loudoun had handed the defence of New York to Daniel Webb, leaving him two regular regiments and 5,500 untried provincials. Fort William Henry, at the head of Lake George, was already vulnerable because in January a scout against Fort Carillon, conducted by 100 of Major Robert Rogers' Rangers, had been badly mauled. The survivors returned to Fort William Henry carrying a badly wounded Rogers and without a quarter of their original numbers. Meanwhile in March a brief raid had destroyed the fort's supply bateaux and a half-built sloop, leaving it with only one gunboat for waterborne reconnaissance. It was now impossible to determine what the French and their allies were up to, just as hundreds of Great Lakes Indians moved south. Through the spring and into the early summer they and Canadian militia hemmed in the garrison and attacked convoys on the road from Fort Edward. It was June before two escaped prisoners brought news of the 8,000-strong force gathering at the foot of the lake, and in July an attempted British raid was ambushed. On 3 August a huge flotilla of about 400 canoes and cannon-bearing bateaux appeared unopposed on the lake. The siege of Fort William Henry was about to begin.

Because the fort had good stocks of ammunition and because the commander, Lieutenant Colonel George Monro, had taken precautions against fire, it should have been possible for the garrison to hold out until Webb could relieve it. But Webb decided not to relieve the fort, at least not until he had himself received reinforcements at Fort Edward. If that could not be done, he advised Monro, Fort William Henry might have to surrender. Because the messenger carrying the letter was intercepted and killed, however, Monro did not receive it until 7 August, when it came to him courtesy of Montcalm. By that time the French had opened a parallel, established two batteries and sapped to within yards of the palisade, while their mortars and howitzers had the garrison under constant fire. By then half the ten British guns had burst through ceaseless firing, the bastions were seriously damaged, and the ammunition was all but gone. At dawn the defenders saw a new French battery of 18-pounders established close to the west wall. On the morning of 9 August, with the agreement of his officers, Monro sued for terms.[6]

The terms agreed by early afternoon were generous in the tradition of honours granted to a dogged defender. The British troops fit to march would leave for Fort Edward under escort, on condition that they did not serve again within eighteen months. The sick and wounded would remain to be cared for by the French until fit to travel. In return, Montcalm demanded the release of all French prisoners in the North American theatre along with what was left of Fort William Henry itself, its artillery and stores. From a European point of view these were the best and least humiliating terms Monro could have hoped for. Unfortunately, the French-allied Indians did not share that view, nor had they been consulted.[7]

The only substantial rewards expected by the Indians were plunder, scalps as proof of courage and skill, and prisoners for adoption or torture and execution. Montcalm told their chiefs that none of these things could be granted, so the warriors took matters into their own hands. As soon as the last British troops able to walk left the fort, Indians rushed in to kill the invalids and seize whatever else they could. Next morning the column of soldiers, families and camp followers starting for Fort Edward was attacked: before the French escort could restore order 185 people were killed and perhaps as many as 500 taken prisoner. About 500 were protected by the French while others sprinted headlong for Fort Edward. Then almost all of the Indians, laden with loot and trophies, decamped for home.[8]

Montcalm was horrified and in the following weeks he and his officers managed to buy back and release up to 200 of the Indians' prisoners. He and Vaudreuil, the governor of New France, feared that the British would mete out like treatment to French garrisons in the future and that the Indians would now be less willing to serve unreliable French paymasters. Their efforts were in vain: the captives and loot from Fort William Henry carried smallpox into towns across the *pays d'en haut*, and henceforth British officers were disinclined to offer honourable terms to French forces.[9]

Fort Edward was not attacked, partly because Montcalm's Indians had gone, partly because he was critically short of supplies, and also because his Canadian militia were anxious to return home for the harvest. But he had struck humiliating blows at British frontier security, in part because of strategic mistakes in London. Loudoun, who had already done much to adapt his troops to forest warfare, was about to be dismissed for obeying his orders.

9

PITT, RECOVERY AND CONQUEST

The collapse of the 1755 strategy caused alarm in London. Of course, the illusory victory at Lake George had to be played up – when news reached the English capital, Johnson was made a baronet. More urgently, the ministry needed to find a way of continuing the war in North America without precipitating a wider conflict with France. To make things worse, Newcastle's suspicions of Hapsburg intentions and fears for the safety of Hanover had already caused him to reach an understanding with Russia. Now, on 16 January 1756, he turned to Prussia for the same purpose, hoping to maintain some kind of balance that would ensure British immunity from any European war.

Meanwhile, the American situation had to be confronted. Halifax wanted a thoroughgoing reform of the war effort and of colonial administration: a new commander-in-chief, a royal commission for Johnson, a central provisions storehouse paid for directly by the Crown, more regulars for America and more provincials. But even now Halifax could not have it all his own way. On 7 January 1756, the Cabinet, having seen Johnson's criticisms of Shirley and well aware of the latter's significance for Indian affairs, approved the first two proposals but rejected the others on the grounds of cost. At a subsequent meeting, Fox and Cumberland, doubting the discipline and competence of provincial troops, pressed for six more British regular regiments – two to be sent from Britain and four more to be raised in America. They also wanted to appoint Edmund Atkin as Superintendent of Indian Affairs in the southern colonies and send a regular to replace Shirley, who was (unjustly) suspected of being the source of military information leaked to the governor of New France. Shirley was already known to confuse the king's service with his own economic interests, and was in any case an amateur soldier.[1]

Atkin, who had been lobbying ministers since his arrival in London in 1750, had produced three substantial documents on southern Indian affairs. The first was an account of the Choctaw Revolt of 1746, effectively a civil war in which a faction favouring a British alliance was heavily defeated. Atkin blamed the failure upon a triumvirate – two South Carolina traders and the province's governor, James Glen, who had first incited the revolt and then failed to provide the necessary weapons. The other two, both written in 1755, were a detailed report on the state of southern Indian affairs and a plan for their better management. Each of these documents was written for Halifax's Board of Trade, so the fact that his core idea was put forward by the Cumberland–Fox faction suggests a continuing accommodation between the two. In particular, Atkin recommended the appointment of a single superintendent to co-ordinate the southern colonies' relations with the Cherokees, Catawbas, Creeks, Chickasaws and Choctaws.[2]

The outcome was a substantial vindication of the Halifax policy of imperial centralisation. Johnson and Atkin would be Superintendent of Indian Affairs in the northern and southern districts respectively. Loudoun became the new commander-in-chief in place of Shirley with authority over the superintendents, while John Pownall's brother Thomas – who had intrigued against Shirley – became the new governor of Massachusetts.

As we have seen, Shirley's replacement was John Campbell, 4th Earl of Loudoun, a reliable professional soldier and experienced military administrator, who had begun his career in the Royal North British Dragoons, informally known as the Scots Greys. Having led a volunteer regiment against the Jacobites in 1745 and 1746, he could be said to have some knowledge of irregular warfare. It was Cumberland, supported by Fox and Halifax, who offered him the American command, as well as the raising of a new multi-battalion unit, the Royal American Regiment, and the nominal governorship of Virginia.[3]

The French were now known to be assembling two expeditions: a force intended to invade the British Isles was gathering on the Channel coast, and another – guessed to be aimed at Minorca – was preparing at Toulon. Faced with two threats and a slow naval mobilisation – hampered all the more by the return of Boscawen's crews, now ridden with fever – the Admiralty opted for home defence. All available ships were assigned to the Western Squadron in the Channel approaches and it was March 1756 before any could be spared for Gibraltar or Minorca. In that same month the French decided that while a cross-Channel invasion was too perilous, under-garrisoned Minorca was highly vulnerable. The wider war dreaded by Newcastle was thus triggered not by American events but by an attack upon Britain's key naval base in the Mediterranean.[4]

The Toulon fleet sailed unopposed, and on 18 April 12,000 French troops landed unopposed on Minorca, laying siege to the unexpectedly formidable Fort Philip at the entrance to Port Mahon. This would be an unexpectedly slow conquest, allowing plenty of time for relief to arrive. Britain declared war on 17 May and three days later Admiral John Byng fought an indecisive action with the French covering squadron before precipitately retiring to Gibraltar. The abandoned and hungry Minorca garrison surrendered on 29 June. The outcome undermined the credibility of the Newcastle ministry and sowed distrust between its members. Henry Fox resigned in

October, leaving Newcastle without a minister capable of leading the Commons. As William Pitt was the only plausible replacement, George II was obliged to accept Newcastle's advice, swallow his personal detestation of the man, and appoint him Southern Secretary on 4 December. The Treasury was taken by the Duke of Devonshire, but it was Pitt who dominated the new government.

Pitt was an opposition Whig, one of the 'Patriots' who had harried both Walpole and Newcastle, demanding a blue-water foreign policy and denouncing European entanglements, particularly the king's preoccupation with Hanover. Unstable, manic and inclined to hyperbole, Pitt's extravagant speeches provoked more amusement than admiration. By 1757 he had gout which hampered his attention to business. While he had important followers in the Commons, the ministry was largely composed of Newcastle loyalists. Thanks to his weakness he had to approve subsidies for German allies, notably Prussia, and obtained a vote of £200,000 to support an Army of Observation in Hanover. Even then his influence was limited by the presence of Cumberland who, though appointed to command in Germany, was reluctant to leave London with Pitt still in office. Pitt was even unable to put off the execution of Byng, who had been indicted for not doing his utmost to carry out his orders.

None of that prevented Pitt from designing an extravagant and flawed American strategy. Loudoun had wanted to defend the southern and middle colonies' frontiers while launching an overland assault on Quebec, a choice which would ensure the security of New York and the New England colonies. In February 1757, however, Pitt overruled him, ordering a seaborne attack on Louisbourg and thence by the St Lawrence to Quebec. Logistically a much easier option, the scheme assumed British naval superiority in those waters and left the vulnerable frontiers needlessly exposed. On 6 April, long before the outcome of this adventure could be known, George II dismissed Pitt.[5]

In June, however he was back. It was as impossible to form a stable ministry without him as it was for Pitt to do without Newcastle. The latter became First Lord of the Treasury while Pitt resumed his work in the Southern Department. It was once orthodoxy to think of this government as binary – Pitt as war minister, Newcastle as manager of patronage and majorities – but in fact the partnership was more collaborative than divided.

The additional regiments sent to reinforce Loudoun in America were a sore point with Cumberland, now in Germany, heavily outnumbered and, as he saw it, abandoned by an uncaring ministry. On 26 July he was defeated at Hastenbeck and soon after was forced to sign the Convention of Kloster-Zevern, agreeing to disband the Army of Observation and to allow the French to occupy most of Hanover. Hastenbeck and Kloster-Zevern were a godsend for William Pitt. They destroyed George II's faith in Cumberland – 'Here is my son, who has ruined me and disgraced himself' were the words that greeted the duke's return to court – and forced his immediate resignation. Pitt now had no serious rival in the Cabinet and the king was more inclined to listen to him. George II's confidence and his own alliance with Newcastle made Pitt almost politically invulnerable: and in his role as Southern Secretary he was able to veto any unwelcome proposals from Halifax at the Board of Trade, or indeed from anyone else. He was able to insert Lord Ligonier into Cumberland's place at the head of the army, and appoint Lord Anson to lead the Admiralty, two astonishingly capable and loyal men upon whom he could lean for advice. Yet, his decisions were his own and usually based on personal judgement. Moreover, Newcastle's management of finance and parliamentary majorities left Pitt free to pull together the old themes of continental commitment and blue-water strategy into a coherent whole.[6]

Pitt was also flexible, though some of that came from confrontation with the realities of office rather than from intellectual agility. To keep the king's favour he could not abandon Hanover, and, as Newcastle had long argued, France's superior resources meant it had to be diverted by a European ally. That ally was of course Prussia, now under extreme pressure from Austrian and Russian armies; so while Pitt wanted to focus as much military strength as possible upon North America, he was now prepared to support Frederick II with almost unlimited subsidies. Though such financial recklessness could and did alarm the First Lord of the Treasury, strategically there was little choice but to seek out the loans Pitt's plans required.

The 1757 attempt to seize Louisbourg had come undone because the Royal Navy could not yet achieve sustained supremacy in America and home at the same time. Undeterred, the Pitt–Newcastle ministry's strategy for the following year aimed at nothing less than the complete conquest of Canada, an enterprise demanding powerful naval support. There was to be a three-pronged assault on New France that was superficially reminiscent of the plan so tragically foisted onto Braddock. Now, however, the main effort was to be by sea against Louisbourg and Quebec, led by two officers brought in from Europe, Jeffery Amherst and James Wolfe. A third, young Lord Howe, was chosen to second as commander-in-chief. Abercromby – who was to replace Loudoun as commander-in-chief – would push north from Albany to take Ticonderoga and Crown Point, so seizing control of Lake Champlain and threatening Montreal. Meanwhile, a second march on the Ohio country, now demoted to a secondary theatre, was to be led by John Forbes, Loudoun's former adjutant general. There was to be no repetition of Shirley's Niagara expedition, nor of the alternative being touted by Colonel John Bradstreet, namely a raid against Fort Frontenac. To ensure colonial co-operation he reversed the Halifax drive towards some kind of imperial unity, removed the commander-in chief's nascent viceregal powers, and offered the assemblies subsidies in return for their support for the war effort. Indian affairs did not in themselves interest him; they hardly figure in his correspondence. In sum, he placed most of the financial burden upon the British taxpayer and undermined any attempt at a coherent management of Indian affairs. Frontier matters were now in the hands of energetic men on the spot, and they were of course a very mixed bag.

Nor were Pitt's military appointments as inspired as it was once conventional to believe. Cold Jeffrey Amherst and neurotic James Wolfe, neither of whom had American or independent command experience, were promoted over the heads of sound officers already serving under Loudoun. Both came to detest Indians, in Amherst's case with tragic long-term consequences. Pitt also sacked Loudoun, who had laboured to train and equip his men for American conditions, and allowed the mediocre Abercromby to succeed him.

Yet it worked. In 1758 Abercromby was bloodily repulsed at Ticonderoga, but Wolfe and Amherst seized Louisbourg, Forbes forced the French to abandon Fort Duquesne and Bradstreet bounced a chastened Abercromby into permitting a successful assault on Frontenac. In 1759 the French were defeated at Minden in Germany and twin naval victories at Lagos and Quiberon Bay made it impossible for France to reinforce Canada; at the same time, the West Indian sugar islands of Guadeloupe and Martinique, which Pitt thought essential to France's maritime economy and naval power, were taken. Wolfe died in capturing Quebec, and Amherst, now commander-in-chief, took both Ticonderoga and Crown Point. The British at Quebec survived a winter counter-attack, and in 1760 Montreal fell to Amherst. The following year saw the surrender of Canada and the occupation of all but the most distant French posts. Now Britain had a frontier problem of unprecedented proportions, one which Pitt was not equipped to manage.

Ironically, it was Pitt's very success that helped to bring him down. The death of George II in 1760 had brought to the throne a young man well schooled in the ideal of 'Patriot' kingship, fostered by his tutor, John Stuart, Earl of Bute. George III was determined to free himself from what he believed to be the slavery of the old Whig politicians and to choose his ministers by ability, not by party. He was not slow to develop a distaste for both Newcastle and Pitt, whom he blamed for continuing a bloody and now unnecessary war, and a determination to appoint his former tutor to the head of government. Bute, the Groom of the Stole, was admitted to the Cabinet in October 1760 and became Secretary of State for the Northern Department in March of the following year. Meanwhile in the summer of 1761, Pitt hoped to weaken Bute and deflect royal determination to abandon Prussia. To do so, he was about to widen the war still further.

In the summer of 1761 Pitt received intelligence that Spain, deeply alarmed by the scale of British victories, was about to declare war on the side of France. The Spanish government would not move until its annual treasure fleet from the Caribbean was safely berthed in Cadiz, so Pitt wanted to strike it pre-emptively, without a declaration of war. He had a firm ally in his brother-in-law Lord Temple, the Lord Privy Seal, but their Cabinet colleagues were not impressed, and nor was the king. Newcastle and the others had the debacle of Boscawen's 1756 expedition in mind, as well as the vast and spiralling costs of the war, not to mention the opprobrium inevitably associated with an unprovoked act of aggression. Such a stroke would violate the terms of a new loan from the City of London bankers, and it would paint Britain as a wanton aggressor. Far better to respond if and when war did break out. Outvoted, Pitt and Temple threatened to appeal to the king, a move which of course came to nothing, and in October both resigned. Halifax was moved to the Admiralty, Bedford replaced Temple, and the hitherto undistinguished Earl of Egremont became Southern Secretary.[7]

10

THE FORBES EXPEDITION AND THE TREATY OF EASTON

John Forbes (1707–59) was a youngest son who had given up medicine for soldiering. After serving as regimental surgeon in the Royal North British Dragoons (the Scots Greys), where he met his friend Loudoun, he bought an ensign's commission and distinguished himself in combat and as a staff officer during the War of the Austrian Succession. At the end of the war he became the Greys' lieutenant-colonel, but rapid promotion through purchase and the need to live as an officer left him £5,000 in debt and in desperate need of a colonelcy or a staff position. He applied unsuccessfully to be Braddock's quartermaster general and for a lucrative staff post in Ireland, and had at his creditors' insistence to turn down the offer of a battalion in the Royal Americans. In the end he had to accept the command of an infantry regiment earmarked for America, just as his health began to fail and he was looking for a little comfort and ease. The silver lining in this cloud was that Lord Loudoun was commander-in chief there, and on arrival in 1757 Forbes became his adjutant general. While in New York and Albany his mind fizzed with ideas, not all of them to Loudoun's liking: cutting a canal through the shallows on the upper Hudson, preferring provincial Rangers to Gage's new light infantry regiment, urging the building of a new fort on the Oneida Carry. There he also conceived a thorough dislike of Sir William Johnson's self-seeking posturing. In 1758 he became brigadier general commanding the new expedition against Fort Duquesne, the most difficult and least glorious of all the planned thrusts against New France.

Whatever his misgivings and state of health, Forbes took his role very seriously. Before leaving Britain he had read – in the original French, before its translation into English – Turpin de Crisse's *Essay on the Art of War* which advocated the use of light troops to screen the regular army, to gather intelligence and to evade and lay ambushes. This reinforced Forbes's own experiences at Fontenoy in 1745, where he had seen a key British thrust pinned down through fear of irregulars defending a wood, and had later himself been captured by surprise in the middle of the night. Here was a man inclined to value woodland tactics and Indian auxiliaries, as well as diplomatic attempts to detach the Indians from their French ally. He was already convinced that their demands were few and modest.

Crisse also advocated a 'protected advance', securing lines of supply and communication with forts at strategic intervals. That too was a departure from Braddock, whose rear had been constantly threatened by raiding parties.

Before Forbes could apply these principles, he had to assemble an army. When he reached Philadelphia in April there was no sign of Montgomery's Highlanders supposed to be coming from South Carolina, nor of the Swiss mercenary Colonel Henry Bouquet with his battalion of Royal Americans. Nor had the expected provincial troops from Virginia and Maryland arrived, and even those raised by Pennsylvania were few, undernourished and ill-armed. Pennsylvanians were also reluctant to supply the necessary wagons and horses, a situation exacerbated by the eccentric and incompetent Sir John St Clair, the quartermaster general whom Forbes had long known as 'a mad kind of Fool'.[1]

His Cherokee scouts, on the other hand, were already waiting, impatiently demanding arms, equipment and presents that Forbes did not possess. Two self-proclaimed Cherokee experts appeared, but the general rightly expected little from them. One was James Glen, his own cousin and former governor of South Carolina, and the other was Abraham Bosomworth, who really was more intimate with Creeks. Forbes sent Bosomworth up to talk to the Cherokees but more to keep him happy than from any hope of success. In the end, the role of Indian coordinator went to a Virginian provincial colonel named William Byrd who was a plausible gentleman and a friend. It was the first of only two serious mistakes on Forbes's part.

He tried vainly to get the Pennsylvanians to release weapons kept in the provincial arms store and in the governor's palace, and before long the disgruntled Cherokees were drifting home, stealing horses and clashing with Virginian back settlers as they went. It was almost June before the troops were ready and even then he had to delay his own departure, being 'much out of order with a kind of Cholera Morbus'. It was August before he could sort out the advanced camp at Carlisle, decide upon the best route to Fort Duquesne and recover sufficiently to begin the march forward.

Virginia too tended to put parochial aims ahead of imperial goals. Its promised regiment arrived late and even then its commander, George Washington, took it upon himself to dictate the general's chosen line of advance. In July, while Forbes had several officers and 100 men at work evaluating the possibilities of Braddock's Road as opposed to a shorter route by way of Laurel Hill, Washington and Byrd persuaded St Clair that the Braddock road was the only viable option, and St Clair obligingly recommended that way to Forbes. It was arguable, of course, that although it would need clearing of three years of growth it was at least known, and would avoid having to hack a new path through hundreds of miles of forest. Washington neglected to mention that it passed very close to his own land and that once the French were expelled it would give Virginia first and best access to the lands coveted by the Ohio Company – in short, it would deny easy access to Pennsylvanians. To many Virginians that was the main purpose of the war.

Forbes of course took the view that the war was an imperial effort that required provinces to pool their resources under the direction of the king's own appointed commander – and by the end of the month overwhelming evidence showed that the shorter road would be better in terms of time, cost, likely resistance and viability for loaded wagons. Washington arranged a private meeting with Bouquet, who was shocked by the Virginians' partisanship, observing to Forbes that 'most of these gentlemen do not know the difference between a party and an army, and find everything easy that agrees with their ideas, jumping over all the difficulties'. Next Washington abused both Forbes and Bouquet to the speaker of the Virginian assembly as being in the pockets of Pennsylvanian contractors.

At last, perceiving that Forbes, Bouquet, Glen and others had weighed the options and fixed their choice, he wrote to Forbes's own brigade major, Francis Halkett. They had known each other since the Braddock campaign, and Washington had been carefully cultivating him as a confidential friend. Urging Halkett to intervene on behalf of the Braddock road, he added disingenuously, 'I am uninfluenced by Prejudice – having no hope or fears but for the General Good.' Forbes was furious when he came across this letter – presumably the loyal and honest Halkett showed it to him – and described it as 'a scheme that I think was a shame for any officer to be concerned in' and Washington's conduct as 'no ways like a Soldier'. Here were the two clashing views of empire and frontier management which would bring America to revolution. [2]

Logistics and internal bickering were exasperating but they allowed time in which pursue negotiations which might detach the Ohio Indians from their French allies. In theory such approaches should have been made by Johnson, whom Forbes had met in Albany and thoroughly disliked. His feeling was exacerbated by the baronet's insistence on controlling Indian diplomacy while doing nothing to negotiate with the Ohio Indians. Fortunately, Forbes had obtained Abercromby's permission to negotiate with Indians, wording his request so generally he seemed to refer to the Cherokees and Catawbas. He then used that consent to develop his own diplomatic initiative. He made discreet contact with the Quaker leader Israel Pemberton, urging him to sound out the Susquehanna Delawares' readiness to approach their western brethren. The Friends sent one of their own, Charles Thompson, with the Moravian Christian Frederick Post, to Wyoming, but rumours of peace had travelled before them. When they arrived they found waiting Pisquetomen, brother to the Ohio war leaders Shingas and Tamaqua. Post and Thompson brought him back to Philadelphia, where the provincial assembly refused to authorise negotiations on the rather spurious grounds that they were bound by Johnson's authority, but perhaps also sensing that genuine negotiations would require territorial concessions. Forbes, however, used Abercromby's consent to push Governor Denny into action.

Denny, for his part, had to be careful of the proprietors' attitude. On one hand they liked the idea of direct negotiations with the Ohio Indians, so bypassing Teedyuscung and avoiding having to deal with his land claims. On the other they did not wish to give up any land claims they might themselves make in the future. The governor had therefore to insist that the peace proposals must not mention land fraud, that the boundary issue was to be discussed only in vague terms, and that the Quakers must be cut out of the negotiations. Thompson was not allowed to travel with Pisquetomen and Post when they left Philadelphia on 15 July.

The Ohio Indians were desperate for peace but very wary of British intentions. When Shingas met Post at the Delaware town of Kuskusky, about 20 miles short of Fort Duquesne, he was without his brothers and very blunt about his fears of dispossession. Most of the Shawnees did not appear at all. Daringly, Post therefore went to them at their camp outside Fort Duquesne under the noses of the French garrison; but even then the Indians wanted peace without swapping a French occupation for a British one, and wanted nothing to do with whatever might have been agreed with Teedyuscung. Many Shawnees continued to back the French and launch harassing raids against Forbes's slowly advancing column. Some Delawares agreed to cease hostilities for the time being but would not take up the hatchet for the British. They would only agree to send Pisquetomen to meet the Pennsylvanians at Easton. Meanwhile, Forbes had been encouraging the Quakers by letter and it was his interventions that overcame Pennsylvania's and Johnson's hostility to their participation in the coming congress. Unfortunately, he could not be at Easton to ensure that the Quakers were heard when the talks actually began.

Despite all this particularist meddling and the incessant delays, by the end of August the road over the ridge called Laurel Hill was complete. An advance guard of 1,500 men and some artillery was now at Loyalhannon, on the western side of the hill and only 40 miles short of Fort Duquesne. Forbes, though by now being carried in a horse litter, was hopeful of breaking ground before the fort within the month.

Major James Grant, second-in-command of Montgomery's Highlanders and a good regimental officer, was almost comically ambitious, socially, financially and professionally. A younger son of the Laird of Ballindalloch in Scotland's Spey Valley, he was determined to use his service to acquire his own estate and 'an establishment in London'; in 1770, after unexpectedly inheriting Ballindalloch, he said, 'My Intention with regard to futurity, is to have a good house in London, a good Cook, good Dinner, good Claret, and good everything as far as I can to make my Friends Welcome & Merry.' He got on well with Forbes and became a good friend of Colonel Henry Bouquet, the able Swiss mercenary commanding the Royal Americans, whom he had met at Charleston in 1757 when they bonded over a sharp quartering dispute with the colony. Small wonder that when Bouquet wanted a good officer with him at Loyalhannon, he asked for Grant.

Back in Carlisle, Grant had asked Forbes for permission to lead a raid against Fort Duquesne, promising to be wary of ambush and not to launch a premature attack. He had been firmly refused at the time, but now that he was being pushed forward with two companies of Highlanders he saw an opportunity for unauthorised action. His first stop was at a fort named after Loudoun, where some Cherokees had been reported to be restless. Upon arriving he found them agreeable rogues who had done nothing worse than to steal a few horses, and his skill in calming the situation revealed a penchant for the manners and subtle prevarications of Indian diplomacy. Then he pressed on to Loyalhannon and his friend Bouquet.

Here the persuasive Grant seems to have convinced Bouquet that a reconnaissance in force – of the very sort that Forbes had forbidden – might surprise the fort and end the campaign at a stroke. It might also win him glory, promotion and perhaps even that elusive estate. The lateness of the campaign left a very small window before the onset of winter snows, and incoming reports of the garrison's numerical weakness and shortage of supplies were tantalising. And just as Forbes, so remote from his chief, could indulge in forbidden negotiations with Indians and Quakers, so Grant and Bouquet – who had been repeatedly ordered to offer the French no provocation – were tempted to launch a sudden coup which their absent commander would never have permitted.

The result was a perfectly avoidable disaster. Grant's hand-picked force of 850 Highlanders and provincials achieved complete surprise but were puzzled as to what to do next. An outlying Indian camp was empty. An outbuilding was fired in an attempt to lure the garrison into the open, but the French were used to such accidents and ignored it. At dawn Grant was reduced to posting Andrew

Lewis's Virginians in ambush to his rear, while the Highlanders – drums rolling – demonstrated on a hill in plain view of the fort. The gates opened and out poured a torrent of French and Indians, far more than Grant thought could possibly have been in there, and enveloped the little British force on the hill. The Pennsylvanians fled while the Highlanders stood their ground and were shot to pieces. Grant surrendered and was packed off to Montreal, a prisoner.

Forbes was appalled at Grant's foolishness and Bouquet's complicity, observing that 'the rashness and ambition of some people brings great mischief and distress upon their friends'. As for Grant personally, he had 'by his thirst of fame, brought on his own perdition, and run a great risque of ours'. On 12 October a sudden sortie by 800 to 900 French and 100 Indians against Loyalhannon seemed to bring that threat of perdition home. At the very least the raiders could drive off or destroy the army's cattle, horses and wagons; at best they might even overrun the camp where Bouquet was building Fort Ligonier. The raiders were detected before they could attack but they drove back three successive waves of provincials sent out against them and, although repulsed from the breastworks by musket and artillery fire, retired with all the post's horses. Forbes was distressed that the marauders were not pursued and routed, although he felt obliged to transform the combat into a victory. 'I puffed up everything,' he wrote, 'and ordered a general *Feu de Joy*', but he knew that everything now depended on the outcome at Easton.

In the midst of these rather faux celebrations, Attakullakulla appeared with forty Cherokee warriors and perhaps as many Catawbas. He was on a diplomatic mission to Williamsburg in Virginia, hoping to check the bloodshed provoked by the clashes between frontier settlers and disappointed Cherokees returning home. He did not make this fact clear in his conferences with Forbes, though he made several speeches warning of a coming Anglo-Cherokee conflict, so when Forbes insisted that they scout for him they demanded a high price in presents. Forbes, naturally

The Forbes Expedition and the Treaty of Easton

assuming that he was being blackmailed, took a disdainful line in public talks, hoping perhaps for a more amicable arrangement behind the scenes. The Indians then volunteered to scout for the army as a favour and as a token of their loyalty. Catawba and Cherokee parties scoured the woods ahead of the army, while Forbes waited and hoped for a settlement at Easton.

When the congress met in October perhaps 500 Indians were present. The ubiquitous Croghan had at last come to represent Johnson and to defend Iroquois claims, as had representatives of the Six Nations. The Western Delawares led by Shingas and Pisquetomen were there, and Teedyuscung arrived claiming to be sole Delaware spokesman and to press his claims of fraud against Pennsylvania. Governor Denny and Richard Peters were keen to avoid making concessions to the Eastern Delawares and to exclude the Quakers led by Israel Pemberton. It was clear that not all these aims could be reconciled or satisfied.

The Pennsylvanians and the Iroquois therefore combined to bypass the Eastern Delawares, a goal assisted by the alcoholism that undermined Teedyuscung's influence and too often clouded his judgement. Denny first promised the return of all lands west of the Alleghenies – that is about half of those gained four years earlier at Albany – but then restored them not to the Eastern Delawares but to the Iroquois. That forced Teedyuscung to change his demands to a request for an Iroquois guarantee of continued possession of Wyoming and for compensation for lands taken by the Walking Purchase, which was ignored. The last business of the congress was to agree a boundary between the Iroquois lands and the Ohio country. With that making the Ohio Indians feel secure and ready to desert the failing French, there was no need for Pennsylvania to appease the Susquehanna Delawares. The outcome concluded on 26 October was not quite what Forbes had wanted, but at least the Lenape and Shawnees had promised to abandon the French. It was some weeks before he knew that the agreement was having its intended effect.

In mid-November, Attakullakulla encountered some Indians who had deserted the French and was told that the French were about to blow up and abandon Fort Duquesne. The campaign was effectively over, and now another crucial mutual misunderstanding rose to the surface. Attakullakulla decided that his presence was no longer necessary, and after reporting their intelligence the Cherokees and Catawbas took horse for Virginia. This was exactly within the rules of warriors accompanying any war party: when you're no longer needed, you can go home. Forbes, ill and anxious, interpreted their departure as desertion, and perhaps even the first event of the Anglo-Cherokee war the Carpenter had predicted. He had them intercepted, disarmed and relieved of their horses, though not of the presents they had received for their service. In this way he hoped to present his action as one of discipline, not of ingratitude, but those who captured the Cherokees took away their goods anyway. The matter was smoothed over but the damage was done: whereas nothing could have appeased Washington and Byrd, humiliating the Cherokees' most prominent diplomat was bound to bring lasting resentment. Cross-cultural confusions could sour the actions of even such well-intentioned men as Attakullakulla and Forbes.

In fact, the Carpenter's intelligence was correct. The commandant at Fort Duquesne had for some time been worried about supplies, the size of his garrison and the deteriorating mood of his Indians: had Forbes struck at once he might have captured the fort intact. Days after the Cherokees' departure, three prisoners taken near Loyalhannon confirmed their story. Forbes at once pushed his light troops forward but too late: on 24 November the sound of a gigantic explosion was followed by a huge plume of black smoke. That evening the Catawbas led the first British troops into the smouldering ruins of Fort Duquesne.

From this moment on every move made by Forbes and Bouquet was meant to secure the trust and loyalty of the Ohio Indians so lately allied with the French. The fort they built there and called 'Pittsburgh' was nothing like the huge fortification later called Fort Pitt. A plain palisade with four rudimentary bastions, it was designed to do no more than repel a sudden French raid – and certainly not to overawe the Delawares, Shawnees and Mingos. There is no sign that either Amherst or the home government had anything larger planned at this stage, and Forbes wrote repeatedly to his commander-in-chief to stress that the whole British position depended upon honouring the Treaty of Easton. Forbes was building not just a new fortification but an entire Indian-centred frontier policy.

It remained for Post and Pisquetomen to convince the Ohio nations to accept the deal hammered out by their leaders at Easton. Even Pisquetomen was uneasy about British ambitions, asking publicly why such a large army and such wide roads were needed to drive away the French, whose security had depended upon having Indian allies. A detour to visit Forbes did nothing to mollify him or the Indians who joined him en route, especially when at Lancaster they were jeered by angry Scots-Irish frontiersmen. On 25 November, the day Forbes's men occupied the ruins of Fort Duquesne, Shingas and Tamaqua met them at Kuskusky.

Forbes, all too well aware of Indian fears, wrote repeatedly to Amherst, urging him to come personally to reassure them with solid guarantees, ruthlessly playing on their old comradeship in Flanders and repeatedly addressing the commander-in-chief as 'dear Jeff'. All was in vain. Amherst certainly had other matters on his mind, but nor did he have much patience for placating recently hostile Indians – an attitude which would later provoke the greatest Anglo-Amerindian war of them all.

In the depths of a bitter winter, John Forbes, who might have led Indian policy to a much happier place, was carried over the mountains to die in Philadelphia. He was given a warm welcome and a hero's funeral, and consigned to an unmarked grave.

11

SOUTHERN CRISIS

Attakullakulla had been brought to Virginia by repeated reports of violence between frontier settlers and Cherokee warriors who were returning from the Forbes expedition bitter at the lack of equipment, presents and action. By June, all but the fifty-seven Cherokees recruited by Byrd had departed, some plundering houses and stealing horses as they went. Armed Virginians pursued them and there were firefights with deaths on both sides. By the Cheroke law of vengeance, their own losses needed be wiped away with an equal number of scalps from the other side. There was already a danger of a war with Virginia, and it would not be long before the reciprocal violence spread southward. So the Carpenter set out for Williamsburg, where despite his treatment at Forbes's hands he made conciliatory speeches and even apologised for what Lieutenant Governor Francis Fauquier was pleased to call his 'scandalous Behaviour'. When he returned to the Cherokee country in March 1759, he counselled peace rather than war and travelled on to Charleston to placate the governor, William Henry Lyttelton. At three meetings from 17 to 21 April, he convinced Lyttelton that he was a friend and had bound himself to keep the Cherokee nation at peace.

On 25 and 26 April 1759, three Cherokee war parties struck at settlements on the Yadkin and Catawba rivers inside North

Carolina, killing and scalping at least twenty settlers, nearly half of them children. The Cherokees' principal leader was Moitoi of Settico, who had set off on his raid the very day he received a message from Attakullakulla urging Cherokees to wait quietly because he had already settled matters with Virginia. This was more than ritualised revenge killing: it was a deliberate attempt to provoke war in the Carolinas. Other headmen were appalled: Connecorte, his heir Standing Turkey and Oconostota met the commandant at Fort Loudoun to offer reassurances.

Lyttelton too was shocked at this first strike within South Carolina's sphere. He and his council wanted to reassert the colony's supremacy in Indian affairs and to pre-empt any criticism for being slow to protect settlers. They therefore insisted that the killers be surrendered at once, thereby refusing to accept that Cherokee headmen could not surrender warriors who took revenge, just as the Cherokees failed to realise that Lyttelton could not overlook the killing of women and children so close to home. The demand alienated the Cherokees most anxious to remain on good terms with him, and their refusal fuelled his own darkening suspicions. His fears were further fed by reports that a persistently hostile Creek leader known as the Mortar had been urging the Cherokees to take up the hatchet. By July, worried that a Creek–Cherokee onslaught would coincide with a slave revolt, he turned for aid to the Catawbas.

This small nation, now a congeries of broken coastal tribes, boasted no more than 150 warriors. Frequently raided by Iroquois, they now faced a Cherokee conflict after a Cherokee woman was killed in one of their towns and the Cherokees had returned the compliment. Despite North Carolina's unfulfilled pledge to build a fort for their protection, the Catawbas' leader, King Hagler, knew he need support from South Carolina as well. He wanted Lyttelton to build a protective fort and send a trader with supplies of powder. If the price had to be involvement in a Cherokee–South

Carolina conflict, so be it. Lyttelton accepted, though he implied that he would be the one to choose the moment for open conflict, not his ally.

From here the situation rapidly deteriorated, partly due to Lyttelton's perceived obtuseness and arrogance, but also because the young officers at Fort Prince George had crossed the line between Cherokee women's sexual freedom and outright rape. At Fort Loudoun, a junior officer who sold rum to Indians was merely reposted to Fort Prince George. In August Lyttelton's council cut off traders' supplies of ammunition, provoking in the Cherokees a fear that the British were trying to destroy them. When the Cherokees objected, he responded disdainfully, saying he would only deal with a properly accredited delegation sent down to Charleston. The Cherokee reaction was to blockade Fort Loudoun while an embassy of leading headmen went down to Charleston to have one last try for peace.[1]

The delegation, comprising thirty-eight headmen including Oconostota, represented a brave effort by the more responsible Cherokee leaders to snatch peace from the jaws of war. Lyttelton, however, already convinced that war was inevitable, did not wait for them to arrive. On 30 September, having refused Amherst's offer of a small force of redcoats, he called out the provincial militia. Half of those mobilised were to march on Keowee, without the assistance of other colonies or of regular troops. The expedition was clearly designed to assert South Carolina's primacy in Indian affairs, and to assure the assembly that the troops would remain within the province. It was less effective as a means of conducting diplomacy.

When the delegates arrived in October, Lyttelton refused their overtures and made demands for the surrender of murderers – a one-sided offer that the Cherokees were never really expected to accept. He would not give them time to consult the nation because he was determined to use the militia while it was still assembled.

He led the little army himself as it began to march on Keowee, taking the Cherokee emissaries with him: before very long they found themselves to be hostages. The governor's inability to conceive of treating Indians on anything like equal terms had made war inevitable.[2]

The Lower Cherokees now faced a difficult decision. The more emotionally satisfying option – which appealed to most of the young men – would be to ambush him at the difficult crossing of the Twelve Mile River. The headmen, however, pointed out that this would probably mean the deaths of the hostages, and it was their view which prevailed. Lyttelton was allowed to reach Keowee in safety, but there he found Attakullakulla, now under extreme pressure to join the war party, speaking conciliatory words without offering the satisfaction South Carolina demanded. With an army never more than 1,300 strong and with smallpox ravaging his camp, Lyttelton was in no position to threaten fire and sword. Instead, on 24 December he released three of his hostages, including Oconostota, and lodged the rest in Fort Prince George as security against the handing over of the Cherokee killers. In theory the Cherokee prisoners were to be released one by one as the guilty warriors came in. It was in fact a recipe for war.[3]

12

THE ANGLO-CHEROKEE WAR

The Treaty of Keowee was both humiliating and unenforceable. The warlike leaders launched raid upon raid on the Carolinian settlements. At Raeburn's Creek some twenty-seven settlers were slaughtered and on 1 February about a hundred warriors killed more than fifty Long Canes refugees at a river crossing. Frontier forts were attacked: Fort Loudoun was isolated; Fort Prince George, where Lyttelton's hostages were left confined, was encircled; lower down the country, Ninety Six was attacked. Fort Augusta on the Savannah was blockaded, and Fort Dobbs in North Carolina withstood assaults. Within weeks the Cherokees had swept the frontier of settlement 100 miles towards the sea. In desperation, Lyttelton turned to Amherst for the help he had earlier so easily spurned.[1]

Then came one last disastrous atrocity. At Fort Prince George, Oconostota, having failed to persuade Ensign Coytmore to surrender his captives, lured the officer out of the fort to his death in ambush. The infuriated garrison then massacred the prisoners, most likely by firing down into their crowded prison through holes in the roof. When the besieging Cherokees realised what had happened, they tightened their investment and fired into the fort from the neighbouring hills. What was left of Attakullakulla's influence evaporated: now the nation would fight until all their losses were fully avenged.[2]

Amherst's relief force of 1,373 seasoned regulars, a battalion each from the 77th Highlanders and the Royal Scots, reached Charleston in the spring of 1760. Its leaders, the 77th's Colonel Archibald Montgomery and Major James Grant – the same who had suffered disaster at Fort Duquesne in 1758 – had orders to conduct a swift campaign so as to be back in New York in time for the summer's drive on Montreal. For that reason their transport ships would wait in Charleston harbour. These orders did not even mention the relief of Fort Loudoun, which by implication was to be attempted only by a Virginian expedition advancing overland under the command of William Byrd. Yet even the means to achieve such limited goals were lacking. Lyttelton was packing his bags for his long-desired promotion to the governorship of Jamaica, and Lieutenant Governor William Bull, dreading a Creek war and a slave rebellion, offered Montgomery only half of the 400 Rangers he needed. The South Carolina Regiment, on paper 1,000 strong, could muster only eighty sickly recruits. There were few supplies and barely any wagons to carry them.[3]

These conditions confirmed Montgomery's jaundiced views of Carolinians, acquired in Charleston during a 1757–58 quartering dispute. '[S]uch a Set of People,' he railed, 'I never saw; 'tis my opinion that if there were no [regular] troops in the Country that a dozen of Indians might go the Charles Town, tho' in conversation they are for putting all the Cherokees to Death, or Making Slaves of them.' Grant, meanwhile, who in August 1758 had had to deal with unruly warriors at Fort Loudoun in Pennsylvania, thought of Cherokees as engaging rogues who were decent enough if dealt with honestly. If confirmation was wanted, it came from the obnoxious Ensign Miln, who on 7 May repeated Lyttelton's treachery by seizing eight warriors during a conference at Fort Prince George. Worse still, Bull's peace terms reflected the aggressively vengeful attitude of the province's assembly: fifteen Cherokee ringleaders were to be executed, four more hostages handed over, and all remaining prisoners – white or black – were to be released. When the Cherokees failed to contest the difficult crossing of the Twelve Mile River, barely a day's march from Keowee, Montgomery and Grant were convinced that the Cherokees wanted peace but were too frightened to ask for it, and that the colonists did not want peace at all.

Montgomery now thought that a little pressure would produce the peace talks he wanted. A rapid night march surprised Little Keowee where, to the commanders' dismay, rampaging troops bayoneted women and children as well as warriors. Next day, Estatoe went up in flames, a dozen Cherokees dying as they fled for the woods and more perishing in the burning houses. Qualatchee, Toxaway and Sugar Town were empty when they were sacked. By the time they reached Fort Prince George at Keowee, between sixty to eighty Cherokees had been killed and forty were prisoners.

Both officers, experienced soldiers hardened by forest war, were appalled at what they had done. Grant found it 'pretty severe' while Montgomery thought Estatoe and Sugar Town 'more considerable than can be imagined, their Houses Neat and Convenient and Well Provided with every necessity of life'. Surely the Cherokees would now negotiate a reasonable peace: significantly, the soldiers had left the sacked towns' crops intact. Arguing, spuriously enough, that invading the Middle Towns would be 'next to impossible', they left the remaining Lower Towns alone and sent two of Lyttelton's prisoners, Tistoe and the Wolf, into the mountains with a message: the Middle Towns would be spared if Attakullakulla came down to treat. Then they settled down to wait.

They were still waiting three weeks later. The Cherokees' bitterness and distrust ran too deep to be mollified by what Montgomery saw as his generosity and moderation. The invitation to talks must be a trap. The treacheries of Miln, Coytmore and

Bell were yet to be avenged. The Carpenter's position was now so weak that he moved into Fort Loudoun and the hardliners led by Seroweh, the charismatic Young Warrior of Estatoe, were bent on resistance and revenge. By 24 June, Montgomery and Grant had to accept that their policy had failed. Without the supplies for a long campaign, with no intention of relieving Fort Loudoun, and probably intending no more than a swift punishing raid, they advanced into the mountains.

By now Seroweh had assembled most of the Lower and Middle Towns warriors, as well as a few Creeks. There was no point in trying to hold Etchoe, the first town in Montgomery's path; it was unfortified and in any case the Cherokees knew of the uselessness of native palisades against a powerful European force. The only alternative was to adopt the usual Indian horseshoe formation, in a place where rapid movement and dense cover would minimise the British advantage in numbers and firepower. At Crow's Creek, 6 miles from Etchoe, he found the ideal place.

Here the soldiers would have to pass between a steep mountain on one hand and low hills and a river with high muddy banks on the other, through a ravine choked with dense forest and undergrowth, where it was impossible to see more than 10 feet ahead. Here a strong blocking force could confront the British vanguard while other warriors descended on the column's flanks and baggage train. Montgomery's men might share Braddock's fate: hemmed in and hampered by their habit of firing by platoons, they would be shot to pieces and forced to flee. Even should the regulars break through, their precious baggage train might be crippled, forcing Montgomery to turn back before he could attack the Middle Towns. At 8 a.m. on Friday 27 June, Montgomery's advance guard collided with Seroweh's blocking force.

As a Ranger company advanced to probe the thickets, the hidden warriors opened fire, routing the Rangers and killing their commander as he tried to rally them. Montgomery sent forward his light infantry and grenadiers and a fierce close-range firefight ensued. An infantry captain was shot down, a surgeon trying to reach him was severely wounded, and two soldiers died trying to recover the captain's body. Only the smoke from the Cherokees' firing and the abuse they hurled at the soldiers betrayed their positions, and everywhere Seroweh could be heard urging his men to stand firm. The redcoats reeled back into the open, where they were raked by fire from Cherokee riflemen using pieces that greatly outranged the soldiers' muskets.

But the Highlanders were woodland veterans and reformed to meet an expected Cherokee counter-attack. Montgomery extended his line, pushing his rearward Highland companies out to the left and the Royal Scots to the right. Their flanks turned and their retreat threatened, the Cherokees found themselves being driven out of the ravine. As they retreated to a low hill out of reach of the advancing Scots, their flanking parties fell upon the exposed pack and cattle train, threatening to disable the army entirely. Then the Cherokees retreated under fire, the ravine was passed and the battered column reassembled on open ground.

Montgomery had won the field but he now had fifty-five wounded to carry and had lost many horses. A great quantity of flour had to be destroyed to free enough animals for horse litters. This in turn reduced his potential radius of operations and limited the time he could stay in the mountains. He reached Etchoe next day, only to find that the Cherokees had gone. Burning this one empty town could not bring the Cherokees to their knees; perhaps not even the destruction of all the Middle Towns could have done so. As Montgomery told Amherst, 'The destroying of an Indian town when the Savages have time to carry off all their Effects' was a futile exercise, and 'this one cost us rather too Dear'. He really had no choice but to retire, and he was probably happy to go. On 30 June the expedition began its withdrawal to Fort Prince George, harassed by Cherokee parties at every step, and thence all the way to Charleston. And at Charleston, with Amherst's orders pressing, they boarded the waiting troop ships and sailed for New York. The Cherokees had scored a significant strategic success.

The Cherokees certainly thought so and even claimed a tactical victory in their triumphant message to the Creeks and others. Conversely, the sight of tough British troops in retreat appalled Charleston. Lieutenant Governor Bull was frightened that 'the imaginary triumphs of the Cherokees' would encourage the Creeks to fight and the French to execute 'their long concerted plan against this province' supported by the Choctaws, 'always at their disposal'. The prospect of a Franco-Cherokee-Creek-Choctaw coalition existed chiefly inside Bull's own head, but was no less terrifying for that. South Carolinians saw in Montgomery's departure yet another sacrifice of southern needs to northern interests and to imperial strategy. A tortuous compromise, by which Montgomery left four companies of the Royal Scots behind, did little to assuage their anger and fear.

Very soon those fears appeared to be realised. The siege of Fort Loudoun was tightened so that by June the troops had only what little food could be brought by their Indian wives and mistresses, who were permitted to visit. These brave women responded to Seroweh's threats of violence with promises of clan vengeance if they were killed. The last message from Charleston arrived on 4 June, and the Cherokees began to boast that they had annihilated Montgomery's force. Weak and ill, in ones and twos the soldiers began to slip over the palisade at night, perhaps hoping to walk through the forest to safety, or perhaps to join the Cherokees. On 5 August those remaining threatened to go too, unless the officers capitulated on terms.

Captain John Stuart, popular among the Cherokees and a friend of Attakullakulla, took Lieutenant James Adamson into Chota to negotiate. On the surface, the Cherokees' offer was generous: the whole garrison with all its women and children were to be escorted either to Virginia or to Fort Prince George by warriors who would hunt game for them. The sick and disabled would be cared for and sent on afterwards when well enough to travel. Each man could keep his arms, ammunition and baggage, but the cannon, spare ammunition and forge were to be given up. On 6 August the surrender document was signed, and next day the British colours were struck and the troops marched out.

Perhaps the Cherokees had always planned treachery. More likely the young warriors were now out of the control of the more sober headmen, and driven by the need to avenge the murders at Fort Prince George. Or perhaps the garrison were found to have hidden some of what they ought to have handed over. Whatever the cause or causes, the Cherokee escort quickly melted away: when the column halted for the night it had no protection at all.

At first light the camp was attacked by hundreds of warriors. Four officers, twenty-three rank and file and three women were killed. Stuart was seized and dragged to safety as a headman cried out to stop the killing: the Cherokee hostages had now been avenged. About 120 men and women were taken captive and ritually humiliated: slapped in the face with fresh scalps, they were taken to their captors' towns, beaten and made to dance, and one man was slowly tortured to death. After that there was no more killing, though the captives still had to dance in the evening, and on one occasion they were even taken to Chota to entertain the visiting Mortar and his Creeks. There was some talk of forcing Stuart and a handful of sailors to haul the captured artillery over the mountains and employ it against Fort Prince George. That came to nothing when the Carpenter allowed Stuart to escape.

Attakullakulla had purchased Stuart from his captor and on 8 September announced that he would go hunting with his family. Others probably expected that he would allow Stuart to get away, and they certainly made no effort to stop him. After all, now that the Fort Prince George victims were avenged giving Stuart back must have seemed a sensible conciliatory move, by Oconostota and Ostenaco if not the militant Seroweh. Once in the forest the little party hurried towards the Great (or Long) Island in the Holston River, reaching the Virginian camp on 8 September 1760, where Attakullakulla opened talks with Byrd. At home, Ostenaco and Oconostota made their own overtures, even arranging a mutual exchange of prisoners at Ninety Six. A whiff of peace seemed to be in the air.

It was not to be. Byrd offered draconian terms, Ostenaco and Oconostota were still angry and wary, and Seroweh wanted to follow up his 'victory' over Montgomery. In Charleston, Bull, unable to withstand Carolinian demands for revenge, wrote urging Byrd to burn the Overhill Towns while he put together an army of his own. Appealing to Amherst for more regulars to join the four Royal Scots companies, he prepared to take the offensive once again.

In New York, Amherst ordered Grant, promoted lieutenant colonel and now in command, to return to South Carolina and crush the Cherokees once and for all. Grant, however, much preferring Indians to settlers, pointed out that the Cherokees might simply retire to their own forbidding country and refuse to treat. Moreover, what was to be done if they did offer peace and the military commander was the only man on the spot to deal with them? Amherst at once saw through this attempt to get control of the peace process: Grant was not to return to New York until 'you have compelled them into a Peace, or you receive orders for so doing'. Moreover, the terms of peace were to be set by South Carolina. Grant accepted his orders for the time being, but when he reached Charleston in January 1762 he was still looking for a way to subvert them. At about that time he received a letter informing him that Henry Ellis, the former governor of Georgia, had called on Amherst to insist that either the Cherokees must be speedily accommodated or Grant must be given a much more powerful army. The likely alternative would be a general Indian war in the south, driven by a pan-tribal fear of extirpation. Grant at once wrote to Amherst, making the same points as Ellis, and when that failed he set about opening his own unauthorised diplomacy. In apparent collaboration with Bull, he had presents and an offer to exchange prisoners sent up to Fort Prince George.

Very quickly leading Cherokees came to the fort to seek fair terms. Attakullakulla was first, but by early April even Seroweh and Ostenaco were making overtures. Grant was impressed and allowed Tistoe, the hitherto hostile headman of Keowee, to resettle at his hometown. As Grant said, by 'putting himself entirely in our Power, [Tistoe] deserves Protection, I shall give him no Trouble when we march up', adding that 'the Lieut. Governor should not insist upon hard Terms & from what he has told me, that is not his Intention'.[4] He then pointed out that it would be necessary for him to have a copy of Bull's terms, to ensure that military operations did not cease until the Cherokees had accepted them. This was both common sense and a tactic to prepare Amherst's mind for a compromise: to his relief, the commander-in-chief gave his grudging assent. When Grant reached Fort Prince George in May he had written permission to both obtain the terms from Bull and conduct the preliminary peace process.

When the terms did arrive they turned out to be harsh indeed. Despite Grant's urgings in private, it was clear that Bull, who had to mind the temper of his assembly and wider public opinion, could only go so far. True, whereas he had originally insisted upon the executions of fifteen named Cherokees he now wanted only the deaths of four to eight warriors, chosen by the Cherokees themselves from across the four regions. Why the Cherokees would accept any retributive deaths was not explained. All white prisoners must be released at once – under Grant's prodding Bull had already obtained the assembly's approval to ransom them with trade goods – but Cherokee captives would be retained until the peace term had been carried out. The Fort Loudoun guns were to be returned and South Carolina was to have the right to build whatever forts it desired in Cherokee territory. The Lower Towns were to surrender all land between Long Canes Creek and the Twenty-Six Mile River, bringing the boundary (and settlements, with their destructive livestock) to within 30 miles of Keowee. Attakullakulla was the be proclaimed emperor of the Cherokees, an impossible attempt to impose a puppet ruler. In future, Cherokee killers of whites were to be executed by the nation, while colonial authorities would deal with white transgressors. Trade would be resumed only when the preliminaries agreed by Grant had been ratified in Charleston. It was a high price to ask for peace.

Bull himself hinted that, while he would not budge on the executions, he might be flexible about the territorial demands and the emperorship proposal, which he expected to be contested by Ostenaco and Standing Turkey. Grant therefore attacked both problems with vigour: the boundary demand was 'unreasonable and improper', especially as the colonists already had more land than they could settle. By return, Bull gave way on both points, a transaction he wisely concealed from the assembly until September, when Grant's campaign was over. Amherst, whom Grant failed to inform until the last moment, was obliged to accept the colonel's *fait accompli*.

The hoped-for Cherokee delegation did not appear. Chota was awaiting the outcome of negotiations with potential allies – the Senecas and the French at Fort Toulouse – and for a separate peace with Virginia. Meanwhile, the war faction played for time, holding out the prospect of peace if only South Carolina would offer real concessions, while some towns found the prospect of peace and food too tempting to ignore. Ransomed white prisoners – 113 in all – trickled into Fort Prince George, along with thirteen returned bullocks. Even a vicious and unauthorised raid on Keowee by Grant's Chickasaw scouts did not halt this process. But the core of the war party remained firm, convinced they could see off Grant as they had done Montgomery.

The Cherokees' diplomatic efforts all failed: the French gave Oconostota no more than a commission and eight packhorse loads of ammunition; the Senecas gave nothing; Onondaga was ostentatiously preparing to fight *against* the Cherokees; Virginia refused to make a separate peace. If that were not bad enough, by the end of May Grant was approaching Fort Prince George with 2,800 men – regulars, Rangers, the South Carolina provincials, Chickasaws, Stockbridges, Mohawks and Catawbas. Attakullakulla used the crisis to halt a plan to attack the British en route and to justify a last approach to Grant on Oconostota's behalf. When Grant arrived on 27 May, the Carpenter and five companions were there to greet him. At a private meeting that evening Attakullakulla asked for time to consult the nation, offering take one of Grant's officers with him and to have the troublemakers put to death. But his tiny following betrayed his weakness within the nation, and Grant, who was disobeying specific orders by talking to him at all, would not budge. All he would say in public next day was that any executions should be with the Cherokees' consent, carried out by themselves and 'not extorted', hinting that he might not insist upon any executions at all. Moreover, he promised to advance on the Middle Towns as soon as the wagon camp was properly entrenched and pack saddles and flour bags were made. These were preparations that would take at least a week: in plain language, Attakullakulla could have his ten days. The overture was so transparent that Grant's disappointed Chickasaws and Catawbas had to be reassured that the invasion would continue.

The Carpenter left on 29 May but failed to make much progress. Oconostota still believed he would be in danger if he went to Grant, Seroweh remained inflexibly hostile, and others would not release more captives as long as there were Cherokee prisoners in Charleston. The arrival of the French ammunition provided the means for battle and about 1,200 young warriors from every Cherokee region flocked to Seroweh. They had about half Grant's numbers and firepower, and the speed of Grant's advance forced

The Anglo-Cherokee War

them to fight in the last defile before Etchoe. But a sound plan on Indian terms might just allow them to do to Grant what had been done to Braddock.

The path the British would have to follow passed between a steep mountainside on their right and a swift, deep river on the left, the waterway protecting the Cherokee gunmen on that flank. This time, learning from the first battle of Etchoe, they would not meet the British head-on but only harry them from the flanks, fighting at long range to minimise casualties and forcing Grant to hurry forward to open ground, leaving his pack train behind. As soon as the packhorses entered the ravine they would close in to kill as many animals as possible. That this was the Cherokee plan can be deduced from the events of the battle, but the outcome was not what Seroweh hoped.

As the British vanguard approached the ravine, their scouts detected a Cherokee outpost and both sides began firing. Grant had no option but to press on and as his main column entered the defile the shooting became heavier. A platoon of light infantry engaged the Indians across the river and on the right skirmishers pushed back the Cherokees. Ahead, like the light at the end of a tunnel, lay a ford and open country beyond. Just as the first troops forced the ford, the pack train entered the ravine. At once the Cherokees stormed it, killing six Rangers, wounding many more and slaying up to sixty horses. So far the Indian tactics had worked beautifully, but Grant was not caught. Sending back 175 provincials to rescue the baggage, he drove his main force on. Light infantry carried the fords against thin opposition, the attack on the pack train was beaten off and by mid-morning the whole army was across, drawn up ready for a battle in the open. The Cherokees kept up a distant fire for a while until they ran out of ammunition and withdrew.

The Cherokees had done well. By skirmishing and refusing to be drawn into a close-range firefight they had escaped with only thirty dead and one prisoner taken, dramatically better than at the first Etchoe. It was true, however, that Grant's larger force had suffered even lighter losses – twelve dead and fifty-two wounded – and he still had enough pack animals for the wounded and supplies. He could now press on and the Cherokees, lacking powder and ball, could not stop him. But if he could not catch the retreating Cherokees and win a decisive victory, he might have to withdraw with nothing accomplished. Time was against him.

For three weeks his men marched around the valleys, burning fifteen towns containing 800 houses, and destroying crops and orchards – work which Henry Laurens said 'often makes my heart bleed'. Perhaps 5,000 Cherokee men, women and children were driven into the Valley and Overhill Towns, where food supplies could hardly sustain them. Yet the Cherokee warriors would not give Grant his decisive battle. By 2 July the soldiers were exhausted, over 300 were already ill or disabled, over half the men had worn out their shoes, and the food was all but exhausted, and the Catawba and Chickasaw scouts had left to claim the Carolinian bounties on their scalps. Should Grant drive them on for a few more days, enter the valley, and sack a couple of towns there before retreating? There was no evidence that such additional destruction would make a strategic difference and much that it would cause greater misery. On Saturday 4 July, the army began its withdrawal to Fort Prince George.

The decision ignited a long-brewing quarrel with the commander of the provincials, Colonel Thomas Middleton, who from the start had been irked by having to serve under a lieutenant colonel. As early as April he had obtained Bull's permission to leave the expedition should it become 'irksome and disagreeable' to him, a permission which he now exercised. Grant's autocratic style of leadership may have been a factor, but the real issue was his alleged tenderness towards Indians. Soon after Middleton reached Charleston it was common talk that by sparing the Valley Grant had only encouraged the Cherokees to attack the settlements again. Middleton was soon feeding his accusations to Peter Timothy, the radical publisher of the *South Carolina Gazette*, including the false claim that it was Middleton who had saved the baggage train on 10 June and that Grant could then have enveloped and crushed the Cherokees. While Grant waited at Fort Prince George for peace seekers, in Charleston the anger grew and spread.

It was seven long weeks before Attakullakulla could come to Grant. At the beginning of July he had persuaded the Chota council to negotiate, but Oconostota insisted that the first approach should be made to Virginia, not to treacherous South Carolina. But when the Carpenter reached the Virginian camp on the Holston, he found that Amherst had ordered Byrd to leave the peace preliminaries to Grant. While he was away the Great Warrior sent an intermediary to Grant, who insisted on meeting only with 'the first voices' – Attakullakulla, Oconostota, Standing Turkey and Ostenaco. But when Seroweh reappeared with stolen horses and a kidnapped Georgia Ranger, Oconostota dared not appear in person. By now hunger had made the decision: the Chota council despatched Attakullakulla with eight supporting headmen to meet Grant. Private talks opened on Saturday 29 August.

Both the emperor clause and the territorial demand had gone when Grant read out the peace terms the following day. There was more of a ritualised dance around the execution: when Attakullakulla asked for time to consider it, Grant promptly gave him twenty-four hours. When the Carpenter returned, he refused to accept even four executions without consulting the nation first – meaning Oconostota and Standing Turkey, who were waiting not far away – and Grant promptly gave him another twenty-four hours: both men knew perfectly well what the answer must be, and that Grant had neither the will nor the means to enforce ritual killings. Attakullakulla then accepted everything else, and they agreed that the Cherokee delegation would go to Charleston for ratification. Grant then wrote to Bull and prepared to withdraw his army to the coast.

Grant's actions divided the South Carolina capital and sent Bull into a panic. While many people came out to welcome the returning army, Middleton continued to publish his inflammatory diatribes. In the end Grant and Middleton fought a duel in which, it would appear, Middleton missed his shot and Grant fired over his tormentor's head. In 1762 Timothy continued to publish attacks on Grant, obviously derived from Middleton but written by another Charleston radical, Christopher Gadsden.[5] Already, although the lines were not yet clearly drawn, the frontier was raising the issues that would lead to revolution. Fearful of public opinion and of his assembly, Bull quietly reinstated the boundary clause removed at Keowee, giving the assembly the impression that the gain in land was a trade-off for dropping the executions.

The result was predictable: the assemblymen objected vehemently but came round when they realised that without Grant's army they were powerless. The Treaty of Charleston, signed on 18 December 1761, fixed the boundary at the Forty Mile River, a considerable concession on the colony's part. There would be no emperor, nor any retributive executions. Trade would be resumed when all white prisoners had been returned. Though imperfect, these terms ensured the peace for the time being and far better imperial–Cherokee relations. They certainly relieved Ostenaco, who now travelled north to treat with Virginia and, upon seeing George III's coronation portrait, insisted upon on going to London to meet him. At one level that request was perhaps a bid to outdo Attakullakulla's rather dated prestige as the man who had gone to London and knew the British. At a deeper level his embassy was probably a reflection of his understanding that a fresh relationship with the Crown was his people's best hope. Whether that visit was a triumph or a disaster would turn on his reception and what ministers had in mind for frontier relations.[6]

13

LORD EGREMONT DRAWS A LINE

Charles Wyndham was fifty-one years old and one of the richest men in Britain when he accepted the seals of Southern Secretary. Son of a Jacobite baronet who had been arrested in 1715, and a graduate of Oxford, he had completed a prolonged Grand Tour of Germany, France and Italy before securing a seat in the Commons in 1735. Five years later his father's death freed him to abandon opposition to the Walpole government and to ingratiate himself with the governing Whigs, a process eased by his sister's marriage to George Grenville in 1749. The following year he inherited his uncle's title and estates to become the 2nd Earl of Egremont and moved from the Commons to the House of Lords.

An infrequent and undistinguished parliamentary speaker, he was better known for affability (and diligence) than for brilliance. His overeating and distaste for exercise caused him to suffer strokes in 1761 and 1762, but even then he ignored doctors' advice to modify his behaviour. He might even be said to have enjoyed indifferent health. In November 1760 he had confided to Hardwicke that he might not be fit for office as 'my health is more precarious than other Peoples'. A month later he excused himself from a meeting with the King 'to preserve my health against

Friday' (to which George III pencilled his assent 'as the weather is so very sharp'). He had no previous ministerial or diplomatic experience. Yet this plump, pleasure-loving trencherman proved to be one of the most perceptive, hard-working and creative ministers of the time.

From the first Egremont faced the problem of a vastly expanded North American empire and its complex and volatile borderlands. He knew that the key to a sustainable North American peace would be a stable Anglo-Amerindian frontier, which would require elimination of the Bourbon threats from Canada, Louisiana and Florida; conciliation of Indians through a continuous limit to white settlement and properly regulated trade; and a centralised system of administration. He was assured independence of judgement through an Order in Council of May 1761, which gave him direct control of correspondence previously filtered through the Board of Trade. In that way he had access to all the information coming in from the colonies, as well as to the filed correspondence going back over decades. He also sought the able advice of Henry Ellis, the former governor of Georgia and resident in London since March. Egremont, aware of his own lack of expertise, met him, was impressed and asked him to be his adviser on American affairs.

He read papers on frontier matters going back to the 1730s, including the question of the Florida–Georgia border. Not only did Florida present a constant threat to Georgia and South Carolina, but there was a potentially disruptive dispute between the two British colonies over possession of land to the south of Georgia. He also studied a 1738 proposal for a fixed Cherokee boundary, James Grant's 1761 conciliatory peace negotiation and correspondence about the release of prisoners at Fort Prince George. He knew that Amherst and Johnson had been planning an Indian congress at Detroit and that Amherst had sent an expedition via Niagara and Detroit to reconnoitre lakes Michigan and Huron. On 12 December, the day the peace preliminaries with the Cherokees landed on his desk, Egremont instructed Amherst to treat conquered Canadians and Indians with equal consideration and deplored the effects of dishonest commerce:

> The shameful Manner in which Business is transacted between Them and Our Traders, the latter using every Low Trick and Artifice to over reach and cheat those unguarded ignorant People in their Dealings with them, while the French by a different Conduct, and worthy of Our Imitation, deservedly gain their confidence.[1]

That same day he obtained an order in council forbidding land grants for white settlers until a more permanent plan could be worked out.

Thus, by the end of 1761, Egremont was committed to a stable boundary line and to honest regulation of trade. And he had shown that to achieve these goals he would have to add a third condition: a paternalistic, metrocentric system of government.

In January 1762, war broke out with Spain. Egremont was deeply involved in the planning of the expeditions against Spanish possessions in the Caribbean and the Philippines, and he asked Ellis to advise him on which American targets to choose. Ellis convinced him that the capture of Havana, the key base in the region, would leave Florida and other Spanish colonies isolated and hopelessly vulnerable. While Cuba could not be held permanently, it could be exchanged at the peace conference table, perhaps for Puerto Rico, which would command the windward approaches to the Caribbean and where there might be less local resistance. Egremont was torn between Florida and Puerto Rico, but as early as 3 March Ellis persuaded him to demand Florida. Havana fell on 13 August and Manila surrendered to an India-based expedition in September. Now the victors had to decide how much they could prudently demand from the defeated Bourbons.[2]

Egremont and his brother-in-law George Grenville opposed the generous concessions favoured by George III, Bute, Newcastle and Britain's chief plenipotentiary the Duke of Bedford, particularly the return of Havana without territorial compensation. For Egremont, Florida was as essential to the security of Georgia and South Carolina as Canada was to that of New England and New York.

Then there was the question of the boundary between the settled regions and the Indian territory, and the problem of how criminal justice was to be administered. Violations of the Easton frontier were alarmingly frequent. The problem was illustrated by reports of Bouquet's efforts at enforcement around Fort Pitt, including a prohibitory proclamation, and the use of troops to intercept intruders and to burn squatters' cabins. Effective enforcement would cost money and require an America-based income stream. There was also a question of legality. Garrison commanders might be made justices empowered to try first instance cases, and as the Quebec capitulation gave the proposed reserve to Britain by right of conquest, English-style courts could be created for trials by jury. But who would form the jury? The alternative would be to transport the accused to a neighbouring colony, where they would face juries already disposed towards acquittal.[3]

In the midst of at all this, on the morning of Saturday 19 June 1762, Egremont received six unexpected visitors at his London home in Piccadilly. They were Lieutenant William Blake, master and commander of British sloop *Épreuve*, which had brought the party across the Atlantic; two Virginians, Lieutenant Henry Timberlake and Sergeant Thomas Sumter, who had been emissaries to the Overhills; and three Cherokees from the Overhill country, led by Ostenaco, dubbed the Mankiller of Tomotly. The problem of a long and volatile North American wilderness frontier had literally come home.

The Cherokee embassy was a nuisance. Months earlier, the treaties of Charleston and Great Island had successfully ended the war and therefore it had no obvious purpose. Communication was awkward, for the Cherokees' interpreter, William Shorey, had died on the voyage. Worse still, the king was ill – an early bout of the porphyria which would later destroy his sanity – and could not receive even distinguished ambassadors. Yet the peace of the southern frontier might turn on how these three warriors were treated in the next few weeks. Egremont played for time. He handed them over to a senior king's messenger – a diplomatic courier and, effectively, political policeman – named Nathan Carrington, who found them a house with servants and a carriage in Suffolk Street, and saw to it that they were royally entertained while they waited for George III to recover. They were quickly fitted out with magnificent clothes, thought to be 'in the mode of their own country', and taken to parade in them in Kensington Gardens, perilous by night but a fashionable place to see and be seen in daylight. Somebody, perhaps Egremont, commissioned Joshua Reynolds to paint portraits of two of them, and Francis Parsons, another London artist, to paint the third. The outfits and portraits reflected growing knowledge of Indian cultures: in 1730, Attakullakulla and the other visitors had been dressed up in the jackets, breeches and stockings of English gentlemen.

They were taken to the Tower of London, St Paul's Cathedral, the Houses of Parliament and Westminster Abbey. Their audience with George III on 7 July was magnificent though stilted, none of the Cherokees speaking much English and Timberlake's Cherokee being rudimentary at best, but in any case it was a diplomatic triumph for both sides. In the following weeks they were taken to lunch at the Lord Mayor's residence, the Mansion House; by boat to Greenwich, past dockyards where ships of the line were being built; to a military parade at St James's; and to see an artillery exercise in Hyde Park.

At the same time, Egremont used the visit to his own political advantage. On the Monday following their arrival, he entertained his sister and her husband George Grenville to a dinner followed by a visit to the Cherokees at Surrey Street. Grenville, though on Egremont's side over Havana, was unsure that extending the British boundary to the Mississippi (and acquiring four formerly neutral West Indian islands into the bargain) was adequate compensation for the return of Guadeloupe and Martinique: islands which Pitt and his followers considered to be essential to French naval power. Pitt also had a new and awkward devotee, the young, aggressively ambitious and devious president of the Board of Trade, William Petty, Earl of Shelburne, who was demanding equal access to the king. Perhaps it was the Surrey Steet meeting that changed Grenville's mind.

Between them Grenville and Egremont persuaded the Cabinet to successfully demand Florida in exchange for Havana, thus eliminating the Bourbon presence on the frontier of Georgia. The negotiators also obtained the cession of all eastern Louisiana except New Orleans, which with Louisiana west of the Mississippi went to Spain. The moderates agreed to return Guadeloupe and Martinique to French rule, much to Pitt's disdain but partly to appease British planters' fears of competition within the Navigation System. The preliminaries of 8 November 1762, followed by the final Peace of Paris in February, confirmed these gains.

The agreement focussed Egremont's mind even more intensely upon the burgeoning frontier problem. On 15 December, Henry Ellis pointed out the dangerous situation created in the southern colonies by Britain's takeover of the forts in Florida and Louisiana without Indian consent. In his view war could be averted only by the immediate demolition of forts Loudoun, Tombigbee and Toulouse. Trade would have to be guaranteed and settlement prevented. Finally, these measures must be explained to Cherokee, Choctaw, Chickasaw and Catawba leaders by the southern colonial governors and the southern Superintendent of Indian Affairs. Egremont digested these ideas and made his decision. When in February he asked the Board of Trade for its opinion, he made it very plain he wanted a report endorsing his own proposals. On 16 March he despatched two letters. One was to Amherst, asking for suggestions as to what might be said at the southern conference, and another to the southern governors and John Stuart, Atkin's successor as superintendent, instructing them to arrange the congress forthwith.[4]

In April his position was further strengthened first by Shelburne's resignation (and his replacement by the more amenable Lord Hillsborough), and then by Bute's departure and Grenville's appointment as First Lord of the Treasury. Grenville was now committed to a metrocentric approach to North America and wanted to deploy 10,000 troops in the West Indies, Florida and Canada and along the new proposed Appalachian line of settlement. Paying for them would be difficult in the face of a Parliament expecting a peace dividend in the form of a lower land tax, but surely the colonies could be asked to pay a proportion of the cost. The vast area between the Appalachians and Canada was to be an Indian reserve forbidden to squatters, speculators and unlicensed traders, but it was not clear how these prohibitions could be enforced. When in June Egremont put the problem to the king, George III presciently suggested assigning the reserve to Quebec, where a new civil government would have to be established. His idea was not adopted as the thorny question of exactly how to govern Canada was yet to be determined. In addition, the Board of Trade wanted to maintain the fiction that the British claim to the region was based on the Covenant Chain with the Iroquois, not from cession by the French. It was also thought that the Indian trade would be monopolised by French Canadian voyageurs. By August it was decided to fix the new boundary at the heads of the eastward-flowing Appalachian rivers, subject to survey and the established rights of Amerindians. At the time it seemed like the most sensible decision. Eleven years later it would turn out to be a vital opportunity lost.[5]

By now Egremont was anxious to get his colourful visitors safely back across the Atlantic, both to avoid embarrassments and to test the effects of the visit upon Cherokee opinion. While the official programme had been worthy and uplifting, the Indians had become a public spectacle. The climax came at Vauxhall Gardens on a night when, it was claimed, 10,000 people turned out to see them. Ostenaco and his companions took refuge in the orchestra where they played with the organ and a violin, and downed large quantities of sweet white wine. At about two in the morning Ostenaco's cloak caught on the hilt of a tipsy gentleman's dress sword; cold steel flashed as the lethal jewellery was drawn. Ostenaco gripped the blade and broke it with his bare hands, afterwards holding them up to display his lacerated palms. He then lay down on the ground and refused to move. Timberlake and his companions had to lift the Mankiller into the coach and fold his legs in after him.[6]

Egremont at once ordered that the Cherokees be kept away from public entertainments and arranged a passage for them to Virginia with Blake – whom they trusted – on *Épreuve*. While Charleston was a more convenient naval destination, the Cherokees were not anxious to go there. Only at the last minute were they somehow persuaded to go via South Carolina. With Blake went Egremont's instruction to Governor Thomas Boone to find out via an interpreter whether the Cherokees had been offended by their recent treatment, and if so to attribute the mishaps to Shorey's death. On Friday 20 August they set out for Portsmouth.

Egremont died suddenly the following day at Egremont House. He had still not taken his doctors' advice, even though he knew his overeating might kill him. In August he is supposed to have observed that 'I have but three turtle dinners to come, and if I survive them I shall be immortal'.

His passing left an unfortunate break in the direction of American policy and his successor Halifax was not appointed until 13 September. Halifax, however, saw to it that the momentum of all these months of preparation was maintained. Within days he was able to inform the Board of Trade of the king's wish that 'the lands which, for the present, are to be reserved for the use of the Indians' were to be separate from all of the colonies, including Canada – that is, there was to be a continuous fixed boundary line – and to be free of intrusive settlements and land grants. The boundaries of Canada were to be exactly as the Board had recommended – along the height of the Appalachians – and settlement of ex-soldiers there and in Florida was to be encouraged.[7] The hope, then, was that settlers would flood into the new colonies instead of into the Indian reserve. While Indian matters came last in the final document, no minister regarded the boundary as a secondary matter: it occupied 40 per cent of the entire text.[8]

In fact, of course, there were plenty of squatters west of the proposed line who would be hard to remove, and land speculation associations like the Ohio Company were likely to object to being deprived of their existing grants. Soldiers who believed they had been promised lands west of the new line, notably Washington's Virginia Regiment veterans, were likely to be upset. Traders and their suppliers, who wanted Indian lands in payment of debts, would feel deprived. Nevertheless, it was a workmanlike attempt to secure a firm boundary.

To put all this into action, Halifax chose the vehicle of a Royal Proclamation issued by Order in Council, thus circumventing the need for a long public debate and the passage of a bill through the Lords and Commons. On 16 September he obtained the sanction of the Cabinet, only Grenville objecting to the Indian reserve not being placed under one or another of the colonial governments. The draft proclamation was then passed to the Board, where Hillsborough and his staff prepared the final draft. By 5 October it had passed the Privy Council, and two days later it received the royal assent. It was rapid work by eighteenth-century standards, but still it came too late to prevent the catastrophe Egremont and Ellis had feared. Days before it was to be signed and issued, news arrived of a major Indian war in the Ohio and Great Lakes region.[9]

14

WYOMING TRAGEDY

In the spring and summer of 1762, Teedyuscung lost almost everything. First, he lost his wife, his sister-in-law and her husband to dysentery. Then he went to the June conference promised at Easton in 1757 and 1758, where a Crown representative would decide whether the Walking Purchase had defrauded the Eastern Delawares. If the official found in his favour, he might recommend awarding them permanent title to the 2.5 million acres restitution first promised in 1757 but in 1758 made subject to Iroquois approval. Unfortunately, the official was Sir William Johnson, whose authority rested upon his relationship with the Six Nations and who could see personal advantages in pleasing the Penns. Perhaps because of his bereavement, Teedyuscung's chronic alcoholism was worse than usual and he was unable to make a coherent case. Even an angry intervention by the Quaker Israel Pemberton ended when Johnson asked him by what authority he interfered in matters of state. In the end the Delaware king had to settle for a paltry sum in compensation: £200 worth of goods and £400 in cash. A second conference at Lancaster in August, to make peace between Pennsylvania and the Ohio nations, also produced nothing. Hamilton and the Penns, though they wanted to halt the New England speculators even now penetrating the Wyoming

Valley, and were happy enough to see them blocked by the Eastern Delawares, wanted to keep the promised reservation open for their own people. The Iroquois were preoccupied with giving away lands alarmingly close to the Eastern Delaware claim. Once again, Teedyuscung had to accept a cheap buy-off: £100 cash and £440 in goods. Worse was about to follow.[1]

As early as the autumn of 1760, twenty settlers from Connecticut had built a village on the Susquehanna and announced that more people were on their way. Meanwhile the Susquehanna Company's surveyors laid out three villages on the Delaware preparatory to hacking a road over the mountains to the Susquehanna itself. By the summer of 1762 that road was nearing completion and in September – when all but a dozen warriors were at the Lancaster treaty – 119 settlers appeared at Mill Creek a few miles from Wyoming town, well enough armed to ignore the few Delawares who warned them to leave. They cut hay, and built blockhouses, cabins and miles of road, clearly preparing for the larger numbers to follow. On 22 September, *sachem* Tom King and the Iroquois delegation travelling home from Lancaster came across them and ordered them to leave. They did so, but left their tools and equipment hidden in the woods and boasted that they were going to meet the Six Nations at Albany and would be back in the spring 1,000 strong and with two pieces of artillery. Tom King stayed behind to wait for Teedyuscung, who arrived about a week later, and advised him to wait for a decision from Albany. After this he had gone north after his comrades, the Wyoming Delawares, wary of trusting the Iroquois again.

At this point 150 Yankees appeared in the valley, followed in October by another fourteen with the tools to build a sawmill about a mile from Teedyuscung's home. When Teedyuscung warned them off, they again buried their tools and gear in the woods and promised to be back in the spring 3,000 strong. Some Delawares wanted to leave Wyoming altogether. Then yet another party came, returned Teedyuscung's horse after stealing it, and like the others left promising to return in the spring. The Delaware chief went down to Philadelphia to complain personally to the governor, 'Brother Onas'.[2]

Hamilton was hostile to the Connecticut invasion of his colony, and believed that the British government and the Penns would support him. To be quite sure he took his case to Amherst, remarking that the New Englanders had come 'to force a settlement at Wyoming', a valued Delaware hunting ground. Governor Fitch of Connecticut denied all official connection with the company but Hamilton knew that Fitch and his sons had been involved in it since 1754. He quickly issued a proclamation forbidding the settlements, and advised Teedyuscung not to kill white men, but neither Hamilton nor Amherst sent the Delawares military help.[3]

Teedyuscung was embittered and desperate. That winter an Eastern Delaware council considered removing to the Ohio country, but instead sent a war belt there, hoping for armed support. Whatever reply he was given was strong enough for the Eastern Delawares to abandon all thought of leaving Wyoming. Then in March came the news that the Iroquois had refused to meet the Susquehanna Company representatives at Albany, and in their absence Johnson had told the New Englanders that the Six Nations would never agree to their settlement. When their bribes failed to move him, they declared that they would settle Wyoming, come what may.[4]

Had the New Englanders not withdrawn in 1762, Hamilton told Amherst, they would have been wiped out by the Delawares and a new Indian war would have begun. He was nearer to the truth than he knew.[5]

On the evening of 19 April 1763, the inhabitants of Teedyuscung's town entertained some visiting Mingo Senecas who distributed copious quantities of strong drink. Later that night, arsonists – whether Susquehanna Company agents or Senecas acting for them is still unclear – set fire to parts of the village, including the cabin where the Delaware king lay sleeping off the effects of the alcohol. Teedyuscung died in flames, and the now leaderless Eastern Delawares scattered. When the New Englanders returned there was no one to oppose them.[6]

It was a short-lived success. Even as Teedyuscung died, a great Indian rebellion had broken out in the north and when the news came to Wyoming most of the invaders fled in fear. On 15 October 1763 the forty or so who remained were attacked by Teedyuscung's son, Captain Bull, and their defences destroyed. Nine men and a woman were tortured, killed and scalped on the spot, and the remainder were pursued north and captured. Two day later, the mutilated bodies were found by a band of armed militia.

Scots-Irish settlers around the town of Paxton – many of whom were squatters on Indian lands – had come under attack from Shawnee and Delaware parties, and created their own defensive militia, thereafter being known as 'Paxton Boys'. Now they surveyed the deliberately shocking injuries inflicted upon the dead – a roasted body, eyes gouged with awls – and wanted revenge upon whatever Indians they could find. On 14 December they descended upon the Conestoga Indians, who had been living peacefully on a Penn family manor for decades but whom they suspected – without much evidence – of collaboration with the raiders. Attacking at dawn, they killed the only six Indians they found there, and a fortnight later slaughtered the survivors sheltering in the workhouse at Lancaster. In February they marched on Philadelphia to murder still more refugees sheltering in the barracks and were only deterred when the citizenry raised a considerable defence force. None of the Paxton Boys were ever put on trial – they even sent written justifications of their behaviour to the provincial government – and their example inspired others.[7]

Weak frontier government had failed everyone. A belief in righteous violence was now baked into the frontier consciousness, as was a deep suspicion of formal government. It was a mindset that could easily turn from defensive retribution to outright revolution. It did not even deter the Susquehanna Company: in the same year one Eliphalet Dyer went to London to petition for a land grant. Later, their people returned to the Wyoming lands vacated by the Delawares and fought a little war with Pennsylvania for its possession. Meanwhile, from the Great Lakes to the Ohio, Indians were battling for their survival and independence.

15

PONTIAC'S WAR OF INDEPENDENCE

As early as the summer of 1761, just as the Cherokee war was coming to an end, two Seneca chiefs were planning a pan-Indian war of resistance against the British. Tahaiadoris and a Mingo called Kiashut intended an attack by the 'three Fires' – Ottawas, Wynadots and Potawatomi – upon Detroit, which would yield essential supplies of guns and ammunition. Next the Ohio nations were to capture all the posts between the Alleghenies, Lake Erie and Fort Pitt, including Presque Isle, Le Boeuf and Venango. The Six Nations were to seize all the posts connecting Albany and the Mohawk Valley including Oswego. With the British all but expelled from the trans-Appalachian country, Niagara and Pitt could be starved out rather than risk bloody assaults. With luck the beleaguered Cherokees and other southern nations – traditional enemies, but also deeply worried by British victories – could be drawn in as well. The pair assumed that the French, who still held the Illinois country and Louisiana, would come swiftly to their aid with ammunition and troops from France. As long as the Seven Years War continued, it was possible to believe that Louis XV would come to rescue his beloved children and so restore European–Amerindian relations to the harmony and mutual respect characteristic of the 'middle ground'. As a strategic plan it was coherent, well thought out, ambitious and – on the surface – feasible.

The problem was to persuade the intended actors to take up their assigned roles. In the course of 1761 Tahaiadoris and Kiashut sent war belts to nations as far away as Illinois and in July summoned the nations around Detroit to a conference at Sandusky. But the Detroit peoples distrusted the Iroquois and were still uncertain as to how the new relations with the British would turn out. As insurance they allowed an informer to reveal the scheme to Donald Campbell, the captain commanding at Detroit, who took it seriously and passed on the news to Amherst. Amherst, however, thought mere savages incapable of putting so elaborate a plan into action and did nothing to win the waverers' trust. His immediate reaction was to restrict the supply of presents, particularly weapons and ammunition, which he expected would force the Indians to purchase what they needed from traders. That would oblige them to concentrate on their hunting for survival and so keep them in penury and dependency. Presents, of course, were seen as pledges of sincerity and friendship, and in this case of rent for the posts taken from the French, and the result was to drive nations otherwise ambivalent about the British into hostility. Indeed, over the next two years Amherst and Johnson took further actions which only confirmed that the 'middle ground' was gone forever, and the very existence of the western nations was at stake.

A peremptory demand for the return of all white prisoners – many of whom had by now been adopted by their captors and were regarded as replacements for the Indians' own losses – was bound to arouse resentment. Insisting that Indians who committed crimes against whites must be tried under British law and British procedures was no less offensive. Worst of all was the British failure to evacuate the posts they had taken from the French:

to Indians this was a unilateral occupation, which, with the restrictions on presents of guns and ammunition, had particularly sinister connotations.

By the beginning of 1762, as Native fears mounted and war belts circulated, the French at last got involved. The governor of Louisiana, Louis Kelérec, had obtained the approval of the Marquis de Choiseul – the new French foreign minister – for a plan to draw Indians into an attack on the British. The bait was to be the promise of a regiment of regulars and plentiful trade goods. Though his main concern was for the southern nations bordering on Louisiana, Kelérec sent one Louis de Lantagnac to persuade the northerners to protect the Illinois country. Reaching the Ohio country in the spring, he found the Senecas welcoming but cautious, offering to join in should the Delawares and Shawnees accept Lantagnac's war belt. The Delawares in turn sent to the Great Lakes nations, many of whom sent delegates to a conference near Detroit. That conference, in the summer of 1762, showed that despite their suspicions of the British, the Algonquian peoples were not yet convinced that war was necessary. Early in 1763, however, their readiness was increased with the news of the Peace of Paris which was taken as a ruse by British officers to divide the Indians from their allies the French. If an inspiring leader could be found, he could ignite war throughout the region.

Obwaandi'eyaag, otherwise known as Pontiac, was an Ottawa leader of exceptional charisma and ability. British contemporaries such as Amherst thought he had unprecedented political authority over most of the Ohio and Great Lakes nations, a view reinforced by the nineteenth-century historian Francis Parkman, who thought him 'almost despotic'. Mid-twentieth scholars were sceptical, even asserting that he was little more than a local leader, and that 'Pontiac's War' was really several interlocking conflicts. More recent scholarship has challenged both views, showing that although Pontiac had few direct followers, his intelligence, oratory and strength of personality did indeed wield a considerable influence over disparate nations.[1]

Born of an Ottawa father and Ojibwe mother, he was connected with two of the strongest of the Great Lakes nations and already had a reputation for oratory and leadership. Almost certainly a participant in Braddock's defeat in 1755, at the Ohio Forks in 1757 he had spoken forcefully in favour of the French alliance. When Canada fell to the British he was at first willing to believe their initial promises but by early 1761 he had come round to favour war. Though he apparently said nothing at the war conferences of 1761 and 1762, he may already have begun to try to provoke war himself. At two conferences in April and May 1763 he put forward both his own version of the Seneca plan and the prophet Neolin's nativist doctrine to support it.

Since at least October 1761 Neolin had been preaching that by adopting the ways and sins of the whites, the Indians' pathways to heaven had been blocked. To achieve redemption, his people must reject all European culture and learn to live as their ancestors had done. For now peaceful relations with the British must continue, but in the end only war would bring salvation. By March 1763 he was teaching that boys must be raised to hunt with bow and arrow, and that women and old men should eat only corn. Trade with whites would end when the fasting and purification had been completed, allowing converts to continue to use guns and to trade as usual. He may even have argued that, though Indians had done wrong in relying upon French goods, the war that would eventually come would be against the British alone. That was certainly the view of a number of his followers.[2]

Pontiac's plan was triggered when some Ojibwes ambushed a military surveying party, forcing him to move quickly before his intentions were uncovered. On 1 May he and forty others appeared at the gates of Fort Detroit offering to do a traditional dance for the garrison. With all other eyes on the dance, ten Indians noted the locations of the magazines, stores and barracks. Pontiac then arranged for a council with Major Gladwin, the commandant, in six days' time, creating an opportunity for warriors with concealed weapons to enter the fort and attack the garrison. Pontiac would signal the attack by holding up a white wampum belt and turning it to show its green side. Accordingly, on 7 May, some 300 warriors entered the fort with sawn-off muskets hidden under their blankets.

Unfortunately for Pontiac, someone had leaked the plan to Gladwin. His garrison was already on the ramparts, weapons pointing inwards. Pontiac was forced to hold a real council, pledging his men's love and friendship for the British. When Gladwin announced that he had had intelligence of intended treachery, Pontiac speculated that some malicious person had been spreading false rumours about them. Gladwin never revealed his sources, but the Indians scoured their town for suspects. They lighted on an old woman, a Catholic, whom Gladwin disclaimed but who was then beaten almost to death. If, as later rumour had it, Pontiac administered the lashing himself, he had good reason to be angry. He had failed to capture the fort's stores of munitions and a siege, the Indians' least favoured military activity, was now inevitable.[3]

Next day Pontiac arranged a new council of reconciliation, but on 9 May he demanded admittance for himself and some 400 followers. As expected, Gladwin refused, thereby seeming to confirm his contempt for Indians. That afternoon, warriors began to fire on the fort.

By late June, thirteen other forts and outposts had either fallen, come under assault or been evacuated. Sandusky and St Joseph fell when warriors were admitted for councils, yielding huge quantities of goods and munitions. At Ouiatenon most of the garrison obligingly came out for a parley. At Fort Miami the tiny garrison surrendered when their commanding officer was lured out by his Native mistress and shot, and his sergeant who followed was captured. At undermanned Michilimackinac the soldiers were induced to watch a lacrosse game alongside a crowd of Indian women. When one of the players lobbed a ball over the palisade, the others poured in after it as the women passed out the bladed weapons concealed under their blankets. If surprise had failed at Detroit, at these posts it succeeded beyond all expectations.[4]

Then every post on the road from Fort Pitt to Detroit was assaulted and taken by force. At Le Boeuf and Venango fire arrows proved decisive. At Presque Isle the attacking Ottawas, Ojibwes, Wyandots and Senecas dug approach trenches, tunnelled beneath the palisade, and set fire to most of the interior buildings. When the beleaguered blockhouse surrendered, most of the surviving soldiers were murdered and the rest made prisoners. The investment of Fort Detroit was tightened and on 31 July a night sortie was ambushed at a stream known afterwards as Bloody Run, crippling Gladwin's capacity to mount offensive operations and encouraging up to 1,000 more warriors to join Pontiac. In the autumn Senecas repeatedly raided the Niagara portage at a place called Devil's Hole – reducing the flow of supplies to Detroit, killing seventy redcoats and seizing horses and munitions. The major forts apart, Pontiac and his allies had cleared the region of British troops and almost secured the Appalachian frontier. It was an astonishing achievement.

It was nevertheless a fragile and short-term success. Forts Pitt, Niagara and Detroit were far too strong, both in defences and in the sizes of their garrisons, to be attacked frontally and the plundered munitions would not last forever. An assault on Forts Ligonier and Bedford, on the old Forbes Road to Pennsylvania, were repulsed. The French at Illinois, the only possible non-British source of munitions, refused to violate the Peace of Paris.

Moreover, as we have already seen, the Indians were divided. The Wyandots attacking Presque Isle pleaded that they had been forced into hostility by Ottawas; there and elsewhere Indians helped some soldiers to escape. The garrison of Fort Edward Augustus at Green Bay, on the far coast of Lake Michigan, were escorted safely to Montreal. While three principal Delaware leaders, Tamaqua, Shingas and Weindohela, told a trader headed for Fort Pitt that Detroit had fallen, another secretly told him the true state of affairs there. The southern nations, mollified by the Congress of Augusta and ever suspicious of northerners, failed to appear. Worst of all, despite all Pontiac's efforts, Detroit could not be fully isolated.

The key was British possession of two gunboats, *Huron* and *Michigan*, which conveyed essential supplies and protected the shore facing the fort. Determined attempts to take or destroy them, including the use of fire rafts, were unsuccessful; and in July they were reinforced by four row-galleys, armed with swivel guns and mortars, able to regularly run the Indian gauntlet along the Detroit River to the fort. Even after 28 August, when foul weather wrecked the *Michigan*, the surviving vessels were more than sufficient for defence and resupply. The Senecas who lived around the Niagara portage remained neutral, so the Indian pressure could not be sustained. Although the garrison suffered casualties and was often short of supplies – Gladwin had to evacuate some of his men in order to make his stores last – it never came to starvation and surrender. In the autumn, with the hunting season upon him, Pontiac recognised reality and loosened the siege. If he could not force the fort to surrender, and if the arrival of a British relief expedition was inevitable, at least he could meet it well away from the gunboats.

Meanwhile, Fort Pitt was being isolated by raiders who penetrated the Pennsylvanian, Virginian and Maryland back settlements. Parties of between fifty and seventy Ohio, Mingo and Delaware warriors hit selected targets along the Forbes, Braddock and Virginia Roads. Woodcutting parties, express messengers, isolated settlements, field workers – even convoys when the raiders had enough men – were struck repeatedly, tying down British forces which might otherwise have marched towards Fort Pitt. Even the Eastern Delawares were drawn in, beginning by taking their revenge on the Susquehanna Company's Wyoming settlement. Shawnees sacked the Virginian Greenbriar farms and villages, sending an unmistakeable message to those hungry for lands west of the Appalachians. As panic spread even as far south as South Carolina and as far north as New York, and the larger settlements became crowded with refugees, the Indians kept the Fort Pitt garrison penned up without intelligence and with precious few supplies. Shingas and other headmen tried to undermine the garrison's resolve by continuing to falsely report that Detroit had fallen.[5]

The first attempt at relief was made by Henry Bouquet at the head of about 500 men from his Royal American Regiment. The Indians handicapped him by raids designed to empty the countryside of people and supplies, while parties carefully watched his movements. Bouquet, on the other hand, had no idea of his enemies' motions and was obliged to weaken his force to strengthen forts Bedford and Ligonier. On 23 July at Edge Hill, near a stream known as Bushy Run, the mixed force of Mingos, Shawnees, Delawares and Wyandots attacked.

The battle of Bushy Run followed much the same pattern as Montgomery's and Grant's encounters near Etchoe. The Indians' first main effort was to break in upon and destroy the baggage train, and when that failed they encircled the British force and kept it motionless until next morning. The Indians were, however, short of powder and ball. With the repulse of a final attack – which some historians choose to interpret as a major British victory – they withdrew, leaving about 110 of Bouquet's 460 dead or wounded. Like Mongomery in 1760, Bouquet had to abandon almost all his flour in order to carry the wounded to the relative safety of Fort Pitt. Not only was the fort not resupplied but Bouquet was now too weak to attempt planned offensive operations towards Presque Isle, Niagara or Detroit. It would be late 1764 before he was ready to move again.[6]

Raids on frontier settlements subsided over the winter but revied again in the spring, by which time the British were preparing a new and multi-pronged offensive. Colonel John Bradstreet was to advance by way of the Niagara portage and Lake Erie towards Detroit; meanwhile Bouquet, now back in Pennsylvania, would march to Fort Pitt and thence down the Ohio and into the Delaware towns in the Muskingum Valley. While they prepared their armies Johnson negotiated, inviting the Genessee Senecas, Ohio Indians and Great Lakes nations to a council at Johnson Hall. Only the Genesees, working through their eastern Seneca brothers, responded – but by August they had formally agreed to release ten prisoners, and pledged a token twenty-three warriors to accompany Bradstreet. Most importantly, they ceded the use of the Niagara portage to the king, meaning that the British could use it for military purposes but not for settlement. With the portage secure, Bradstreet, the half-Acadian veteran of the Seven Years War, set off up Lake Erie in a flotilla of sturdy keel boats carrying about 1,200 provincial regulars from New York, Connecticut and New Jersey, accompanied by 650 Iroquois assembled by Johnson. He had also Gage's orders to seek a peace acceptable to both sides, and an expectation that Pontiac's authority had been seriously undermined.

Like James Grant, Bradstreet was a junior officer with an independent mind, a fairly autonomous command and a determination to make the best peace he could. But unlike Grant, with Gage's instructions behind him, he had no need to prevaricate. When foul winds obliged him to stop at a place called L'Anse aux Feuilles and he was approached by a mixed delegation of Ohio Indians, he moved quickly to secure a deal honourable to both sides. The Indians granted possession – not ownership – of existing and future forts in their country and all lands within cannon shot of their walls. They also agreed to meet Bradstreet again at Sandusky to hand over prisoners; that anyone who committed hostilities in future should be tried by juries of whom half should be Indians and half white; and to leave six prominent hostages as pledges of good faith. For his part Bradstreet agreed to send to Fort Pitt to stop any offensive action on Bouquet's part and gave the Indians twenty-five days in which to make good their obligations. Revenge and punishment did not come into the equation.

Gage and Johnson would have none of it. Both were upset at Bradstreet's failure to consult them and – noting that none of the Indian delegates had been prominent leaders – suspected deception and treachery. Gage was particularly annoyed by the lack of penalties in the agreement. Johnson convinced him that any negotiations – especially terms relating to Ohio land – should have been made through himself and the Iroquois, so sustaining the Covenant Chain. Bradstreet's treaty was cancelled and Gage ordered Bouquet to crush Pontiac's people and if necessary to wipe them out. Whether Bradstreet had really been deceived, or whether Bouquet's preparations kept the Ohio Indians in their own country, their non-appearance at Sandusky within the allotted time confirmed the commander-in-chief's suspicions.[7]

From Sandusky, Bradstreet pushed on to conclude a second treaty at Detroit. Pontiac did not appear but the Indians who came were probably anxious to conclude because they knew that Bouquet was now on his way via Fort Pitt, and they had no desire to be caught between the two armies. Nor had they any wish to see their towns and cornfields set aflame. Bradstreet was then able to relieve Fort Detroit, get a vessel up onto Lake Huron and regarrison Michilimackinac before returning to Niagara. Not a single Indian house or cornfield had been destroyed.

Bouquet was less accommodating. When in October some Delawares offered to confirm Bradstreet's agreements, release their prisoners and give hostages, he demanded that all prisoners be given up before peace talks could even begin. Moreover, he could only agree to a truce because *treaty* making belonged solely to Johnson. That caused some anger but by November the two sides had reached agreement. The Shawnees were slower to agree to talks – some of their important headmen were even in the Illinois country soliciting French aid. Nevertheless, by the end of the month the Delawares, Ohio Senecas and Shawnees had all agreed to the truce. All three nations would surrender hostages and deliver up all prisoners. In the spring, they would send delegates to a formal treaty-making meeting with Johnson. In return they saved their towns and fields from attack and avoided any land cessions. Significantly, when he marched back towards Fort Pitt Bouquet did not regarrison the old forts. These terms were confirmed during a congress at Albany in April and May 1765, where the Indians also accepted the notion of an Allegheny boundary line running from Oswego via the Susquehanna and the Ohio to the mouth of the Tennessee. Arguably, the military balance of power had delivered a significant proportion of the result envisaged in the Proclamation of 1763.[8]

That summer Pontiac moved towards negotiation as his influence waned and that of a militant Shawnee rival, Charlot Kaské, grew. Despite an attack on his escort, Croghan reached the Illinois country where he met Pontiac himself. Instead of burning Croghan – as Kaské wanted – Pontiac agreed to travel to Fort Ontario for talks with Johnson. Despite rumours of false promises and treachery, Pontiac was this time determined to reach an accommodation with the British. In late June 1766 he was at Detroit whence he travelled by British schooner to Niagara and then on to Fort Ontario near Oswego. The negotiations there resulted in a treaty agreed on 25 July 1766. No land cessions were involved, no hostages exchanged, and no prisoners returned. The boundary question was not even discussed. Johnson would not yield on the question of restricting traders to specific posts, but the

Indians were pleased by his proposal to send blacksmiths to their towns. The status of Indians in relation to British rule – as subjects or allies – was not aired. Significantly, Pontiac and his fellows refused to ratify any terms until they had been discussed in the western villages. On both sides it was a recognition of deadlock.[9]

The treaty did not put an end to violence, discontent or suspicion of British intentions. Afterwards many western Indians saw Pontiac as a turncoat, a tool of the British, and that may be what ultimately led to his murder in 1769. It did not address the real grievances of Indians, nor prevent repeated attempts to weave together another pan-Indian coalition for independence. Nor did it address the complex military, administrative and judicial problems inherent in the Proclamation of 1763 and the Plan of 1764 which succeeded it.

16

PLANS AND BOUNDARIES

Pontiac's War made the permanent implementation of Egremont's reforms an urgent matter. Confirmation of the proposed Appalachian boundary, the core issue, would bring with it significant jurisdictional and financial implications. The North American garrisons alone would cost about £20,000 a year, without considering the expense of regulating trade throughout the Indian reserve, enforcing the ban on trans-Appalachian settlement, and providing a workable system of justice. It was to address these issues that the Board of Trade produced a comprehensive draft plan, which it sent out to American governors, the superintendents of Indian affairs and the commander-in-chief on 10 July 1764.

There would be a fixed, agreed Appalachian boundary between Indians and whites. Just as Johnson, Stuart and Gage had wanted, the superintendents were to be freed from military supervision and colonial interference and be responsible only to London. As before, they were to correspond directly with the Board and the Secretary of State, but now they were to be allowed to appoint deputies, commissaries and smiths to manage their vast regions and to regulate trade. The garrisoning of the frontier was to be through the posts as they were before Pontiac's War. The Plan of 1764 recommended that although the Indian trade was to be limited to specified posts, it should be open to all the king's subjects without distinction. All traders were required to have licences from at least one colonial government. They would be overseen by the superintendents and their deputies, who would become justices of the peace – civil magistrates with a legal authority unavailable to military officers.

It was far from a perfect arrangement: it now became almost impossible for a colony to refuse a licence, while the very people charged with enforcing licences could not revoke them and those charged with serious offences would have to be tried in colonial courts. Not only were those courts far distant from the Indian country, but their juries would be most unlikely to convict traders indicted for cheating or murdering Indians. In the south it was impossible to confine trade to the few existing posts, and it was unlikely to meet with the approval of frontier settlers, traders and wealthy speculators. To make it work, many more frontier garrisons would be required and the Indian department would have to be generously funded. Yet in London there were powerful political forces demanding economy.

Thus, under the Grenville ministry, and after Egremont's death, Indian relations were ultimately governed by the dual – and contradictory – needs for tighter control over a vastly expanded empire and to reduce expenditure. In 1762 a net income of £9.4 million was dwarfed by a net expenditure of £17.7 million. By 1763 the national debt had reached an unprecedented £132.6 million as opposed to £72.2 in 1754, and it remained at that level until 1770, when it fell very slightly. At the same time the country MPs were keen to celebrate the peace with a significantly lowered land tax, and their defection could, and did, bring down governments. Headlong military and naval demobilisation helped but could only go so far, especially in view of the estimated 10,000 soldiers would be needed to defend the West Indies, Florida and Canada, as well as to man the Indian frontier.

From London it seemed perfectly reasonable to tax the American mainland colonies, partly to pay for the war from which they had benefitted and to bring the burden of American taxation more nearly in line with that borne in Britain, where wages were significantly lower. It is true that the American colonies suffered from a shortage of hard currency, but that in itself did not make taxation inequitable.

The Plantation Duties Act (or Sugar Act) of April 1764 was a modest attempt to tighten up the navigations system, most famously halving the duty on foreign sugars, while making enforcement much more rigorous. This offended American sensibilities on several levels. First, it was an attempt to raise a revenue as well as to regulate trade, one which might ultimately undermine the elected colonial assemblies. It also affected those New England merchants so accustomed to smuggling foreign molasses that they regarded it almost as a right. Finally, as much of the imported molasses was distilled into rum, the efficient collection of duties would push up the cost of a key item in the frontier Indian trade. As might have been anticipated, there were loud protests, including an attempt to boycott British sugars. When the boycott failed, ministers were encouraged to think about internal taxes imposed from Westminster: a stamp duty to pay for about a third of military costs, and further levy to support the Indian Department.

The Plan of 1764 was greeted by Gage with approval and relief. As long as the Indian department had to keep running up unauthorised expenses, the military chest would have to pay out; and if London rejected any of the superintendents' accounts, the commander-in-chief might have to pay out of his own pocket. Thus, while Gage generally approved of measures taken by Johnson and Stuart, he always urged financial caution. The plan for a separate levy would remove the burden on the army and preserve Gage himself from possible bankruptcy.

Even the expansionists and speculators were not unduly concerned. Though the Appalachian boundary laid down by the

Proclamation ran exactly counter to the ambitions of Johnson, Croghan, Washington and others, it was not immutable, and Washington himself regarded it as a temporary expedient. The plan was workable if a mutually satisfied western boundary could be agreed upon.

It was the Stamp Act that upset the apple cart. Passed in 1765, in the fond belief that it would be acceptable to Americans, it imposed a duty, similar to the excise already levied in Britain, on all printed papers in the colonies. This could cover legal contracts, tavern licences, newspapers and even playing cards. From a ministerial point of view, it was merely levelling up the tax burden. Though arguably the shortage of specie in the mainland colonies would have made the tax difficult to pay in cash, this was not an insuperable obstacle. It was therefore a shock and surprise that it provoked violent resistance in the colonies and vocal criticism at home.

Parliamentarians like Chatham who opposed the tax did not deny Parliament's ultimate right to tax any and all parts of the empire. Rather, they argued that a direct stamp duty was inexpedient and unwise, and of course saw it as a wide-open political opportunity. The crisis did not of itself bring down the Grenville administration, but the ministry fell soon after, to be replaced with one led by the Earl of Rockingham. In 1766 the Stamp Act was repealed, though an accompanying Declaratory Act affirmed Parliament's right to levy taxes if it chose. It was now unthinkable to propose a tax on the fur and skin trades and therefore no hope of independently funding the Indian Department. Worse still, London having been caught without adequate troops to keep order in the cities, there was a case for shifting the frontier garrisons to the coast. By now Lord Barrington, the new Secretary at War responsible for troop deployments, was trying to persuade Gage to recommend the withdrawal of all posts west of the 1763 Proclamation Line. Before any decision could be made, George III dismissed the

Plans and Boundaries

Rockingham ministry and appointed a new government nominally led by William Pitt, now Earl of Chatham.

The new government was disunited and weak. By accepting a peerage Pitt had sacrificed his seat in the Commons, where majorities had to be coddled and persuaded and swayed by rhetoric, but also a great deal of his moral popularity. Moreover, he was unwell and spent too much of his time taking the waters at Bath. The result was a leadership divided between the ineffective Henry Conway, Leader of the Commons and Northern Secretary, Lord Grafton at the Treasury, Shelburne as Southern Secretary, and the Chancellor of the Exchequer, an impulsive and ambitious young man named Charles Townshend.

In January 1767, during a debate on the American army budget, Townshend rashly claimed that he could find a new way to tax America and defray the cost of maintaining the interior forts and Indian Department. By March he had proposed to withdraw the troops to the coastal cities, make the colonies pay for the Indian Department, and levy customs duties upon certain imports into the American colonies. Ill advised by Benjamin Franklin, now the Virginian agent in London, ministers decided that while many colonists would not accept an internal tax, they would agree to an external levy. After all, the furore over the Sugar Act had been limited and short lived. Accordingly, in 1767, Townshend persuaded Parliament to impose import duties on a variety of products: paper, glass, paint, lead and tea. These would not only supply the funds for military purposes but provide a civil list as well. But far from accepting the impositions, radicals in the port cities rioted and a decision was taken to send two regular regiments to subdue Boston. Meanwhile Shelburne repeatedly put off a frontier policy decision until he had adequate information from America.

Nor was he very encouraging to the speculators. Phineas Lyman of Connecticut now wanted an inland colony at the mouth of the Ohio, just as the Mississippi Company put in a new proposal for a settlement in the same region. Lyman's ally Richard Jackson, the Connecticut agent in London, was involved with the Illinois Company formed by Croghan and his partners in 1766. In May Johnson was secretly given a ninth share of the eight-man company in return for his promise to use his influence with the ministry, while in London Benjamin Franklin lobbied ministers face to face. But while the secretary made moderately encouraging sounds, he hinted at Hillsborough's opposition to inland colonies, the region's remoteness and vulnerability to attack, and to the Treasury's reluctance approve the costs of its defence. Such delays were frustrating for men whose fortunes depended upon frontier expansion. By the summer of 1767 Lyman wanted to settle the Illinois without government sanction while Washington, not necessarily for lofty constitutional reasons, began to contemplate armed resistance. Already the Illinois Company was changing its focus from the Mississippi to the Ohio, where Croghan wanted to make good a deed he had obtained from the Iroquois, so combining its interests with those of the 'Suffering Traders' backed by Johnson. Yet their arguments were useful in his quest to economise on the colonial military commitment and therefore on the need to tax the colonies to pay for it. Would not inland colonies provide cheap security in themselves and so reduce the military budget? Might they minimise dependence upon long trails and waterways by feeding the small garrisons which would remain? [1]

Indeed, Shelburne was increasingly pushed towards revision by both political and financial factors. Financial pressures – not to mention the need to pacify land tax consciousness among the independent gentlemen on the cross benches – indicated economy by sacrificing the frontier posts. Order, and the need to be seen to be moving against mob rule, proclaimed that those same forces should be deployed to the coast. Withdrawal would satisfy Barrington, while in early September 1767 Townshend's death removed its most articulate opponent. Hillsborough at the Board of Trade was hostile to inland colonies but he had voluntarily given up the Board's advisory powers. Within a week of Townshend's demise, Shelburne presented a plan which would return trade regulation to the individual provinces, create two inland colonies at Detroit and in the Illinois country, and abandon all but a handful of western posts: only Crown Point, Frontenac, Michilimackinac, Fort Pitt and three new forts on the Mississippi would remain. That would enable the immediate reduction of the North American garrison from fifteen battalions to four and eventually to just two.

For the speculators this was all good and well, but useless without a boundary settlement which would give them legal title. Nudged by Franklin, in February 1768 Shelburne requested, and the Board produced, past correspondence showing that a modified boundary had already been discussed with the tribes. John Stuart had already agreed part of its southern portion with Cherokees and Creeks, which ran from the Kanawha River's junction with the Ohio; and rather than disturb Stuart's line, the ministry agreed that the northern section should run only as far south of the mouth of Kanawha. Orders to enter final negotiation were despatched to both superintendents.

Thus in September 1767 Shelburne was able to produce, unopposed, a scheme which superficially solved all the frontier problems, rejected the Proclamation and the Plan of 1764, and abandoned the Halifax-Egremont vision for good. The frontier posts would be all but eliminated and the whole American garrison reduced to a fragment, at the very moment when armed settler resistance became a reality. In October, Shelburne passed the scheme to the Board of Trade, taking a leaf from Egremont's book by pointing out what he wanted in its report, and getting the qualified assent of Lord Clare, the new president. More importantly, nudged by Benjamin Franklin, he raised the question of a definitive boundary. It was his last contribution.

All this delayed and even precluded a firm determination of frontier policy. The Indian Department, much to Gage's distress, remained dependent upon military funding, and there was no clear authority for trade regulation or the appointment of the superintendents' deputies. If the 1763 border was to be moved substantially to the west, it would further separate the Indians from the advancing tide of settlers. Of course, that could only be a temporary solution unless the new line could be enforced, and enforcement was very far from Shelburne's mind. On 28 February 1768 responsibility for the colonies was transferred to a new secretaryship, and it was given to that arch-opponent of inland colonies, the Earl of Hillsborough.

17

JOHN STUART'S EMPIRE

Trouble was brewing in the Creek country. This nation was a confederacy of Muskogean-speaking peoples settled along the rivers and streams flowing southwards into the Gulf of Mexico. By 1763 there were about fifty-nine villages, thirty-nine belonging to the Upper Towns on the headwaters of the Alabama River and twenty to the Lower Towns further to the south-east. The Upper Creeks were in turn divided into three main groupings – Alabamas, Talapooses and Abeikas.

At town level, the leading man was the *mico*. It was thought that there could be a many as three or four to a town, and they were chosen mainly from the sons of the last headman but also based on experience and achievement. The *mico*'s authority depended upon his ability to persuade a council of the older men and war leaders to adopt his own view: only after they arrived at a consensus were the young men involved. Between them the *mico* and councillors appointed the *tastanage*, or senior war leader, who in turn was expected to consult younger but distinguished warriors and retired head warriors.

The most important of the *micos* led the four towns traditionally regarded as the founding communities of the nation. When one of these towns became more important or highly regarded than the others, its *mico* was the senior of the four. From 1748 this distinction was held by Coweta, one of the Lower Towns, where the *mico* Malatchi was grooming his son Togulki for the succession. Togulki seems to have seems to have taken over from his father soon after but, being very young, he never achieved his father's degree of authority and the influence of Coweta declined. In any case, like the Cherokee *uku*, the First Man or 'Emperor' of the Creeks was regarded as only the first among equals and could not compel obedience. In the uncertain situation of French defeat and the British arrival, stronger men contended for power. In the Upper Towns, Coweta's primacy was strongly challenged by the conciliatory Gun Merchant of Okchais, while the headman known as the Mortar pursued a nativist, anti-British agenda.[1]

Thus, when Pontiac's war erupted in May 1763, the Creeks were already unsettled. The forts and settlements which Spaniards and French had been allowed to build and occupy in their territory were on Indian land – reportedly the British had already landed troops at Mobile and Pensacola – yet they were being transferred as freehold to a third party, the British, without Creek consent. Worse, armed Carolinian and Georgian settlers were already spilling onto unceded land on the Savannah River above Augusta, and roaming around the disputed zone south of Georgia. As for trade, the Creeks were now more than ever dependent upon the British but were offered worse prices than the defeated Cherokees. They had also lost their role as commercial middlemen between the British and the Choctaws. While most headmen saw the folly of provoking a war, among the Upper Creeks the Mortar was particularly incensed and instigated attacks on British traders, threatening to kill any attempting to reach the Choctaw country. When messengers came from the north urging them to take up the hatchet with Pontiac's warriors, some of the young men began to strike settlements close to the Cherokees. In August they killed a man and two children on the Catawba River, and on the

25th they ambushed and killed Hagler, the Catawba leader. Once again frontier settlers were cramming themselves into hastily built stockades for safety. There was a serious prospect their being joined by Cherokees still suspicious of the British, so leading to a general Indian war from the Great Lakes to the Gulf of Mexico. Much would hang on the congress which Egremont had ordered Atkin's successor to convene at Augusta.

John Stuart was Egremont and Halifax's idea of an imperial viceroy. Born in Aberdeen in September 1718, as a young man he worked for a merchant company in London and later in Spain, and served as clerk, purser and midshipman on Anson's voyage around the world. In 1748 he emigrated to Charleston in South Carolina, married, and made a business partnership with Patrick Reid. The venture failed soon after Reid died but Stuart rebuilt his fortunes and became a respected member of Charleston society. Election to the South Carolina assembly led to a commission as captain in the colonial militia, his posting to Fort Loudoun, and so to his friendship with Attakullakulla, respect among the Overhill Cherokees, and eventually to three half-Cherokee children. He had been marked out as a coming man during the Anglo-Cherokee War and was made superintendent in the Southern Department in 1762. Augusta would be his first high-profile test in that office.

Out of his earlier experience emerged Stuart's ideology of empire. He saw Indians becoming full subjects of the Crown, their lands protected by fixed boundaries, with private purchases of their lands forbidden and white traders strictly regulated. As (in his view) colonists were on the whole greedy, unreliable, dishonest and often violent, such an outcome would mean giving the king absolute power over the frontiers, a power to be exercised through his appointed superintendents and their deputies, and not through trader diplomats enlisted by colonial authorities. Unlike Johnson, although not averse to acquisition, he never confused his personal interest with the public good.[2] Such an inflexible approach made him many colonial enemies and most colonial governors were unenamoured of the prospect of losing local control. Governors Johnstone and Grant of West and East Florida were reasonably sympathetic and Wright of Georgia may have had similar goals, but they all had to take note of the internal provincial politics which Stuart chose to ignore. Worst of all was Virginia, where not only did Boone insist upon his independent right to manage Indian affairs, but his assembly introduced its own trade system without consulting Stuart at all.

Egremont's instructions reached him on 6 June. He at once wrote to all the governors and then to all the southern nations convening a meeting at Augusta on 15 October. Boone had already suggested an earlier date but fell into line with Stuart because the Indian delegates would need plenty of time to reach the rendezvous and all except the Creeks would have to pass through hostile territory. The Choctaws would have to cover 700 miles, much of it through Creek lands, and in the end decided to risk the lives of only two delegates pretending to be Chickasaws. The Chickasaws also faced a long trek and the Cherokees were nervous after two of their people were killed by Creeks.

So much could not be said for three of the colonial governors who assembled at Charleston. Dobbs of North Carolina, who was ill and disinclined to go all the way to Georgia, persuaded Boone and Fauquier to change the place of rendezvous to Dorchester, about 20 miles from the South Carolina capital. Stuart was adamant that he must keep his word to the Indians and pushed on to Augusta alone. There on 15 October he met the Chickasaw, Choctaw, Catawba and Upper Creek delegates. When Stuart put the proposed change of venue to them – no doubt implying his own disapproval – they refused to go a step further. Stuart then summoned the errant governors, and while he waited for them the Lower Creeks and Cherokees appeared. When Boone, Fauquier and Dobbs arrived on 1 November they were greeted by over 840 men women and children.

All the Native delegates were nervous of British intentions. Oconostota declined to come in person, though he conferred with Attakullakulla and Ostenaco, who did appear, while the Valley Towns declined to send anyone at all. On the other hand, a total of fifteen Cherokee headmen attended, including Attakullakulla, Ostenaco and that younger former champion of armed violence, Seroweh. During the formal talks Seroweh acknowledged Ostenaco's prominence by inviting those who had been to London to speak first. It seemed that the Cherokees had reached a consensus: while the British were not to be relied upon, and the settlements above Long Canes were an issue, the nation was in no condition for another war. As for the Creeks, all but two Upper Towns leaders – even those friendly or neutral, like the Gun Merchant – were too wary of the mood in their towns and refused to come, fearing with reason that the conference was a British scheme to annex their lands, but probably aware that a large cession to Georgia was now inevitable.

The delay had been used by traders such as George Galphin and Lachlan McGillivray to persuade the Creeks to make a major land cession, and the four-day gap between Stuart's arrival and the opening of the congress doubtless allowed for more private conversations. Stuart and Governor Wright of Georgia found that the Creeks were willing to cede land on the upper Savannah, already polluted by settlers and their livestock and where hunting was sparse, in compensation for hostile acts against settlers and traders. In return, they hoped, they would get guaranteed borders, a steady trade at reasonable prices, the demolition of Forts Toulouse and Loudoun, and an undertaking that no new forts would be built.

The treaty agreed on 10 November was imperfect: the Upper Towns did not endorse it until April 1764 and even then they expressed resentment at the land cessions. Frontier violence continued, especially in the Long Canes area. However, it did lay the groundwork for improved relations. The Creek-Georgia boundary was successfully defined, while that with Florida was to be determined later on. The Creeks would expel illegal settlers and dispossess rogue traders, but only after consultation with the relevant colonial governors. As for justice, the treaty reiterated the long-standing convention that Indians who murdered whites would be executed by Indians in the presence of whites; while whites guilty of murdering Indians would be tried in colonial courts attended by Indian witnesses. The Cherokees, who had contended that their real boundary was still Long Canes Creek, secured the Forty Mile River boundary, but with mutual access for hunters between there and Long Canes. The Catawbas gained all they could have hoped for and what they most needed: a promise of a definitive survey of their borders and a guarantee of the integrity of their tiny 15-mile square reservation. None of this settled all grievances or engendered deep trust, but it did prevent Pontiac's War from spreading into a huge pan-Indian conflagration.

The open question of the Floridas' frontiers of course left plenty of room for trouble. Stuart's first congress there was at Mobile, where he and the newly arrived William Johnstone of West Florida conferred with the Choctaws – for so long within the French orbit – and Chickasaws. Johnstone was an interesting character, a brave but obstreperous thirty-six-year-old naval captain, who arrived – like many a new governor – full of ambition his province.

At first surprisingly clever at Indian relations, Johnstone wanted a boundary settlement that would allow his colony to grow. Stuart was afraid that the Choctaws might be seduced by Pontiacs' agents; and both wanted a peaceful relationship which would prevent them from allying with the Creeks. Most urgently of all, Gage wanted to clear the way for the occupation of the Illinois by way of the Mississippi, two military expeditions by that route having been turned back by the hostile Small Tribes and Arkansas. For their part, the Choctaws, though feeling neglected, and still

1. George II. The military-minded monarch whose favourite son had a significant effect upon British intervention in North America. (Detroit Institute of Arts, CC0)

2. Thomas Holles, 2nd Duke of Newcastle. Newcastle was a veteran statesman with an acute awareness of the interdependence of European and colonial policy. (Yale Center for British Art)

Left: 3. Charles Wyndham, Second Earl of Egremont. Plump, pleasant and hitherto inconsequential, Egremont turned out to be the imaginative architect of post-war frontier policy. (© National Portrait Gallery, London)

Below: 4. Lord Halifax and his secretaries. Poses more painterly than practical reflect Halifax's serious work ethic. (© National Portrait Gallery, London)

Above: 5. Fort Necessity. The faithful reconstruction shows the vulnerability of this undersized fortification. (EWY Media/AdobeStock 765203688)

Below right: 6. Hendrick. British clothing and Mohawk hatchet symbolise Hendrick's role as cultural go-between. (John Carter Brown Archive, Creative Commons CC-BY SA 4.0)

Below left: 7. Military officer. A young Virginian who might have been sent packing by Braddock in 1755 shows off his new uniform in 1756. (National Gallery of Art, Washington, CC0)

Above: 8. Pipe tomahawk. Ceremonial pipes like this were used at the 1758 Easton conference and other congresses. (Etnografiska Museet, Creative Commons CC-BY SA 4.0)

Left: 9. George III. This idealistic young man supported the 1763 Proclamation and foresaw the Quebec boundary of 1774. (Rijksmuseum)

10. Ostenaco. The Outacite or Mankiller of Tomotly saw the best interests of his people (and himself) in a readjusted relationship with the British. (US National Portrait Gallery, CC0)

Above: 11. A contemporary map showing the geographical distribution of Native American nations. (Library of Congress)

Right: 12. Thomas Gage. Commander-in-chief from 1763, Gage was reasonably sympathetic to Indian grievances, but feared having to bear the cost of frontier management himself. (Yale Center for British Art)

13. Bradstreet. Like John Forbes, as man on the spot, Bradstreet was able to carve out his own Indian policy during Pontiac's War. (US National Portrait Gallery, CC0)

14. Henry Bouquet. Captive children are unwillingly separated from their adoptive families to be handed over to Bouquet, a Swiss mercenary prominent in the British actions of the French and Indian War and Pontiac's War. (Library of Congress)

15. Thomas Penn. Neither Quaker nor pacifist, Penn led Pennsylvania into ruthless competition for Indian lands. (Philadelphia Museum of Art)

16. Benjamin Franklin. The Pennsylvanian expansionist and speculator posing as a man of science and letters. (Philadelphia Museum of Art)

17. Guy Johnson. William Johnson's nephew and successor with a Mohawk friend presented as his servant. (US National Gallery of Art, CC0)

18. George Washington. As he saw himself: the ex-colonel presented as a gentlemanly military hero, defender of frontier conquests, and perhaps as rebel leader in waiting. (Courtesy of Washington and Lee University, University Collections of Art and History)

resentful of the unilateral expulsion of the French, knew that they must now settle with the British: the nearest Bourbon outpost was at New Orleans and, perhaps more importantly, they needed British trade goods. Fortunately, Stuart and Johnstone had ample presents on hand and with Gage's reluctant support were able to buy more: the final bill was for £6,000. The treaty signed on 27 April provided for justice arrangements and pledges of friendship similar to those agreed at Augusta. While the Choctaws agreed to hand a large L-shaped piece to West Florida, and to receive and protect Stuart's commissaries, they promised to provide diplomatic support and escorts for the third British Illinois expedition already preparing at Mobile.

Both sides were as good as their word. Stuart exceeded his powers in appointing commissaries, and obtained Gage's retrospective support, and the Choctaws provided eighty warriors to accompany Major Farmer's little force as it ascended the Mississippi. Their presence made all the difference: the Small Tribes and the Arkansas were reassured and even supplied Farmer as he toiled north. The Illinois posts were peacefully occupied – it was a remarkable piece of diplomacy. The Stuart–Johnstone partnership was working well. (Ironically, two years later Johnstone's pugnacity got the better of him when he answered a Creek's threats of war in kind. He was dismissed and returned to Britain.[3])

Now Stuart urgently needed to meet the Creeks. Already a headman called the Wolf of Mucolossus had visited Pensacola and Mobile, threatening war if the British troops tried to occupy more than the sites of those two forts, or if Fort Toulouse was occupied. The British commanders had responded with commendable moderation, offing him assurances and presents and allowed the Alabamas to take over Fort Toulouse. Stuart followed up with a message to the Mortar, and with a fresh congress at Pensacola in September 1764. On arrival there he repudiated a local agreement giving the British a 10-mile coastal strip between Pensacola and

Mobile, and through the former French commander of Fort Toulouse persuaded the Mortar that he could safely come to the renegotiation. Between 12 and 28 May 1765, Lower and Upper Creeks agreed to cede the 10-mile strip in exchange for guaranteed trade from Mobile and Pensacola. Even the Mortar, politically isolated and aware of the nation's new dependence upon British trade and friendship, allowed himself to be wooed with private counsels, flattery, presents and the status of 'Medal Chief' – that is, he was given a copper medallion symbolising his allegiance to George III. Though he was to throw it away when he next fell out with the British, it was at least a temporary success. Then Stuart was off to East Florida for yet another conference.

In November, Stuart came into contact with Governor James Grant – he of the Fort Duquesne debacle but also the man who had foisted the Treaty of Charleston onto unwilling South Carolina and lately lieutenant governor of Havana. In Britain as temporary colonel of the 40th Regiment, and as ever looking for distinction and lucrative employment, he had applied for the governorship of West Florida and for a permanent colonelcy. He received neither but was offered the eastern province instead. He accepted with enthusiasm and was duly commissioned in November 1763.

East Florida was no sinecure. It was poor, underpopulated, open to attack, and in desperate need of stable relations with its Creek neighbours. From a governor's point of view, particularly one sensitive to Native fears and hopes, its lack of an elected legislature was a definite advantage, meaning he could work with the superintendent towards a stable frontier. Significantly, almost his first act was to appoint Stuart to his executive council. On 1 December 1763 the pair reached an agreement as to the direction of future Indian policy. Stuart or his deputy would preside and diplomacy – by necessity as much as by inclination – would be through peaceful conferences and generous presents. Finally, on 3 October 1765, the pair met to prepare for a meeting with the

John Stuart's Empire

heads of the Lower Creek towns at Fort Picolata on the St John's River to the north of St Augustine.

Stuart's relations with Grant were not to be easy. The latter saw his new province as the guardian of British North America's southern flank and wanted it to replace South Carolina as the centre of southern Indian diplomacy. Upon his arrival in St Augustine he had written to the superintendent, urging him to hold just such a conference to fix a boundary which would allow for provincial development while being acceptable to the Creeks. Stuart was of course occupied with business elsewhere, and by April 1765 Grant had became impatient enough to threaten to call a meeting on his own authority. But wait he did until Stuart arrived from Charleston on 3 October.[4]

From 12 to 15 November, they conferred with the Lower Creeks' representatives at Fort Picolata. The Creeks complained of high trade prices and of settler encroachments beyond the limits set at Augusta. As usual on these occasions, both sides took hard positions in public while haggling in a more conciliatory fashion in private. At the end the Indians agreed to a boundary linking the headwaters of the streams flowing eastward to the Atlantic, giving East Florida a little room to grow and the Creeks ample presents. The exact boundaries were deliberately left vague so that the Creeks would not feel too confined, while leaving open the way for future cessions.

This did not satisfy the self-important Grant, who was amply provided with presents and an Indian fund of £1,000 a year. To Stuart's chagrin he arranged a second Picolata conference with minor Creek headmen unable to do serious business, which the superintendent was unable to attend. Nevertheless, Grant's generosity and anxiety to stick to conference diplomacy was perfectly in line with the ideas of Halifax and Egremont – and even of Stuart.[5]

Stuart could not immediately return to Picolata because there was trouble on the Georgia frontier. Minor scuffles and Creek harbouring of runaway slaves was threatening to provoke the kind of vigilante violence already so prominent further north. Stuart raised these matters at a second Augusta conference intended to agree on trade regulation, but still local hostilities escalated. In the summer of 1767, a Creek cattle raid provoked settlers to burn a town on the Oconee River. Then the Lower Creeks failed to come to pre-arranged boundary conferences at Augusta in September 1767 and again in the spring of 1768.

The final outcome was the loss to the Creeks of huge areas – Georgia alone had acquired 5.5 million acres by 1775 – as well as continued suspicion of British words and motives, and frequent border violence. Because the Plan of 1764 did not allow restrictive licensing – a power Stuart badly wanted – avaricious traders flooded into the region, competition led to unscrupulous methods, and overhunting decimated the herds of white-tailed deer. Even the Choctaws were reduced to poverty and dependency. Stuart was unable to check such ruthless exploitation, but his efforts to do so bred hostility from colonists throughout the south. As Calloway argues, 'Britain's efforts to regulate the frontier and to establish Indian boundaries fuelled anti-imperial sentiments that would lead to revolution and fuelled the revolutionaries' hunger for Indian lands'. Yet Stuart went determinedly his own way, appointing commissaries (deputies) to the southern nations on his own authority and supported, after the event, by Gage.[6]

In 1768, the decision to call in the frontier garrisons and to return trade regulation to the colonies meant the days of Stuart's empire appeared to be numbered. Asked to negotiate the new frontier, he summoned the Cherokees to Hard Labour in October 1768. Knowing that Johnson was likewise about to hold a corresponding congress at Fort Stanwix on the Oneida Carry, he agreed a line which ran along the Kanawha River from its mouth to its source and hence southwards to East Florida. The result cancelled all Cherokee claims north of the Kanawha but protected all other hunting grounds. As we shall see, Johnson and Croghan had their own agendas.

When he was ordered to call in his commissaries and to let the colonial governments manage trade, Stuart found ways to carry on as before. Arguing that the Indians were asking for commissaries, in 1771 he appointed John McIntosh to the Chickasaws and another to the Choctaws, following up in the following year by sending David Tait to the Creeks. In the same way he took advantage of the fact that diplomacy, his official field of activity, was in practice inseparable from trade.

Stuart has been criticised for his inflexibility and his failure to establish a compromise on a 'middle ground' between the southern Indian nations on one hand and white settlers and speculators on the other. There is, however, little evidence that such a middle ground existed. By the late 1760s workable compromises with expansionists, who coveted Indian lands and believed they had a right to them, had become impossible. To protect the Indians' livelihoods Stuart had to insist upon the letter of imperial law – and with support from sympathetic governors in the Floridas and Georgia, and with effective deputies, he was able to achieve a great deal, even without adequate military support. However, the time was coming when, without that military support, that law would be too hard to enforce.

18

SPECULATION, FRAUD, MURDER AND REVOLT

On 3 June 1763, Washington, his brother, four members of the Lee family, twelve other Virginians from the Northern Neck region and a single Marylander formed the Mississippi Land Company. There were to be fifty shareholders at most, each of whom would be entitled to 50,000 acres 'to lye on the Mississipi [sic] and its waters'. The scheme assumed that the British government would not only grant the lands and put a twelve-year moratorium upon all quit rents and taxes, but also provide a garrison of regulars to protect the settlers from 'the insults of the Savages'. Yet the company would 'ignore' any ministerial attempt to impose collective terms of tenure; every investor was to have his 50,000 acres as his own property. The proposed grant was to consist of 2.5 million acres extending east from the Mississippi along both sides of Ohio to the Wabash and Tennessee (Cherokee) rivers.[1]

Clearly the scheme depended upon imperial approval. Accordingly, the collaborators not only reserved eight shareholdings to bribe potential London allies but also appointed a Quaker merchant called Thomas Cumming to present their case to the government. Washington himself penned their petition to George III, which was transmitted to London along with 80 guineas to

Speculation, Fraud, Murder and Revolt

support the agent's expenses. In this letter Cumming was apprised of objections he might encounter, particularly those arising from the dispossession of Indians. The 1758 Treaty of Easton, it pointed out, was made with the Iroquois, not with the distant Mississippian nations, to whom it could not apply. The letter then went on to argue that the outbreak of Pontiac's War had in any case invalidated that agreement. Clearly Washington and his collaborators saw nothing immoral in dispossessing Indians.

Washington at least had been living far beyond his means and at a level he thought appropriate for an independent gentleman, importing wines, expensive clothing in the latest London fashion, furniture and much else – and complaining that his agents charged him too much and paid him too little for his tobacco. Determined to free himself from self-incurred debt and to achieve the economic independence which he thought befitted men of his rank, he turned from tobacco to the cultivation of wheat, and increasingly to speculation in western lands. Indeed, he encouraged other indebted gentry to do the same and there can be no doubt that to him there was no distinction between his Virginian ambition and the destiny and duties of the British Empire.[2] Yet what would happen if ministers in London refused to conform and interfered with colonists' perceived right to expand?

The letter also warned Cumming that one George Mercer was already active in London on behalf of the Ohio Company, and possibly of other ventures, and begged him to have nothing to do with him – which is a little strange as Washington and other members of the Mississippi Company were also investors in the Ohio Company.

The Proclamation of 1763 was a disappointment but did not long deflect the speculators. Washington for one hoped that the Appalachian boundary line was a temporary measure 'to quieten the minds' of the Indians prior to their inevitable dispossession. Therefore, land grants must follow from a revision of the boundary line proposed in 1763 and 1764. The Loyal Company simply ignored the proposed boundary and set about illegal surveys and sales of Ohio Valley lands. There was little sympathy for any of them in the Grenville cabinet as long as Halifax was Secretary of State and the Rockingham Ministry, in the way of weak governments facing complex and thorny decisions, decided it needed much more information. But once the Earl of Shelburne became Secretary of State in August 1766, they vigorously renewed their demands. By the following spring Cumming had been instructed to present a revised Mississippi Company petition.

Croghan, who was campaigning for the claims of the 'distressed traders' who had suffered losses in 1754 and 1763, wanted recognition of a 20,000-acre grant made to him by the Iroquois, either in the Ohio region or failing that on the frontier of New York.

Late in 1764, he joined with the Philadelphia firm of Baynton, Wharton and Morgan to reopen trade with the Ohio and Illinois Indians. Both parties were all but bankrupt and wanted to be first in now that Pontiac's War was over, with the added lure of Indian lands as compensation for their losses. Croghan persuaded Wharton that there would almost no financial risk, because as deputy Indian agent he would purchase large quantities of the goods as Crown presents for the Indians, leaving enough goods to be traded for furs and to make fortunes for the partnership. Bouquet was persuaded to give Croghan a pass, on the understanding that it would all be sold to the Crown at Fort Pitt and Fort Chartres. Croghan even visited New York to convince Gage that he was the man to pacify the Ohio and Detroit nations and to persuade the Mississippi Indians to open the way to another Illinois expedition. Neither officer was wholly deceived by these public-spirited declarations, but both believed that he was key to general peace. It is significant that Johnson, who rarely saw a contradiction between conflict between imperial and private interests, gave the enterprise his blessing.

Speculation, Fraud, Murder and Revolt

Croghan left Philadelphia in February 1765 having spent more than twice the £2,000 credit he had received for presents, in which he owned a secret 25 per cent share. Of course, among these goods – worth £20,000 at frontier prices – were Croghan's own trade purchases from his merchant partners and intended for trade once the diplomacy had opened western commerce once again. Naturally, the whole enterprise stimulated suspicion and rumours that it was illegally carrying ammunition to hostile Indians. A heavily laden wagon train carried the goods to Pawling's Tavern, near Greencastle in Pennsylvania, where no less than eighty-one packhorses were waiting for them. This was in Cumberland country, where settlements had been raided again and again during Pontiac's War, and where a volunteer militia, the Brave Boys, already existed. During the transhipment a barrel burst and was found to contain scalping knives: naturally local vigilantes were furious. Thrice they stopped the train, demanded to inspect the goods, and told the packhorse men to turn back. When they were ignored and the packhorses carried on, they took more forceful action. On 6 March, blacking their faces to avoid recognition, and dressed as Indians, 200 lay in wait for the pack train to appear at Sidelong Hill. As the train began to climb the hill, they shot the leading horse and gave terrified drivers fifteen minutes in which to collect their personal belongings and to disappear. The 'Black Boys' (as they would become known) then unpacked and burned sixty-three horse-loads of goods. The rest of the stock, mostly strong drink, was left alone. As Gregory Dowd observes, by destroying but not stealing they reflected an established English type of protest. But they also marked themselves out as American by their Indian dress, blackened faces and their shouting while shooting into the air in celebration.[3]

When the fleeing packhorse men reached nearby Fort Loudoun, the lieutenant in command sent a patrol to investigate. The soldiers took some prisoners and captured nine guns, which they took to Fort Loudoun. The 'Black Boys' now converged on the fort, encircling it, and traded shots with the garrison until the prisoners were released. The vigilantes then established an inspection regime, checking all traveling traders' goods and seizing those they deemed contraband. In May they attacked a trader and fired on a patrol sent to intervene, and later in the month, in a vain attempt to recover the guns lost in March, they kidnapped the Fort Loudoun commandant when he was out riding. In June they again fired on the fort and vanished when the guns were given up. The trouble spread across the border into Virginia where a gang of backwoods settlers – the 'Augusta Boys' – killed six Cherokees, and when their leaders were arrested over a hundred of them stormed the gaol and threatened to march on Williamsburg. This upheaval has been described as most serious challenge to royal authority before outbreak of the War of Independence.[4]

The Sidelong Hill incident exposed Croghan's dishonesty for all to see. Gage was furious, even more so when it came out that Croghan had invited a large number of headmen to trade at Fort Pitt when he was supposed only to meet a few leaders in distant Illinois. Though the deputy superintendent pressed westwards, he was once again on the brink of economic and reputational disaster. All he could do was go forward with his negotiations and hope that some success would redeem him.

Croghan waited eight weeks at Fort Pitt for the suspicious Delawares to arrive. It was May before 500 Shawnees, Delawares and Mingos assembled and he was able to solidify the peace previously agreed by Bouquet. Prisoners were released, deputies were appointed to go to Johnson to make a formal treaty, and Shawnee emissaries were chosen to accompany Croghan to the Illinois. This was a major achievement in itself, but for Croghan it was but a preliminary to his mission to the Mississippi. He left Fort Pitt on 15 May.

At first light on 8 June, the expedition was encamped near the mouth of the Wabash River in the territory of the Weas,

Piankashaws, Twightwees, Kickapoos and Mascoutens, who formed the loose Wabash Confederacy. At first light the camp was surprised by eighty Kickapoos and Mascoutens: Croghan himself was tomahawked, two servants and three Shawnee delegates died and almost everyone else was wounded. When the attackers realised that they had assaulted a diplomatic mission and slain Shawnees they were alarmed and confused – but that did not prevent them from dragging Croghan and the other survivors to Vincennes and then on to the village of Ouiatenon. At both places his captors were rebuked by Indians who already knew Croghan. More importantly, they realised that they risked a descent by the Ohio nations and just possibly a major British expedition too. When the French commander at Fort Chartres instructed them to let Croghan go they did so – but they preserved their dignity by accepting 64 gallons of rum in exchange.

Now that the Wabash tribes needed his forgiveness, wounded Croghan was able to negotiate a treaty allowing the British access to Illinois. In July he received Pontiac and delegates from the Illinois nations, who agreed that British troops could take over the former French posts and thus open the Illinois to a British military presence. It was not an invitation to build more forts, less still permission to found a colony, but it did allow troops to descend the Ohio to take peaceful possession. Returning via Detroit, he concluded a second treaty in the presence of the fort commander and delegates from the Illinois nations. He came back to Philadelphia not to condemnation as a frontier fraud but to adulation as a diplomatic saviour. In New York he won over Gage by playing the aggrieved victim and allowing Bouquet's pass to be misinterpreted. Far from being shunned, he was sent back to the Illinois to further reconcile and report.

Naturally his preliminary recommendations included a proposal for a British settlement in the Illinois, brazenly claiming that the Wabash and Western confederacies had no objection whatever to more British forts and British settlers. He told Johnson that trading posts there would be necessary there to compete with the Louisiana traders beyond the Mississippi and even persuaded him to push the Board of Trade to sanction an inland colony. Meanwhile he wooed his old commercial partners, desperately out of pocket after the 1765 venture but anxious to recoup losses, of the inevitability of an Illinois colony. The military garrisons, he argued, would lead to settlement, and the French settlers and Indians would be eager to sell land. Crohan was never less than persuasive.

On 26 April 1766, Croghan and his allies formed the Illinois Company to agitate for land cessions once a new colonial government was established there. William Franklin, illegitimate son of Benjamin and now governor of New Jersey, was secretly promised a large share in whatever could be obtained, and his father supported the plan to compensate the 'Suffering Traders'. Other participants included (of course) Baynton, Wharton and Morgan, Johnson and Joseph Galloway, Croghan's own lawyer and speaker of the Pennsylvanian assembly. Johnson discreetly refused to sign the agreement though he endorsed it, and Croghan signed for him. (Significantly, the agreement specified that the Illinois land was to be purchased from the Iroquois – not the Indians who actually lived there.) In due course Bejamin Franklin presented the ministry in London with a proposal, probably penned by his son, broadly hinting that Croghan should be the new colony's first governor.

Then he was off to the Illinois country via Fort Pitt, where he narrowly succeeded in preventing Indian hostilities against murderous squatters, and travelled downriver to the Scioto, where on 24 January 1767 he opened a conference with the Western Confederacy. Now the limitations of the earlier agreements were exposed. Their leaders were prepared to allow the British to occupy the French forts to facilitate trade, but resented Iroquois claims and would not countenance settlement without ample compensation. That could not happen until a new boundary was fixed, so speculators like Croghan made the most of Indian unrest to start a war scare. War, it was contended, could not be avoided until the boundary was fixed far to the west of intrusive whites.

Frontier violence seemed to substantiate these claims. On 10 January 1768, one Frederick Stump and his servant John Ironcutter entertained four Indian men and two women at his Susquehanna home, got them thoroughly drunk, and killed them. Next day they travelled 14 miles to murder a woman and two children and burn their camp. Stump was incarcerated at Carlisle but, in true Black Boys fashion, he was freed by a frontier mob. As Indians gathered to seek vengeance, frontiersmen took hostage some Tuscaroras. A frightened Pennsylvania assembly offered a £200 reward for Stump's apprehension and £2,500 in condolence presents, a necessary move which naturally angered frontier settlers even more. A new boundary seemed to be the only viable solution.[5]

19

THE ROAD TO FORT STANWIX

Meanwhile, Johnson had been working to uphold the fast-fading authority and friendship of the Six Nations, which was vital if they were to be persuaded to cede more of the lands they claimed but did not occupy. His lever was the still-unresolved matter of the Kayaderosseras patent, which particularly annoyed his closest friends, the Mohawks. If that was cancelled, and if the Iroquois could be assured of a fixed norther border, huge western cessions might be forthcoming and the 'Suffering Traders' might be offered something on the Ohio. With that in mind, in May 1765, at a peace conference called to discuss and settle the peace terms Bouquet had agreed, he took the chance to raise the boundary issue.

After several days' discussion, the Onondaga spokesman suggested a line running along the north and south branches of the Susquehanna and on to the Ohio, and down the Ohio to the mouth of the Tennessee or Cherokee River. In short, they were pushing the boundary to the south bank of the Ohio and impinging upon Cherokee hunting grounds. This was acceptable to Johnson and was later confirmed by the Board of Trade. But when Johnson spoke of extending the line northwards they were careful. Should a line be negotiated in future, it should cross the Mohawk no higher than German Flats, but that was for later consideration. It was not going to be easy to talk them into yielding the Oneida Carry, but in return for security on the New York frontier they would make major concessions elsewhere. Persuading the patentees to yield up their claims would be critical.

In the summer of 1768 a series of Johnson Hall congresses tackled this very issue. In June two Kayaderosseras heirs produced a transparently forged version of the original cession, which was laughed out of court by the Mohawk spokesman, Abraham. A month later two more claimants appeared, according to Johnson with a legitimate-looking copy of a patent giving them a smaller portion of the contested area. Here at last was a ground for compromise, especially as this cession would not affect Johnson's own claims. Abraham agreed to accept the claim while Johnson promised to secure a new boundary line that would protect the remaining Mohawk lands. The way was clear for the coming boundary congress between the Iroquois and Johnson at Fort Stanwix.[1]

Johnson was still genuinely concerned that that the military vacuum and failure to restrain dishonest traders would produce serious frontier disturbances. However, the long delays in London and the substantial dismantling of the Plan of 1764 had led him, not for the first time, to give priority to his own interests. It is notable that he, Samuel Wharton, William Trent and William Franklin conferred for a month at Johnson Hall before apparently travelling to Fort Stanwix together. Croghan spent three months with Johnson before he too appeared at Fort Stanwix.[2]

As usual, Johnson's concerns were with the Iroquois claims to suzerainty, not with the allegedly subordinate nations such as the Cherokees. If he could get the Iroquois to give up claims as far south as the Tennessee, they might be willing to provide land elsewhere for Croghan's cronies. That was at least part of his reason for inviting the leaders of the Ohio nations to Fort Stanwix, not as participants but merely as observers.

The Virginian representatives, Andrew Lewis and Thomas Walker, of the Greenbrier and Loyal companies respectively, had personal interests in obtaining a generous border settlement. Aware that Stuart had just drawn a line ending at the mouth of the Kanawha, they encouraged Johnson to work for a much more generous boundary, extending far south to the mouth of the Tennessee. That would not only embrace most of the Cherokee country protected by the Hard Labour agreement, but might – in the view of at least one historian – set the scene for a major landgrab when the superintendents fell out.[3] Their aims, however, differed from those of the largely Pennsylvanian interests close to Johnson and Croghan, who wanted to create 'Vandalia', which would stand in the way of unfettered Virginian expansion westward. New York was represented to ensure that the Oneida Carry was ceded and that the governor's own speculations were respected. There were even Congregationalist missionaries in attendance, determined to protect their Oneida flock.[4]

Johnson had to balance these different interests while looking after his own. How he did so is far from clear because, as usual at these conferences, the most important negotiations took place out of public view, 'in the bushes'. However, he seems to have done his best to reconcile the goals of provinces, speculators and merchants, while establishing a defensible boundary and without provoking a new Indian war. However, buying Iroquois co-operation meant ignoring his orders from London and the claims of the Ohio nations and Cherokees.[5]

No fewer than 3,000 Indians – almost all men, the women and children staying at home to secure the harvest – appeared for the opening of the congress on 24 October 1768. Three issues predominated: the Iroquois claim to lands as far south as the Tennessee River, Pennsylvanian claims at the Forks of the Ohio, and the notion of a clear boundary between the Mohawk River settlements and the Oneida lands.

The question of the northern boundary extension arose almost at once. An Onondaga spokesman, after expressing doubts as to whether whites could be trusted to respect any border, asked what was the point of agreeing a boundary with Virginia and Pennsylvania if there was not to be one designed to check settler encroachment into Iroquois homelands. He then suggested drawing a line from Owego on the Susquehanna, the terminal point of the agreed 1765 line, to definitively separate the Six Nations from New York. In return, Mohawk spokesman Abraham announced that the Iroquois wanted the Crown to grant them a clear title to all Ohio lands down to the mouth of the Cherokee River. Clearly no amateurs in the real estate business, they were asking for as much as they could possibly hope to be given. They could then cede these lands used by Shawnees and Cherokees in exchange for trade, goods, cash and the northern boundary.

Johnson then deliberately deviated from his instructions and agreed, knowing that it would benefit his and Croghan's private interests – as well as proving a clear borderline to the south. He could thus claim to have carried out his core duties as a Crown servant. From the Iroquois point of view, it would deflect land speculation to a place far away from themselves. Neither side flinched even when it became clear that the Ohio nations would forcefully resist any incursion upon their hunting grounds.

There was hard bargaining over the Oneida Carry. The Oneida chiefs suggested that the line should begin at the launching place on Wood Creek near Fort Stanwix. This would yield the actual portage but keep the waterway in Indian hands. Johnson, surprised, demanded a starting point much further west, but the Oneidas pointed out that with their hunting grounds so degraded they would have to depend on portage fees for their sustenance. They would only offer a very slight adjustment to the west, and that for $600 more than had already been agreed in private, a concession which Johnson was obliged to accept.[6]

The Iroquois leaders then asked for $10,000 for the immense area they would cede to Pennsylvania. This committed both Johnson and the Six Nations to Pennsylvania's side in the jurisdictional dispute with Virginia over the south side of the Ohio and the claims of the 'Suffering Traders'. Yet all parties thought it well worth the trouble and cost. As well as acquiring a huge swathe of territory, Pennsylvania would see its borders confirmed by the Iroquois and the Crown; both the Penns and the Iroquois would see the final extinction of claims by Connecticut; and the Indiana Company, representing those who had bought up the 'Suffering Traders' claims, had their own cession – to the west of Pennsylvania's – written into the agreement. As an individual, Croghan did even better: he was assigned over 100,000 acres in two lots, in New York and on the Ohio. As for the Six Nations, they had won a fixed boundary which protected most of the lands of the eastern Iroquois. As for the now-isolated Mohawk castles, the land belonging to them was deemed to be their own property to use or dispose of as they saw fit. Furthermore, the Six Nations received a further £10,460 7s 3d for the Ohio lands down to the mouth of the Cherokee River, which were of course occupied and used by others. That was in addition to over twenty boatloads of gifts. The Ohio nations were assigned a princely £27 in trade goods, while the Cherokees were wholly ignored.

The Virginian and Connecticut speculators were of course horrified. Virginia challenged the cessions to Pennsylvania as unjust, while in February 1769 the Connecticut men rested their case for making inland settlements upon a supposed private agreement. In Connecticut there was talk of a large body of settlers going to take Wyoming by force. But the real victims were the Ohio nations, who might well be expected to take armed umbrage at having their hunting grounds sold from under them. Wharton even suggest that the Crown should place settlers on the ceded lands without delay, so that their militias could strike back at any attempted Indian violence.⁷

The treaty concluded on Friday 4 November 1768 departed from Hillsborough's orders in three significant respects. The most egregious of these was the extent of the southern boundary, yielding to settlement about 110,300 square miles, much of it Shawnee hunting grounds and some of it already ceded by the Cherokees at Hard Labour. The northern extension, though not fraudulent, was also unauthorised. Finally, the inclusion of private claims was a blatant breach of diplomatic protocol. In Johnson's defence it could be argued that he had simply faced up to diplomatic realities and made the best bargain for the king that could possibly be had. As for Pennsylvania and the 'Suffering Traders', it was better that these interests be satisfied than left to cause disruption later.⁸

It remained to be seen whether the Secretary of State would agree.

20

LORD HILLSBOROUGH STANDS HIS GROUND

Wills Hill, Earl of Hillsborough, knew a lot about colonies. An unremarkable but ambitious Irish peer and English MP, he first experienced responsible office in 1763 as president of the Board of Trade under his friend Grenville. He was not a distinguished policy maker (unlike Halifax, another friend) but it was in this period that he began to form the views towards empire that would mark his later secretaryship. As early as 1751 he had written a pamphlet in favour of Anglo-Irish union, and – perhaps under Halifax's influence – he developed a metrocentric mentality towards colonies. While he thought the Stamp Act unwise, he did not countenance the resistance it provoked. Significantly, though dismissed when Rockingham took office in 1765, he endorsed the Declaratory Act in 1766. He returned to the Board under Chatham, but – curiously for an ambitious man with a deserved reputation for administrative diligence – he insisted upon giving up his Cabinet seat and that the Board should confine itself to writing reports. When at the end of the year he moved to the Post Office – almost a sinecure with a salary of £2,900 a year – he was seen by some Americans as lax, lazy and harmless. They were sorely mistaken.[1]

Lord Hillsborough Stands His Ground

When he became the first Secretary of State for Colonies in 1768, Hillsborough had strong ideas about colonial expansion, new colonies and colonial unrest, all of them negative. He had little choice but to approve Shelburne's decision to agree a new boundary line far to the west of the 1763 Proclamation Line, but his orders to Johnson and Stuart were very specific: the northern part of the line should run no further than the mouth of the Great Kanawha. Consequently, he was infuriated by Johnson's behaviour in running a line right down to the mouth of the Cherokee and incorporating the demands of Croghan's cronies. As we shall see, his orders for rectification were executed by Stuart at Lochaber, the subsequent alterations by Colonel Donelson bringing the line back to Stuart's own recommendations. To Johnson's chagrin, Hillsborough's orders obliged him to leave the grants to Croghan and the 'Suffering Traders' out of the Fort Stanwix treaty when he and the Iroquois ratified it July 1770. The Secretary of State had marked out his position and held it.[2]

He still had to deal with the 'Suffering Traders', represented at first by Trent and Wharton, who in July 1769 arrived in London to lobby for a share of the Fort Stanwix cession. Franklin convinced them that the best way forward would be to involve prominent British figures with political influence. The result was the Walpole Associates formed in July of that year with seventy-two shareholders. They included the usual suspects, such as Wharton, Trent, Croghan, Johnson, Benjamin and William Franklin and Richard Jackson, but also a number of new British figures. John Sargent, a merchant and former MP, was a friend of Benjamin Franklin. Thomas Walpole and his nephew Richard, both London bankers, Sir George Colebrooke, Chatham's nephew Thomas Pitt, and Shelburne's friend Lachlan Maclean all had seats in the House of Commons. On 24 July the company petitioned the king, asking to be allowed to buy 2.4 million acres of Ohio land, free of quit rents for twenty years, for the same price as was paid to the Iroquois.³ The Privy Council passed the petition to the Board of Trade and at a meeting in December Hillsborough, who was usually strongly opposed to such proposals, seemed to be sympathetic to the scheme.

Hillsborough, however, had not changed his views. He was isolated in the Cabinet, so tried a gamble. Instead of simply trying to block the scheme he suggested that they should ask for 20 million acres – enough for a new proprietary colony – calculating that the Treasury would ask for almost ten times the £10,460 paid for the original Fort Stanwix purchase. He believed, or hoped, that the Walpole Company would be unable to afford £100,000 and the venture would collapse. To his horror, on 14 January the Treasury gladly agreed to the expanded claim at the old price.

There were, however, other sources of opposition. The boundaries outlined by Wharton included land west of the Great Kanawha claimed by Virginia; so, when one of the Treasury commissioners leaked the details, Edward Montague, agent for the Virginian assembly, lodged a formal protest. Existing Virginian venturers were also alarmed. George Mercer, representing the Ohio Company of Virginia, William Lee of the Mississippi Company and the Penns all protested. It took five months to defeat the Mississippi Company and to seduce Mercer into joining the Walpole Associates in what now became the Grand Ohio Company. But Hillsborough was not done yet: as both Secretary of State and President of the Board of Trade, he was able to delay action for five weeks. When Walpole protested and claimed that Virginia was making illegal grants coveted by his company, Hillsborough obligingly referred the charges to Virginia for comment. In that way he was able to postpone the affair for two more years.

Lord Botetourt, the governor of Virginia, had just died, so the colony's reply came from William Nelson, president of the executive council. Predictably, Nelson claimed that all pre-war grants had been properly sanctioned and there had been no large transmontane patents since then, and reminded Hillsborough that the new Walpole colony would clash with the claims of Virginian officers. He enclosed Washington's complaint on this point, presumably unaware that at the same time Washington – with his usual duplicity – was trying to buy Croghan's share in the Walpole Company. Also on Hillsborough's desk was an objection to the Walpole plan written by the governor of New York, Lord Dunmore, later to become governor of Virginia; and he may also have been aware that the Loyal Company had entered its own protest. That allowed him to assure Virginia that London would honour all legitimate claims predating the Walpole petition, and to ignore the Walpole Associates' subsequent cry of anguish. Then he took himself off to Ireland, effectively preventing the Walpolers from getting a favourable decision from the Privy Council.[4]

There was plenty of incoming evidence to confirm Hillsborough's original fears that to move the 1763 boundary would be to invite an Indian war. Johnson warned him that the Fort Stanwix treaty had alarmed the Ohio nations and John Stuart reported that an anti-British intertribal coalition was in the making. Yet, even as the indications mounted, Johnson still maintained that the ceded lands belonged not to the actual occupiers but to the Iroquois. The Donelson additions, and Dunmore's eagerness to take advantage of them, were therefore deeply alarming. By early summer of 1772 Hillsborough was more certain that ever that the scramble for land triggered by the Fort Stanwix treaty had brought the frontier to the brink of a bloody, difficult and expensive war.[5]

Meanwhile, Samuel Wharton had been recruiting more influential investors as levers against Hillsborough. At least three Treasury officials were on his books, as well as Temple, Lord Camden and Lord Hertford, and perhaps the cash-strapped Lord Rochford, the Southern Secretary. All of course wanted to make money out of western lands, but the politicians were also motivated by a desire to unseat Hillsborough and thereby his ally the new premier,

Lord North. Rochford was probably scheming to take over colonial patronage for his own department, Lord Gower wanted the premiership, and the Earl of Suffolk, the Northern Secretary, wanted to remove a possible obstacle to his own advancement. Whether they were able to persuade the king to drop a hint to Hillsborough at a levee is unknown, but at all events their pressure worked. On 20 March 1772, the Board met to consider the Walpole petition, and quickly decided that the matter was sensitive enough to require a Great Board, involving the key ministers of state. A meeting was rescheduled for 22 March but the ex-officio members refused to attend, prodding Hillsborough into openly condemning the proposed new colony. He based his arguments upon the Board's 1768 report rejecting Shelburne's proposal for inland colonies. The Board then passed the issue to the Privy Council, where Gower, its lord president, allowed the Walpole Associates to present their own evidence. A committee heard Trent, Wharton and Mercer testify that there were already tens of thousands of settlers in the region concerned, that it was impossible to remove them by persuasion or force, and that both Williamsburg and Philadelphia were too distant to provide effective government. Mercer denied that the dearth of easy waterborne communications would hinder commerce, and a Mr Robinson solemnly claimed that a sample of American silk from the region – supplied by none other than Benjamin Franklin – was as fine as anything from Italy. The petition was approved and returned to the full Privy Council.

Hillsborough, finding himself isolated, threatened to resign if the petition passed the full council. North, whose main political skill was conciliation, tried to smooth things over, and Suffolk suggested that they first seek a compromise. Hillsborough remained obdurate and resigned on 13 August 1772, to be immediately replaced by North's pious half-brother, Lord Dartmouth. Next day the council approved the Walpole petition – political calculation and economic ambition had triumphed over principle.[6]

Lord Hillsborough Stands His Ground

The decision had been taken in the teeth of Gage's evidence and the opposition of Barrington, Secretary at War, but with Hillsborough gone the speculators thought the way was clear. While the Board of Trade drew up a constitution for the new colony, Wharton was delighted by his first meeting with Dartmouth, and arranged to send Croghan a cargo of presents to mollify the restive Ohio Indians. The Board worked slowly, causing Wharton to press Dartmouth on the matter, but finally completed its work on 6 May 1773.[7]

The name chosen for the new colony – not 'Pittsylvania' as originally envisaged but 'Vandalia' in honour of the queen's supposed descent from destructive early medieval barbarians – was unintentionally comical, but other elements of the proposed charter were more serious. Its inclusion of the Donelson line cession within Vandalia was a greater block than ever to Virginians' expansion and guaranteed their continued opposition. The Crown law officers objected that allowing the investors joint tenancy as proposed would make it extremely difficult to collect quit rents from individual settlers, adding that the colony's boundaries were far too ill defined. Dartmouth struck down both objections, and the Attorney and Solicitor General were ordered to produce a final draft of grant. It looked as though Hillsborough's last stand had been in vain. But in London, disillusionment at the chaos arising from the decisions of 1768 pointed towards an upheaval that would bury Vandalia forever.[8]

21

THE PATH TO LOCHABER

Croghan's scheming and Johnson's disobedience at Fort Stanwix had quite undermined Stuart's Hard Labour settlement with the Cherokees. There could be no going back to the original Hard Labour line, but Johnson's annexations could not be permitted either. On 10 October 1770, on Hillsborough's orders, he met 1,000 Cherokees, including Oconostota, Attakullakulla and the Wolf of Keowee at Lochaber, Alexander Cameron's plantation near Ninety Six in South Carolina. Also present were Virginian representatives led by Colonel John Donelson, who would not accept a reversion to the Hard Labour line.

There a line was agreed to run from the northern tip of the Virginia–North Carolina boundary at 36° 20' N to the Holston, 6 miles above Long Island. Thence it continued in a straight line to the mouth of the Great Kanawha on the Ohio. This was better than the Fort Stanwix line but was nevertheless intrusive, bringing the boundary uncomfortably close to the sacred Long Island, where the Cherokees in the past had not even allowed a trading post – partly out of fear that the building would turn out to be a fort. Stuart was offered other land in compensation, which he refused ostensibly on the grounds that it 'was not within the Limits of my Instructions', but perhaps also as part of his plan to 'avoid all cause from the Cherokees of Complaint of Jealousy' which might lead them into alliance with the Shawnees. It also sliced through very difficult country where the line would be difficult to survey and mark. Yet it was markedly better than the Fort Stanwix proposal, giving away their most distant and degraded hunting grounds while keeping the core of their country intact. That may be why sixteen leaders from all the Cherokee regions, including Oconostota, Attakullakulla and the Wolf of Keowee, put their marks to this agreement.[1]

That, however, was not the end of the matter. The Cherokees had put their marks to the treaty with great reluctance, Oconostota sadly remarked that the young warriors would never accede to it, and complained bitterly of a Virginian who hunted at the head of fifty men and threatened to shoot Cherokees who complained. Attakullakulla waxed lyrical, asking whether the just 'great one above' would approve of what the Virginians had done, and suggesting that their actions were illegal in the highest sense of the word. There was no question of driving the Virginians into the sea, but surely peaceful and respectful co-existence was possible.

In March 1771, Oconostota summoned Cameron to Chota in an attempt to revise the agreement. Cameron would not budge. He knew that Stuart wanted to avoid further wrangling with Virginia, and also that Virginians thought they should have been given at least the Long Island to allow for their further expansion to the south-west. Cameron refused to take back the beads he had given at Lochaber. For his part Oconostota refused to help with the boundary survey. That disagreeable task fell to Attakullakulla.

In May 1771, the Carpenter and a small number of Overhills joined Donelson and Cameron for the survey. The country was rugged and Attakullakulla, who by now must have passed seventy, found the journey wearying. Perhaps, as one recent account has it, he was now so tired of difficult diplomacy that he was open to bribes. He proposed a more easily marked and traversable route by way of the Louisa (Kentucky) River, and received £500 in return for his co-operation. Virginia could now add a further 10 million acres to its acquisitions, but the Cherokees had salvaged more than they had lost. If it had not restored the Hard Labour agreement, the so-called Donelson Line was a significant improvement upon that imposed at Fort Stanwix.[2]

22

DUNMORE'S LITTLE WAR

While the Ohio peoples wanted a fixed boundary that was honoured by all parties, there was a widespread suspicion among them that it would soon be breached. Even the Mingos thought that the Iroquois had given away too much, while the Delawares and Shawnees felt betrayed. It was not just that they had not been consulted or invited to the private meetings where the real business was done. It was not even only that a large swathe of their hunting grounds, their means of livelihood and their safety barrier against advancing settlements, had been taken away. What made all this hurt more was that the Iroquois had made off with the goods and cash given in compensation – a point which also irritated the Cherokees. Both Johnson and the Six Nations were now deeply distrusted and all the Ohio peoples sought ways to ignore them both.[1]

Moreover, Ohio Indians held that even had the Fort Stanwix treaty been legitimate, it could only have transferred the land, not its resources. As one headman put it, when a European sold a farm he gave up the land, not his livestock, unless it was paid for separately. In the same way Shawnees, Delawares and Mingos claimed the right to hunt on the ceded land and to exact rent in the form of cattle, horses and traders' hides. This was not a petty distinction for the danger of starvation was real and enormous. By

1771 there were perhaps 25,000 settlers west of the mountains, placing unsustainable pressure on the local resources. Settlers painfully clearing land and competing with Indians for less and less abundant game also experienced both hunger and poverty.

It is hardly surprising that acts of border violence did not decrease after 1768 but grew in intensity. Indian seizures of horses, cattle and hides were met with retribution. Clashes between Indians, intrusive hunters, traders and settlers developed into a spiral of raids and revenge, like a Native mourning war but less restrained. In one incident Senecas slaughtered a trading party travelling in five boats, apparently in payment for a single murder. The conflict was complicated by clashes between whites and Iroquois war parties going south to raid the Cherokees and by Cherokee parties coming north to attack the Six Nations. Meanwhile settlers fearing raids, sure of their right to occupy land and feeling abandoned by colony and empire, built makeshift stockades and formed their own militias. The likes of the Paxton Boys and Black Boys reappeared, plundering and threatening all traders trying to do business in Indian country. Bands led by Daniel Greathouse and Michael Cresap were particularly active. Revolution – not just another Indian war – was already in the frontier air.

How should Native societies respond? Resistance might bring on another destructive and unwinnable war, yet passive acceptance seemed to promise annihilation. Many Delawares opted for patience and peace but most Shawnees and Ohio Senecas decided otherwise. By 1770 the Seneca leader Guyasuta was weaving a pan-Indian alliance rather like Pontiac's. He approached the Wabash and Illinois peoples, stirred up kinsmen to raid around the Niagara portage, and encouraged cattle killing and horse stealing.

The Shawnees were even more active. From as early as 1769 they drew in the new Wabash Confederacy, old friends now increasingly suspicious of British intentions. Their attempt to reach out to the Cherokees, already at war with the Wabash nations, was more difficult: in 1770 at German Flats, and in Johnson's presence, they instead allied with their old foes the Iroquois. That was bound to be a difficult connection to sustain but even the possibility of a Six Nations–Ohio–Cherokee combination was a major threat to the British. Yet to disrupt it would ensure the continuance of north–south raids and intensify the warfare along the Ohio frontier. Instead, Johnson urged the Six Nations to abstain from joining Cherokee raids and instead to warn the Wabash nations to remain at peace. The grand scheme, so like that of the early 1760s, was becoming unravelled before it could be securely knitted together.

Nevertheless, the Shawnees persisted and had some success among the Cherokees who were feeling the pressure of settler expansion upon their own frontier, and who were worried by Johnson's abrogation of the Hard Labour agreement. Headmen favourable to peace, including Attakullakulla, were once again losing ground to the more belligerent *sachems*. The Cherokees, however, insisted upon Shawnee and Wabash aid against the Chickasaws before attacking whites; and Wabash approaches to Creeks and Choctaws were rejected. Even among the Ohio nations, jealousies and past tensions worked against the Shawnee plan: in 1771 they specifically excluded the cautious Delawares from a planned conference.

War became much more likely when in 1772 royal troops were at last withdrawn from Fort Chartres and Fort Pitt, leaving only fifty men west of Detroit, at Kaskaskia on the faraway Mississippi. Pennsylvania and Virginia rushed to fill the jurisdictional vacuum. Pennsylvanians created a new county, Cumberland, as far along the Ohio as Kentucky, thus unilaterally asserting their predominance in the west. Virginian settlers and speculators responded angrily: not only was the prospect of Pennsylvanian taxes resented, but men like Washington stood to lose fortunes.

The latter had, however, a key friend and ally in John Murray, 4th Earl of Dunmore, ex-Jacobite and ex-army officer, governor of Virginia from 1771, and himself a keen speculator in western lands. During his governorship of New York, the earl had taken pains to secure large estates and even from there he had shown an interest in Virginian land issues. Washington himself frequently corresponded with Dunmore about securing patents for land already marked out by his surveyors. Unlike Washington, however, he was Crown servant first and a property developer second: by the summer of 1775 they would find themselves on opposite sides.[2]

Dunmore's key agent in securing Virginian claims was Dr John Connolly, who was also associated with William Crawford, Washington's chief surveyor and land scout. While Connolly had a stake in the Vandalia project, which clashed with Virginian ambitions, he was won over by Dunmore's opposition to Pennsylvanian claims in the same region: to say nothing of a promised of 2,000 acres at the Falls of the Ohio in addition to his patent for military service. Early in 1774 Connolly seized the abandoned Fort Pitt, called out a recently formed local militia, declared the region part of Virginia and appointed civil magistrates. Then on 27 April, as war brewed between Virginia and Pennsylvania, Daniel Greathouse's gang enticed Mingo hunters into their camp at Yellow Creek (or into a nearby settler's house) and slaughtered thirteen. The victims included the Shawnee wife and the pregnant sister of Tachnechdorus, otherwise known as John Logan, a Mingo chieftain who had hitherto good relations with the local settlers. The sister, Koonay, wife of a Pittsburgh trader, was hung by her wrists, her belly was cut open and her unborn child was ripped out and impaled on a stake. Inexplicably, they did not kill Koonay's two-month-old daughter, who was later rescued by Crawford and returned to her father. Michael Cresap's men attacked a band of traders on the same day, killing one of its Shawnee escorts.[3]

Yet Logan's retaliation was remarkably restrained, being at first limited to taking an equal number of white scalps, after which he declared himself satisfied. Meanwhile the Shawnee headmen worked hard – and not always successfully – to restrain their own young

Dunmore's Little War

men. Their main spokesman was Hokoleskwa or Cornstalk, also known as Hard Man, who had been one of Bouquet's hostages at the end of Pontiac's War. When Connolly asked Cornstalk not to mind the misdeeds of a few, he answered (through an intermediary) that Connolly should not mind the actions of the young Shawnee men, adding that he would protect traders moving between their country and Fort Pitt. It was a promise that he and his kin strove to keep.[4]

This was disappointing for Dunmore and Connolly, who hoped for a war which would allow Virginia to clear Kentucky of both Pennsylvanians and Shawnees while saddling the Indians with the blame. It was certainly Connolly's cries of alarm that in June 1774 led the Pittsburgh militia to attack Shawnees escorting local traders to Fort Pitt. Shawnee patience snapped at last and raid upon raid was launched against frontier settlements.[5]

Dunmore's response was to organise an offensive against the Shawnee towns. A temperate observer might note that when he arrived at Fort Pitt (renamed Fort Dunmore) on 10 September he seemed genuinely surprised that the violence had been provoked by the Virginians. A less charitable interpreter might suggest that it was what he and Connolly had intended all along. Two days later, when the Delaware chief White Eyes – the usual go-between – and other headmen came offering to mediate peace, he kept them waiting two more days for a reply. Then he solemnly acknowledged their good offices but, reciting their alleged crimes, stated that the Shawnees could not go unpunished. Meanwhile he pressed on with his preparations for a war of territorial conquest. Then there was ambition: as an officer he had always coveted military glory, but his active service consisted of a few raids on French ports during the Seven Years War, and he had never held an independent command. He may or may not have deliberately provoked the coming war against the Shawnees, but the situation offered an opportunity not to be missed.[6]

Dunmore received no imperial support. Johnson's last action was to try to persuade the Ohio nations to restrain the Shawnees, but he collapsed and died in the midst of the conference. Meanwhile, the British regular garrisons at Detroit and Niagara refused to send help. But that did not inhibit Dunmore, who pressed ahead with only the Virginian militia. His force advanced in two columns, Dunmore himself leading about 1,200 militia westward from Fort Pitt, Andrew Lewis's smaller contingent marching overland to the headwaters of the Kanawha and thence to its junction with the Ohio. There seemed to be no clear plan or communication between the two except a vague intention to rendezvous somewhere near the Kanawha. While on 7 October Lewis encamped at Point Pleasant at the mouth of the Kanawha, Dunmore unexpectedly veered inland to threaten the Scioto towns, offering the watching Indians a chance to attack Lewis. Lewis, with no more than 600–1,000 men, and a 200-strong rearguard still some distance behind, was vulnerable.

Cornstalk was already making a bold strategic gamble. Should Lewis's rearguard arrive, and should Lewis and Dunmore unite, the Virginians would have a three-to-one numerical advantage. But at that moment their forces were days apart. A swift blow against Lewis's column would dramatically shorten the odds and perhaps bring in more allies against the Virginians. Even if he could not destroy Lewis, his warriors could inflict losses heavy enough to dismay Dunmore's force and compel the governor to retreat. His fighters, mostly Shawnees but with some of Logan's Senecas and even a few Ottawas, assembled north of the Ohio River.

In the small hours of 10 October, Cornstalk brought between 500 and 800 warriors across the Ohio on about eighty rafts and canoes. Landing perhaps 6 miles upriver from the Virginians, they advanced through the woods to abandoned Old Shawneetown, within 2 miles of the sleeping soldiers. At dawn they would close in, silently kill the sentries and rapidly overrun the camp. There was a tactical gamble involved here too: trapping the militia against the rivers would oblige the Indians to attack frontally, rather than laying an ambush in traditional crescent formation.

But surprise might make all the difference. The warriors may have had fewer rifles than their enemies, but smoothbore trade muskets, loaded with ball or buckshot, could be devastating at close range. If they could suddenly close with the unprepared militia, Lewis's whole force might be annihilated. At first light the Shawnees and their allies moved in silently to attack.

Almost immediately they lost the element of total surprise when they were sighted by two pairs of unauthorised hunters straying from the camp. One hunter was killed and the survivors fled back to raise the alarm, causing the sleepy militiamen to hurriedly arm themselves. Cornstalk sent his whole force into the attack, hoping he could still overrun the camp. But Lewis, thinking he was facing only a scouting party, sent out two weak columns to deal with it. They were slowly driven in as the Indians strove to keep the two parties apart. As Lewis sent in further reinforcements the Virginians' numbers began to tell, and slowly the battle line stiffened. Shawnees and militia were now locked in a close-quarter battle of attrition, both sides firing, clubbing and hacking.

Even now Cornstalk dared not retire: he needed to inflict as many casualties as possible. Though pushed back for about a mile on their right, on the left the Indians were able to consolidate their defence on a patch of rising wooded ground. Militia officers examining the ground concluded that it would be too costly to dislodge them, and the battled became a stalemate. At about 4 p.m. the Shawnee firing slackened, whether from lack of powder or failing morale it is impossible to know. Then, just before sunset, their shooting ceased almost completely and under cover of darkness Cornstalk withdrew and recrossed the Ohio. The militia had lost seventy-five dead and 140 wounded, against the Indians' at least thirty-three killed and an unknown number wounded. Lewis had been mauled but not destroyed.[7]

Meanwhile, Dunmore had marched to within 8 miles of the Shawnee towns on the Scioto and established a strongly fortified base which he named Camp Charlotte. Cornstalk now had to make a difficult choice: should the Shawnees fight, flee or accept Dunmore's terms? His Shawnees had not stopped Lewis, nor had most of his potential allies turned out to fight, and now the Shawnee towns were in imminent danger. The principal town, Chillicothe, standing behind the steep west bank of the deep Scioto, might have been defended: there was only one crossing place lower downstream, the houses were strong and defensible, there was a wide cleared field of fire around them, and they were occupied by up to 700 warriors. Yet the stakes were too high: Dunmore already had over 1,110 men on hand and Lewis's battered division was known to be on its way. If the defence failed all would be lost; if it held, from Camp Charlotte the Virginians could raid and burn every other town and its crops. Retreat would produce the same result. With a heavy heart, Cornstalk advised a council to accept Dunmore's terms. The Shawnees, and even a lamenting Logan, had to agree.[8]

The terms were less draconic than the Shawnees had expected but the price of survival was high. On 16 October the Treaty of Camp Charlotte obliged the Shawnees to return all their white captives; refrain from hunting south of the Ohio or molesting any boats travelling upon it; accept Virginian trade regulations; recognise the earlier cessions made by the Iroquois and Cherokees; and promise to attend a formal settlement conference in the spring. Kentucky had been cleared of its Native claimants and for the first time the actual occupiers of Indian land had agreed to a cession.[9] No wonder that the Virginians were jubilant. An officer writing a long, triumphant martial poem in his journal included the following telling verse:

> The land is good, it is just to our mind
> Each will have his part if his lordship be kind
> The Ohio once ours, we'll live at our ease,
> With a Bottle & glass to drink when we please[10]

Dunmore's Little War

The Shawnees' Mingo allies were less obliging: Logan agreed to stop fighting and released his prisoners but refused to attend the peace conference. Dunmore received intelligence that the Great Mingo was about to take his people north to the Great Lakes, out of reach of any pursuit. The Virginian response was simple: a patrol was sent to surprise his town far up the Scioto, burn the houses and bring back the erring Mingos. It was a partial success: surprise was lost when the attackers had to kill an Indian sentry hidden behind a log. Six Mingos died and fourteen were captured and all their baggage and horses were taken. But most of the band escaped and all Dunmore could do was to release four prisoners in the hope forlorn hope of luring the others back.[11]

The campaign had reinforced both the Virginians' sense of their own military prowess and also their anger at Lord Dartmouth's announcement that Virginian veterans of the French and Indian War were not entitled to the land bounties promised by Dinwiddie in 1754. On their way home the militiamen halted at Fort Gower on the upper Ohio, where they learned that the Continental Congress had responded to the Coercive Acts with a boycott, and also that Parliament had brought the Quebec frontier down to the Ohio. The officers responded in dramatic fashion by signing the so-called Gower Resolves, affirming loyalty to George III but reserving their right to oppose him with violence should he betray their 'Love of Liberty, and Attachment to the real Interests and just Rights of America'.[12] Given their recent service, there could be no doubt that the just American interest they had in mind went far beyond the bounty land grievance. For a new Quebec Act had denied Canada a representative assembly, enshrined toleration for Catholics and brought Canada's border right down to the Ohio. Frontier land-lust was now firmly wedded to a revolutionary agenda.

23

LORD DARTMOUTH'S INTOLERABLE ACT

Since 1764, ministry after ministry had tried to find a method of equitable taxation that Americans could accept. While few politicians wholeheartedly embraced the Halifax–Egremont conception, the idea that the empire was a collegiate entity, not a loose association of semi-independent polities, was now common currency. Anything less would not only be inequitable but dangerous for the security of both metropole and periphery. While the events in Massachusetts had little directly to do with frontiers it was nevertheless an underlying issue, and the part of the response involving the boundary was the one Americans found least tolerable.

The response was designed by Frederick, Lord North, Prime Minister since 1770. North was the very first premier to work harmoniously with George III and, at the same time, deliver reliable parliamentary majorities through his ability to reconcile rival factions. His advantage was that, though addressed as 'Lord' by courtesy, he had not yet inherited his father's peerage, so he could sit in the House of Commons and there personally manage critical business. His ministry was referred to as 'Tory' but in fact it was a mixed bag: Dartmouth came from a Tory family turned

Whig after the Hanoverian succession; many, like Sandwich at the Admiralty and North himself, were from Whig backgrounds and probably thought of themselves as Whigs. The ministry was 'Tory' only in the American sense of favouring parliamentary supremacy. The critical figure was Dartmouth.

At first, from across the Atlantic, Dartmouth seemed a much more amenable figure than Hillsborough. Though he had served as president of the Board of Trade under Rockingham, he owed his appointment more to his loyalty to North, his stepbrother and close friend, than to experience or knowledge of American affairs. He had opposed the Stamp Act and so had the approval of Benjamin Franklin. His real enthusiasm was for religion: a committed Anglican evangelical, he was acquainted with John Wesley and the Countess of Huntingdon. He was linked to the anti-slavery movement through patronage of the former slaver captain John Newton, who composed 'Amazing Grace'. He was thought to be more favourable to the Vandalia scheme and to inland colonies in general, believing that they would provide stable government in lawless places.[1]

Franklin and others missed two points about Dartmouth's thinking. While at the Board he had formed very clear views about colonial government from which he never deviated. A strong believer in parliamentary sovereignty, he had opposed the Stamp Act as impolitic but supported the Declaratory Act as constitutionally necessary. Though he favoured conciliation, and even conducted a private correspondence with the speaker of the Massachusetts assembly, he was prepared to sanction force should negotiation fail. He also had a genuine concern for the welfare of Indians: his approval of Vandalia was highly qualified and he wanted managed, not unfettered, expansion.

For years he had supported Ebenezer Wheelock's charity school for Indians which became (to secure backing and without his express permission) Dartmouth College in New Hampshire. He embraced the Enlightenment notion of the noble savage. Moreover, by 1773 he was convinced that not even a new frontier colony could halt unauthorised expansion and that it could only result in more warfare. By now, he was listening to arguments against allowing a new and distant colony at all: it would have a tiny population; it would be unable to supply men in a crisis; water routes would not support commerce, so far from being a lucrative market for British goods it would probably develop its own industries; and moreover the permission would not address the problem of violent frontiersmen. When Gage came home on leave in 1773, he was keen to confirm these impressions. The good earl was looking round for a workable alternative solution.[2]

One was already at hand. For some time the Board had been considering the problem of incorporating Quebec, a conquered colony with a predominantly French Catholic populace, into the British Empire. As there were many French settlers between the Ohio and the existing bounds of Quebec, it would make sense, in terms of both frontier management and securing their loyalty, to bring the Quebec boundary down to the north bank of the Ohio.

Action was precipitated by the American reaction to the 1773 Tea Act, which accompanied a separate Act revising the East India Company's charter. The latter introduced a measure of royal supervision of the company's activities in the subcontinent and created the post of governor general to check the territorial recklessness of the individual presidencies. The *quid pro quo* was the Tea Act, intended to provide some relief for the company's very considerable debts by removing the requirement that it should auction its tea imports in London. In effect, it cut out the London middlemen and allowed the company to sell tea cheaply in its destination markets, including the American colonies. The effect would have been to undercut Boston smugglers like John Hancock, even allowing for the fact that the company would pay the tea tax. The result is well known: Boston 'Sons of Liberty' boarded the ships and dumped the tea into the harbour. Less well known are the riots in other ports: lax customs regimes at Rhode Island, New York and Philadelphia had made them even busier centres of smuggling than Boston itself. The Tea Party, however, was the most spectacular protest of them all, an act of lawless defiance that could not be ignored. After a decade of ministerial compromises being met with boycotts and mob violence, enough was enough.

Sensibly, the ministry and Parliament elected to punish only Boston and Massachusetts, either to limit the outrage or because they (wrongly) thought Boston to be the real seat of the trouble. In the summer of 1774, a quartet of coercive laws closed the port of Boston to legitimate trade until compensation was paid; altered the Massachusetts charter to weaken elected institutions and strengthen the governor; allowed the governor to seize unoccupied buildings as quarters for the troops; and finally, to protect soldiers and officials executing their duty, allowed trials to be moved to Britain or another colony. The appointment of the commander-in-chief, Gage himself, as governor was the final touch.

The result was the first Continental Congress, which met at Philadelphia to consider retaliatory measures but at this stage avoided outright rebellion – after all, the British government's own actions had been limited to Massachusetts. What tipped American 'patriots' over the edge of loyalty was not the Coercive Acts (to them the 'Intolerable Acts') but the measure that followed them: the Quebec Act.

Dartmouth had had little to do with the passages of the Coercive Acts, apart from expressing a hope that enforcement would be tempered with moderation. The problem of Quebec, however, fell squarely within his department's responsibility: since the previous summer his two under-secretaries, William Knox and John Pownall, had been busy working out the details and the Solicitor General, Alexander Wedderburn, was now turning their proposals into drafts for a bill. The new American crisis made it a matter of urgency to secure the loyalty of French Canadians, and by April 1774 the third and final draft was ready. Quebec's boundary was to be brought down to the Allegheny and Ohio rivers; the province would have a military governor and a nominated council; and although British criminal law would be introduced, French civil law would remain in force. All tenant farmers remained liable for militia duties, as did a *corvée*, the obligation to work on roads, bridges, fortifications and transport services for an indeterminate number of days per year. The Catholic Church was to have full freedom of worship and priests would still be able to collect tithes; and the semi-feudal privileges of the *seigneur* landlords were confirmed. These included the right to collect dues from their *habitants*, who also had to use his mill and pay for the privilege (*banalités*), and to exercise judicial authority through his manorial court. A *seigneur* could issue licences to hunt, fish and cut wood, and he might insist upon a *corvée*.

Hillsborough and Governor Guy Carleton objected to the boundary for fear that French settlers might create their own Vandalia north-west of the Ohio, but the Cabinet was in no mood to quibble. It was very late in the session when Dartmouth introduced the bill into the Lords where it sailed through; and – partly because many weary peers and members had already left for the country – it was not until its second reading in the Commons that there was any serious debate. There Wedderburn firmly rebutted Isaac Barré's contention that ministers were planning to use the Canadians against the existing colonies. The bill, he asserted, was intended to check westward expansion for the good of the empire as a whole, not to oppress British subjects. Edmund Burke and Charles James Fox regretted the retention of French civil law and the absence of an elected assembly, but even Burke had reservations about giving a parliamentary system to a population unused to it. Both weakened their own arguments by praising its toleration of Catholicism. On 6 June the bill passed the Commons by 56 votes to 20. It then went back to the Lords, where a long, ranting speech by an ailing and unstable Chatham did nothing to prevent it from passing 26 to 7. It received the royal assent on 22 June and was due to come into force on 1 May 1775. It was an extraordinary measure.

In the colonies it met a more robust opposition. George III's support for a law that appeared to establish Roman Catholicism and confirm both an unrepresentative form of government and a quasi-feudal social system – in short something like conditions in France – may have been the tipping point for radicals' relationship to the Crown. By the end of 1775 increasing numbers of Americans were prepared to jettison the monarchy altogether.[3] These provisions handed a massive propaganda weapon to the radicals, who represented it as a plot to arm the Canadians against the English-speaking colonies, strip them of their representative assemblies and impose a popish dictatorship. The First Continental Congress, meeting in Philadelphia to consider retaliatory action, stopped short of secession but authorised preparation for armed resistance, thus clearing the way for rebellion in the spring of 1775 and a declaration of independence the following year. But the reform which moved the border of Quebec was the main reason for elite and backwoods resentment.

Not only was the boundary moved to the north bank of the Ohio, but all private land purchases from Indians there would now become illegal. No more Indian lands could ever be acquired legally and the original British colonies would ever after be confined to the east coast. Enforcement would be partly assisted by denying Quebec a representative assembly and by retaining French civil law, both of which would be unattractive to Anglo-American speculators and settlers. The accompanying Quebec Revenue Act, which attracted far less attention in America, was both a fiscal measure and an attempt to deter illegal traders. The duties it imposed on rum, sugar and molasses were payable only at posts on the St Lawrence and Sorel rivers, places inconveniently remote from the Ohio Valley markets. Moreover, those who ignored the duties were liable to be punished by seizure of the rum and the horses, wagons or boats carrying them, as well as a fine triple the value of the goods.

The Ohio boundary threatened the long-term prospects of wealthy speculators such as Washington, the Lees, Patrick Henry, Baynton and Morgan (who had substantial stakes in the Vandalia project), Trent and even the moderate South Carolinian merchant Henry Laurens. Without clear title they could not sell on their grants and purchases. Washington affected to believe that, like the Proclamation of 1763, the Quebec Act boundary would soon be abandoned, and claimed that his main grievances were with taxation and the Coercive Acts. But beneath that remark he was furious about Dartmouth's denial of the 1754 land bounties and about the new barrier to north-western expansion. The First Continental Congress, summoned specifically in response to the Coercive Acts, revealed militant views from similar quarters. Richard Henry Lee and Patrick Henry, both Virginian representatives with extensive western land interests, thought the Quebec Act the worst thing that Britain had ever done to the American colonies. When Congress established the Continental Association to boycott British goods – on the face of it a protest against the tea duty – it objected not only to the arbitrary government of Canada but also to the barriers against settlement beyond the Ohio.

The speculators scrambled to secure their claims before the Act could come into force. Their allies in the Virginia, New York and Pennsylvania assemblies objected to the new boundary as a violation of their founding charters, meaning that it prevented them from expanding westward. Some took more direct action. As early as May 1774, Wharton – then in London lobbying for the Vandalia project – urged Croghan to secretly secure an Indian cession on the right bank of the Ohio before it could become part of Quebec. He even promised to send £4,000 worth of goods for this purpose, By June two very large shipments had arrived in Virginia, awaiting the end of Dunmore's war so they could be shipped west. Wharton was unaware that Croghan had already bought himself 1.5 million acres, promising not to settle it for fifteen years unless its Indian occupiers moved away earlier. Of course, he was calculating that hunting there would soon become so scarce that the Indians would have to move, and that government would then have to grant him a patent. [4]

On the left bank there was more dramatic and open activity. In August 1774 a North Carolinian lawyer, Richard Henderson, founded the Transylvania Company (as it was eventually named) with the aim of creating a proprietary colony below the Kentucky cessions on the left bank. He seems to have met Attakullakulla more than once early in 1775 and obtained what he thought were offers of large quantities of land. In March 1775 he met about 1,200 Cherokees supporting a number of headmen, including Attakullakulla and Ostenaco, at Sycamore Shoals on the Watauga River. There was an atmosphere of confusion and incoherence about the conference, made more colourful by the presence of traders making money by selling the Indians food and drink: what one historian has called 'a helter-skelter air'. There was no British official there to ensure sobriety and order: John Stuart was stuck in Charleston under the watchful eyes of local radicals, and his deputy Alexander Cameron gave up his journey when his interpreter was poached by Henderson's people. The headmen were mostly drunk when Henderson produced deeds giving his company the illegal purchase of 27,000 square miles of Cherokee land between the Kentucky and Cumberland rivers. Attakullakulla's own son Tsiyu Gansini (Dragging Canoe) was disgusted by the extent of the white men's demand and walked out. Only three signed – Attakullakulla, the Raven of Chota and

Oconostota – and Oconostota immediately had second thoughts. Next morning he was seen with other headmen drawing maps in the soil and contending that the Cherokees had given away only a limited right of way. It was too late: the deal was done and the company employed the frontiersman Daniel Boone to hack a rough track from the Shoals to the Falls of the Ohio, the so-called 'Wilderness Road' intended to channel settlers into the new land and make a fortune for its new proprietors.

Once again it was the story of high trade prices, a shortage of guns and munitions with which to resist either settlers or Native foes, land degraded by settlement and spiralling trade debts. However huge and painful the cession, the £10,000 in goods (mostly guns, lead and powder) and £2,000 in cash that the Cherokees received in return must have seemed irresistible. But this last cession put the Overhill Towns in the direct path of white settlement and the nation was almost surrounded. Pan-Indian militants denounced the deal. In 1776 Dragging Canoe fought enthusiastically against the American rebels and led his followers southward to become the breakaway Chickamauga people.[5]

However, the ultimate success of Transylvania and Vandalia depended upon sales, and land sales, as ever, required legal title. It was now clear that that approval would not be forthcoming from London, nor from the governors of individual colonies: even Dunmore denounced the Sycamore Shoals treaty. Nor would a government already taking strong action in Boston ever be inclined to reverse the Quebec Act. Many men like Croghan and Wharton, whose fortunes turned on schemes like Vandalia and Transylvania, soon moved from lobbying in London to petitioning the Continental Congress for lands north of the Ohio. Entrepreneurs like Henderson and settlers alike knew that their land claims would be void if the British government was ever to reassert its frontier authority – and make the new Quebec boundary effective – and to prevent that from happening many

Lord Dartmouth's Intolerable Act

were inclined to take up arms. In the spring of 1775 Wharton and Trent, hedging their bets, began to appeal to the Continental Congress. Washington was incandescent when Dunmore decided that, because William Crawford was not a qualified Crown lands surveyor, having failed to take the required oath of allegiance, Washington's claim to more than 23,000 acres was void. No wonder that in April, when an Ohio surveying party heard that a Massachusetts militia had clashed with British infantry, they renamed their camp 'Lexington'.[6]

24

COLLAPSE

Was a reconciliation possible after the Quebec Act? Dartmouth appeared to think so. On 1 February 1775 he showed an interest in a draft bill put forward by Chatham in the House of Lords. It proposed that the Quebec Act and all the Coervice Acts should be at once repealed, judges in vice-admiralty courts should be appointed during good behaviour, as in England, and not as at present at the king's pleasure; and that colonial charters could not be arbitrarily changed. Congress could be recognised as a governing body in America and even be allowed, like provincial assemblies, to collect taxes. However, Chatham stopped short of full capitulation, insisting upon the overarching supremacy of Parliament.[1]

Dartmouth seemed inclined to give the bill further consideration, suggesting that debate should be postponed until he had time to consider it in detail. However, it immediately became apparent that others on his side of the House were not of the same mind. Sandwich, the First Lord of the Admiralty, moved that it be rejected out of hand, Lords Gower, Hillsborough and Grafton all supported him, insisting that a rebellion was already in progress, and could only be ended by force. It was apparent that Sandwich's motion would pass, whether Dartmouth supported it or not, and if he did so he would be voting with the opposition against ministerial colleagues. Hillsborough's views may have been particularly influential when he announced that he would now vote for rejection. When Sandwich prevailed by 61 to 32, the author of the Quebec Act may have actually been relieved, but he appeared to be a ditherer. Benjamon Franklin afterwards denounced the Colonial Secretary as weak-willed.[2]

Dartmouth was not done yet. He and sympathetic colleagues entered into a secret negotiation with Franklin, who came up with eight proposals, of which the ministers accepted five. The points of agreement were all to do with the fiscal, judicial and constitutional measures so often assumed to have been at the heart of the American rebellion. Ministers would not accept a colonial veto over the Navigation Acts, nor would they agree that British troops could only be quartered with the assent of the relevant provincial assembly, nor that the Quebec Act should be repealed. When they seemed open to repealing the Massachusetts Government Act, Franklin tried to couple with it with the Quebec Act, arguing that constitutionally they were the same. Unsurprisingly Dartmouth, who had always asserted that the two were unconnected, repeated this assertion now. The boundary of Canada was to remain where George III had said it should be, and its conciliatory constitution would remain in place. If the Quebec Act was not the sole sticking point, it was probably the most important. There would be no more negotiations and no more proposals from Franklin, who took ship for America in March. Before he arrived home, crisis had degenerated into warfare.

Dartmouth would not yet admit defeat. Still on the table was a proposal from Lord North that, should the colonies raise enough revenue to support government needs there, Parliament would not in future exercise its right to tax them itself. In its final form the draft resolution made no mention of compelling obedience by force. Once North's resolution was adopted by Parliament, his stepbrother sent copies to the governors of all the colonies, essentially suggesting that everything but Parliament's supremacy was up for negotiation. For Dartmouth the only alternative was complete independence. Was he now prepared to sacrifice the Quebec Act? It is impossible to say with certainty, but his official silence on that point may be significant.[3]

The opposition argued that it was intended to divide and rule, by tempting individual provinces to negotiate their own terms. In America it had an even more hostile reception. Congress and the individual assemblies would not accept unfettered parliamentary supremacy without a legal guarantee of their perceived rights. The First Continental Congress had already demanded the removal of all objectionable legislation since 1763, which would have included the principle of the 1763 Proclamation and the Quebec Act. The Olive Branch Petition, which offered submission to either taxation or trade regulation but not both, betrayed a yearning for the slack trade and frontier regulations of pre-Proclamation America. Before it arrived in August the ministry was under severe pressure to declare the colonies in a state of rebellion, and Dartmouth (who was on holiday) was informed by both his undersecretaries that French officers were showing an alarming interest in the new Continental Army. The declaration passed the Privy Council two days before the Olive Branch Petition was presented to Parliament and, with the returned Dartmouth's support, soundly rejected. War was declared, and the first major move by the Americans was to invade Canada.[4]

We are not here concerned with the wider causes of the American Revolution, which of course were many and complex, but with a single if important and often neglected theme. Was the containment of frontier expansionism always impossible? Did eighteenth-century Britain ever have the resources necessary to support a metrocentric frontier policy? Financially it was probably affordable: the national debt stood at £134.2 million in 1764, immediately after the Seven Years War, and remained at roughly that level until well into the War of American Independence when in 1782 it reached £214.2 million. One might conclude that the cost of the most catastrophic of eighteenth-century wars was surprisingly modest. Surely it would have been possible to finance an adequate, well-staffed and disciplined Indian Department and an effective frontier military force in peacetime? The estimated annual cost of defending America after 1763 was £30,000: even with the Indian Department's needs added, surely an attainable sum.[5]

But of course, that is not the whole story. Grenville and his successors were deeply alarmed the size of the debt and could not have known that an even greater burden could be successfully borne. During the years of unstable government from 1763, when ministries could be toppled by a slight rise in the land tax, retrenchment was politically essential. It might have been possible to have persuaded Americans to accept taxation in return for an open frontier, but as managing the frontier was largely the *point* of the proposed taxes, that option was off the table. By 1768, ministers had made the worst of all worlds: a theoretically closed frontier without the money or will to enforce it.

Will was a key factor. Halifax and Egremont had will and vision in abundance, and for a time they prevailed. Others, however, were less committed, and the Proclamation of 1763 and the Plan of 1764 were never vigorously tested. Shelburne was at best lukewarm and at worst destructive: the withdrawal of the frontier garrisons in 1768 (though understandable) and the castration of the Indian Department meant the effective end of the experiment. Thereafter, Hillsborough and Dartmouth were fighting rearguard actions. There was also a shortage of suitable men on the ground. Many governors were too attached to the interests of their provinces and most saw no clear distinction between private and public duties. Sir William Johnson was the supreme example of this kind of official, while Croghan represented those who saw public duty as a road to private prosperity. There were others like Stuart who, while acquiring property themselves, were convinced and conscientious public servants, but they were too few. Some soldiers fell into this class – Forbes, Grant, Bradstreet, even at times Bouquet – but these were local mavericks, able and willing to create their own Indian policies whatever the attitudes of distant commanders-in-chief. The commanders-in-chief themselves were less adventurous: Amherst was not interested in frontier affairs and heartily disliked Indians, and Gage was too cautious. One thinks again of the sad fate of George II's elaborate pavilion for the fireworks in 1749.

Thus we come full circle. The plans for a metrocentric empire were in the beginning dangerous but necessary. Subsequent experience showed that the model could work briefly and unevenly, despite 3,000 miles of intervening ocean, before the deficiencies in its execution took hold. Without it the dissolution of the empire in America was probable; with it, survival was possible – and was in part achieved.

APPENDIX 1

The Royal Proclamation of 1763

1763, October 7.
BY THE KING
A Proclamation
George R.

Whereas We have taken into Our Royal Consideration the extensive and valuable Acquisitions in America, secured to Our Crown by the late Definitive Treaty of Peace, concluded at Paris the Tenth Day of February last, and being desirous, that all Our loving Subjects, as well of Our Kingdoms as of Our Colonies in America, may avail themselves, with all convenient Speed, of the great Benefits and Advantages which must accrue therefrom to their Commerce, Manufactures, and Navigation; We have thought fit, with the Advice of Our Privy Council, to issue this Our Royal Proclamation, hereby to publish and declare to all Our loving Subjects, that We have, with the Advice of Our said Privy Council, granted Our Letters Patent under Our Great Seal of Great Britain, to erect within the Countries and Islands ceded and confirmed to Us by the said Treaty, Four distinct and separate Governments, stiled and called by the Names of Quebec, East Florida, West Florida, and Grenada, and limited and bounded as follows; viz.

First. The Government of Quebec, bounded on the Labrador Coast by the River St. John, and from thence by a Line drawn from the Head of that River through the Lake St. John to the South End of the Lake nigh Pissin; from whence the said Line crossing the River St. Lawrence and the Lake Champlain in Forty five Degrees of North Latitude, passes along the High Lands which divide the Rivers that empty themselves into the said River St. Lawrence, from those which fall into the Sea; and also along the North Coast of the Baye des Chaleurs, and the Coast of the Gulph of St. Lawrence to Cape Rosieres, and from thence crossing the Mouth of the River St. Lawrence by the West End of the Island of Antiocosti, terminates at the aforesaid River of St. John.

Secondly. The Government of East Florida, bounded to the Westward by the Gulph of Mexico, and the Apalachicola River; to the Northward, by a Line drawn from that Part of the said River where the Chatahouchee and Flint Rivers meet, to the Source of St. Mary's River, and by the

Course of the said River to the Atlantick Ocean; and to the Eastward and Southward, by the Atlantick Ocean, and the Gulph of Florida, including all Islands within Six Leagues of the Sea Coast.

Thirdly. The Government of West Florida, bounded to the Southward by the Gulph of Mexico, including all Islands within Six Leagues of the Coast from the River Apalachicola to Lake Pentchartain; to the Westward, by the said Lake, the Lake Mauripas, and the River Mississippi; to the Northward, by a Line drawn due East from that Part of the River Mississippi which lies in Thirty one Degrees North Latitude, to the River Apalachicola or Chatahouchee; and to the Eastward by the said River.

Fourthly. The Government of Grenada, comprehending the Island of that Name, together with the Grenadines, and the Islands of Dominico, St. Vincents and Tobago. And, to the End that the open and free Fishery of Our Subjects may be extended to and carried on upon the Coast of Labrador and the adjacent Islands,

Appendix 1

We have thought fit, with the Advice of Our said Privy Council, to put all that Coast, from the River St. John's to Hudson's Straights, together with the Islands of Anticosti and Madelaine, and all other smaller Islands lying upon the said Coast, under the Care and Inspection of Our Governor of Newfoundland.

We have also, with the Advice of Our Privy Council, thought fit to annex the Islands of St. John's, and Cape Breton or Isle Royale, with the lesser Islands adjacent thereto, to Our Government of Nova Scotia.

We have also, with the Advice of Our Privy Council aforesaid, annexed to Our Province of Georgia all the Lands lying between the Rivers Attamaha and St. Mary's.

And whereas it will greatly contribute to the speedy settling Our said new Governments, that Our loving Subjects should be informed of Our Paternal Care for the Security of the Liberties and Properties of those who are and shall become Inhabitants thereof; We have thought fit to publish and declare, by this Our Proclamation, that We have, in the Letters Patent under Our Great Seal of Great Britain, by which the said Governments are constituted, given express Power and Direction to Our Governors of Our said Colonies respectively, that so soon as the State and Circumstances of the said Colonies will admit thereof, they shall, with the Advice and Consent of the Members of Our Council, summon and call General Assemblies within the said Governments respectively, in such Manner and Form as is used and directed in those Colonies and Provinces in America, which are under Our immediate Government; and We have also given Power to the said Governors, with the Consent of Our said Councils, and the Representatives of the People, so to be summoned as aforesaid, to make, constitute, and ordain Laws, Statutes, and Ordinances for the Publick Peace, Welfare, and Good Government of Our said Colonies, and of the People and Inhabitants thereof, as near as may be agreeable to the Laws of England, and under such Regulations and Restrictions as are used in other Colonies: And in the mean Time, and until such Assemblies can be called as aforesaid, all Persons inhabiting in, or resorting to Our said Colonies, may confide in Our Royal Protection for the Enjoyment of the Benefit of the Laws of Our Realm of England; for which Purpose, We have given Power under Our Great Seal to the Governors of Our said Colonies respectively, to erect and constitute, with the Advice of Our said Councils respectively, Courts of Judicature and Publick Justice, within Our said Colonies, for the hearing and determining all Causes, as well Criminal as Civil, according to Law and Equity, and as near as may be agreeable to the Laws of England, with Liberty to all Persons who may think themselves aggrieved by the Sentences of such Courts, in all Civil Cases, to appeal, under the usual Limitations and Restrictions, to Us in Our Privy Council.

We have also thought fit, with the Advice of Our Privy Council as aforesaid, to give unto the Governors and Councils of Our said Three New Colonies upon the Continent, full Power and Authority to settle and agree with the Inhabitants of Our said New Colonies, or with any other Persons who shall resort thereto, for such Lands, Tenements, and Hereditaments, as are now, or hereafter shall be in Our Power to dispose of, and them to grant to any such Person or Persons, upon such Terms, and under such moderate Quit-Rents, Services, and Acknowledgements as have been appointed and settled in Our other Colonies, and under such other Conditions as shall appear to Us to be necessary and expedient for the Advantage of the Grantees, and the Improvement and Settlement of our said Colonies.

And whereas We are desirous, upon all Occasions, to testify Our Royal Sense and Approbation of the Conduct and Bravery of the Officers and Soldiers of Our Armies, and to reward the same, We do hereby command and impower Our Governors of Our said Three New Colonies, and all other Our Governors of Our several Provinces on the Continent of North America, to grant, without Fee or Reward, to such Reduced Officers as have served in North

Appendix 1

America during the late War, and to such Private Soldiers as have been or shall be disbanded in America, and are actually residing there, and shall personally apply for the same, the following Quantities of Lands, subject at the Expiration of Ten Years to the same Quit-Rents as other Lands are subject to in the Province within which they are granted, as also subject to the same Conditions of Cultivation and Improvement; viz.

To every Person having the Rank of a Field Officer, Five thousand Acres. — To every Captain, Three thousand Acres. — To every Subaltern or Staff Officer, Two thousand Acres. — To every Non-Commission Officer, Two hundred Acres. — To every Private Man, Fifty Acres.

We do likewise authorize and require the Governors and Commanders in Chief of all Our said Colonies upon the Continent of North America, to grant the like Quantities of Land, and upon the same Conditions, to such Reduced Officers of Our Navy, of like Rank, as served on Board Our Ships of War in North America at the Times of the Reduction of Louisbourg and Quebec in the late War, and who shall personally apply to Our respective Governors for such Grants.

And whereas it is just and reasonable, and essential to Our Interest and the Security of Our Colonies, that the several Nations or Tribes of Indians, with whom We are connected, and who live under Our Protection, should not be molested or disturbed in the Possession of such Parts of Our Dominions and Territories as, not having been ceded to, or purchased by Us, are reserved to them, or any of them, as their Hunting Grounds; We do therefore, with the Advice of Our Privy Council, declare it to be Our Royal Will and Pleasure, that no Governor or Commander in Chief in any of Our Colonies of Quebec, East Florida, or West Florida, do presume, upon any Pretence whatever, to grant Warrants of Survey, or pass any Patents for Lands beyond the Bounds of their respective Governments, as described in their Commissions: as also, that no

Governor or Commander in Chief in any of Our other Colonies or Plantations in America, do presume, for the present, and until Our further Pleasure be known, to grant Warrants of Survey, or pass Patents for any Lands beyond the Heads or Sources of any of the Rivers which fall into the Atlantick Ocean from the West and North-West, or upon any Lands whatever, which, not having been ceded to, or purchased by Us as aforesaid, are reserved to the said Indians, or any of them.

And We do further declare it to be Our Royal Will and Pleasure, for the present as aforesaid, to reserve under Our Sovereignty, Protection, and Dominion, for the Use of the said Indians, all the Lands and Territories not included within the Limits of Our said Three New Governments, or within the Limits of the Territory granted to the Hudson's Bay Company, as also all the Lands and Territories lying to the Westward of the Sources of the Rivers which fall into the Sea from the West and North West, as aforesaid; and We do hereby strictly forbid, on Pain of Our Displeasure, all Our loving Subjects from making any Purchases or Settlements whatever, or taking Possession of any of the Lands above reserved, without Our especial Leave and Licence for that Purpose first obtained.

And We do further strictly enjoin and require all Persons whatever, who have either wilfully or inadvertently seated themselves upon any Lands within the Countries above described, or upon any other Lands, which, not having been ceded to, or purchased by Us, are still reserved to the said Indians as aforesaid, forthwith to remove themselves from such Settlements.

And whereas great Frauds and Abuses have been committed in the purchasing Lands of the Indians, to the great Prejudice of Our Interests, and to the great Dissatisfaction of the said Indians; in order therefore to prevent such Irregularities for the future, and to the End that the Indians may be convinced of Our Justice, and determined Resolution to remove all reasonable Cause of Discontent, We do, with the Advice of Our Privy Council, strictly

Appendix 1

enjoin and require, that no private Person do presume to make any Purchase from the said Indians of any Lands reserved to the said Indians, within those Parts of Our Colonies where We have thought proper to allow Settlement; but that if, at any Time, any of the said Indians should be inclined to dispose of the said Lands, that same shall be purchased only for Us, in Our Name, at some publick Meeting or Assembly of the said Indians to be held for that Purpose by the Governor or Commander in Chief of Our Colonies respectively, within which they shall lie: and in case they shall lie within the Limits of any Proprietary Government, they shall be purchased only for the Use and in the Name of such Proprietaries, conformable to such Directions and Instructions as We or they shall think proper to give for that Purpose: And We do, by the Advice of Our Privy Council, declare and enjoin, that the Trade with the said Indians shall be free and open to all our Subjects whatever; provided that every Person, who may incline to trade with the said Indians, do take out a Licence for carrying on such Trade from the Governor or Commander in Chief of any of Our Colonies respectively, where such Person shall reside; and also give Security to observe such Regulations as We shall at any Time think fit, by Ourselves or by Our Commissaries to be appointed for this Purpose, to direct and appoint for the Benefit of the said Trade; And We do hereby authorize, enjoin, and require the Governors and Commanders in Chief of all Our Colonies respectively, as well Those under Our immediate Government as those under the Government and Direction of Proprietaries, to grant such Licences without Fee or Reward, taking especial Care to insert therein a Condition, that such Licence shall be void, and the Security forfeited, in Case the Person, to whom the same is granted, shall refuse or neglect to observe such Regulations as We shall think proper to prescribe as aforesaid.

And We do further expressly enjoin and require all Officers whatever, as well Military as those employed in the Management and Direction of Indian Affairs within the Territories reserved as aforesaid for the Use of the said Indians, to seize and apprehend all Persons whatever, who, standing charged with Treasons, Misprisions of Treason, Murders, or other Felonies or Misdemeanours, shall fly from Justice, and take Refuge in the said Territory, and to send them under a proper Guard to the Colony where the Crime was committed of which they stand accused, in order to take their Tryal for the same.

Given at Our Court at St. James's, the Seventh Day of October, One thousand seven hundred and sixty three, in the Third Year of Our Reign.

God Save the King

London: Printed by Mark Baskett, Printer to the King's most Excellent Majesty; and by the Assigns of Robert Baskett. 1763.

APPENDIX 2

An Act for making more effectual Provision for the Government of the Province of Quebec in North America (1774: 14 George 3 c.83: The Quebec Act)

WHEREAS his Majesty, by his Royal Proclamation bearing Date the seventh Day of October, in the third Year of his Reign, thought fit to declare the Provisions which had been made in respect to certain Countries, Territories, and Islands in America, ceded to his Majesty by the definitive Treaty of Peace, concluded at Paris on the tenth day of February, one thousand seven hundred and sixty-three: And whereas, by the Arrangements made by the said Royal Proclamation a very large Extent of Country, within which there were several Colonies and Settlements of the Subjects of France, who claimed to remain therein under the Faith of the said Treaty, was left, without any Provision being made for the Administration of Civil Government therein; and certain Parts of the Territory of Canada, where sedentary Fisheries had been established and carried on by the Subjects of France, Inhabitants of the said Province of Canada under Grants and Concessions from the Government thereof, were annexed to the Government of Newfoundland, and thereby subjected to Regulations inconsistent with the Nature of such Fisheries:

    I. May it therefore please your most Excellent Majesty that it may be enacted; and be it enacted by the King's most

Excellent Majesty, by and with the Advice and Consent of the Lords Spiritual and Temporal, and Commons, in this present Parliament assembled, and by the Authority of the same: That all the Territories, Islands, and Countries in North America, belonging to the Crown of Great Britain, bounded on the South by a Line from the Bay of Chaleurs, along the High Lands which divide the Rivers that empty themselves into the River Saint Lawrence from those which fall into the Sea, to a Point in forty-five Degrees of Northern Latitude, on the Eastern Bank of the River Connecticut, keeping the same Latitude directly West, through the Lake Champlain, until, in the same Latitude, it meets the River Saint Lawrence: from thence up the Eastern Bank of the said River to the Lake Ontario; thence through the Lake Ontario, and the River commonly call Niagara and thence along by the Eastern and South-eastern Bank of Lake Erie, following the said Bank, until the same shall be intersected by the Northern Boundary, granted by the Charter of the Province of Pennsylvania, in case the same shall be so intersected: and from thence along the said Northern and Western Boundaries of the said Province, until the said Western Boundary strike the Ohio: But in case the said Bank of the said Lake shall not be found to be so intersected, then following the said Bank until it shall arrive at that Point of the said Bank which shall be nearest to the North-western Angle of the said Province of Pensylvania, and thence by a right Line, to the said North-western Angle of the said Province; and thence along the Western Boundary of the said Province, until it strike the River Ohio; and along the Bank of the said River, Westward, to the Banks of the Mississippi, and Northward to the Southern Boundary of the Territory granted to the Merchants Adventurers of England, trading to Hudson's Bay; and also all such Territories, Islands, and Countries, which have, since the tenth of February, one

Appendix 2

thousand seven hundred and sixty-three, been made Part of the Government of Newfoundland, be, and they are hereby, during his Majesty's Pleasure, annexed to, and made Part and Parcel of, the Province of Quebec, as created and established by the said Royal Proclamation of the seventh of October, one thousand seven hundred and sixty-three.

II. Provided always: That nothing herein contained, relative to the Boundary of the Province of Quebec, shall in anywise affect the Boundaries of any other Colony.

III. Provided always, and be it enacted: That nothing in this Act contained shall extend, or be construed to extend, to make void, or to vary or alter any Right, Title, or Possession, derived under any Grant, Conveyance, or otherwise howsoever, of or to any Lands within the said Province, or the Provinces thereto adjoining; but that the same shall remain and be in Force, and have Effect, as if this Act had never been made.

IV. And whereas the Provisions, made by the said Proclamation, in respect to the Civil Government of the said Province of Quebec, and the Powers and Authorities given to the Governor and other Civil Officers of the said Province, by the Grants and Commissions issued in consequence thereof, have been found, upon Experience, to be inapplicable to the State and Circumstances of the said Province, the Inhabitants whereof amounted, at the Conquest, to above sixty-five thousand Persons professing the Religion of the Church of Rome, and enjoying an established Form of Constitution and System of Laws, by which their Persons and Property had been protected, governed, and ordered, for a long Series of Years, from the first Establishment of the said Province of Canada; be it therefore further enacted by the Authority aforesaid: That the said Proclamation, so far as the same relates to the said Province of Quebec, and the Commission under the Authority whereof the Government of the said Province is at present administered, and all and every the Ordinance and Ordinances made by the Governor and Council of Quebec for the Time being, relative to the Civil Government and Administration of Justice in the said Province, and all Commissions to Judges and other Officers thereof, be, and the same are hereby revoked, annulled, and made void, from and after the first Day of May, one thousand seven hundred and seventy-five.

V. And, for the more perfect Security and Ease of the Minds of the Inhabitants of the said Province, it is hereby declared: That his Majesty's Subjects, professing the Religion of the Church of Rome of and in the said Province of Quebec, may have, hold, and enjoy, the free Exercise of the Religion of the Church of Rome, subject to the King's Supremacy, declared and established by an Act, made in the first Year of the Reign of Queen Elizabeth, over all the Dominions and Countries which then did, or thereafter should belong, to the Imperial Crown of this Realm; and that the Clergy of the said Church may hold, receive, and enjoy, their accustomed Dues and Rights, with respect to such Persons only as shall profess the said Religion.

VI. Provided nevertheless: That it shall be lawful for his Majesty, his Heirs or Successors, to make such Provision out of the rest of the said accustomed Dues and Rights, for the Encouragement of the Protestant Religion, and for the Maintenance and Support of a Protestant Clergy within the said Province, as he or they shall, from Time to Time think necessary and expedient.

VII. Provided always, and be it enacted: That no Person professing the Religion of the Church of Rome, and residing in the said Province, shall be obliged to take the Oath required by the said Statute passed in the first Year of the Reign of Queen Elizabeth, or any other Oaths substituted by any other Act in the Place thereof; but that every such Person who, by the

Appendix 2

said Statute, is required to take the Oath therein mentioned, shall be obliged, and is hereby required, to take and subscribe the following Oath before the Governor, or such other Person in such Court of Record as his Majesty shall appoint, who are hereby authorized to administer the same; *videlicet*, I A.B., do sincerely promise and swear: That I will be faithful, and bear true Allegiance to his Majesty King George, and him will defend to the utmost of my Power, against all traitorous Conspiracies, and Attempts whatsoever, which shall be made against his Person, Crown, and Dignity; and I will do my utmost Endeavor to disclose and make known to his Majesty, his Heirs and Successors, all Treasons, and traitorous Conspiracies, and Attempts, which I shall know to be against him, or any of them; and all this I do swear without any Equivocation, mental Evasion, or secret Reservation, and renouncing all Pardons and Dispensations from any Power or Person whomsoever to the contrary. So help me GOD. And every such Person, who shall neglect or refuse to take the said Oath before mentioned, shall incur and be liable to the same Penalties, Forfeitures, Disabilities, and Incapacities, as he would have incurred and been liable to for neglecting or refusing to take the Oath required by the said Statute passed in the first Year of the Reign of Queen Elizabeth.

VIII. And be it further enacted by the Authority aforesaid: That all his Majesty's Canadian Subjects within the Province of Quebec, the religious orders and Communities only excepted, may also hold and enjoy their Property and Possessions, together with all Customs and Usages relative thereto, and all other their Civil Rights, in as large, ample, and beneficial Manner, as if the said Proclamation, Commissions, Ordinances, and other Acts and Instruments had not been made, and as may consist with their Allegiance to his Majesty, and Subjection to the Crown and Parliament of Great Britain;

and that in all Matters of Controversy, relative to Property and Civil Rights, Resort shall be had to the Laws of Canada, as the Rule for the Decision of the same; and all Causes that shall hereafter be instituted in any of the Courts of Justice, to be appointed within and for the said Province by his Majesty, his Heirs and Successors, shall, with respect to such Property and Rights, be determined agreeably to the said Laws and Customs of Canada, until they shall be varied or altered by any Ordinances that shall, from Time to Time, be passed in the said Province by the Governor, Lieutenant Governor, or Commander in Chief, for the Time being, by and with the Advice and Consent of the Legislative Council of the same, to be appointed in Manner herein-after mentioned.

IX. Provided always: That nothing in this Act contained shall extend, or be construed to extend, to any Lands that have been granted by his Majesty, or shall hereafter be granted by his Majesty, his Heirs and Successors, to be holden in free and common Soccage.

X. Provided also: That it shall and may be lawful to and for every Person that is Owner of any Lands, Goods, or Credits, in the said Province, and that has a Right to alienate the said Lands, Goods, or Credits, in his or her Lifetime, by Deed of Sale, Gift, or otherwise, to devise or bequeath the same at his or her Death, by his or her last Will and Testament; any Law, Usage, or Custom, heretofore or now prevailing in the Province, to the contrary hereof in any-wise notwithstanding; such Will being executed either according to the Laws of Canada, or according to the Forms prescribed by the Laws of England.

XI. And whereas the Certainty and Lenity of the Criminal Law of England, and the Benefits and Advantages resulting from the Use of it, have been sensibly felt by the Inhabitants, from an Experience of more than nine Years, during which

Appendix 2

it has been uniformly administered: be it therefore further enacted by the Authority aforesaid: That the same shall continue to be administered, and shall be observed as Law in the Province of Quebec, as well in the Description and Quality of the Offence as in the Method of Prosecution and Trial; and the Punishments and Forfeitures thereby inflicted to the Exclusion of every other Rule of Criminal Law, or Mode of Proceeding thereon, which did or might prevail in the said Province before the Year of our Lord one thousand seven hundred and seventy-four; any Thing in this Act to the contrary thereof in any respect notwithstanding; subject nevertheless to such Alterations and Amendments as the Governor, Lieutenant-governor, or Commander in Chief for the Time being, by and with the Advice and Consent of the legislative Council of the said Province, hereafter to be appointed, shall, from Time to Time, cause to be made therein, in Manner hereinafter directed.

XII. And whereas it may be necessary to ordain many Regulations for the future Welfare and good Government of the Province of Quebec, the Occasions of which cannot now be foreseen, nor, without much Delay and Inconvenience, be provided for, without intrusting that Authority, for a certain Time, and under proper Restrictions, to Persons resident there, and whereas it is at present inexpedient to call an Assembly; be it therefore enacted by the Authority aforesaid: That it shall and may be lawful for his Majesty, his Heirs and Successors, by Warrant under his or their Signet or Sign Manual, and with the Advice of the Privy Council, to constitute and appoint a Council for the Affairs of the Province of Quebec, to consist of such Persons resident there, not exceeding twenty-three, nor less than seventeen, as his Majesty, his Heirs and Successors, shall be pleased to appoint, and, upon the Death, Removal, or Absence of any of the Members of the said Council, in like Manner to constitute and appoint such and so many other Person or Persons as shall be necessary to supply the Vacancy or Vacancies; which Council, so appointed and nominated, or the major Part thereof; shall have Power and Authority to make Ordinances for the Peace, Welfare, and good Government, of the said Province, with the Consent of his Majesty's Governor, or, in his Absence, of the Lieutenant-governor, or Commander in Chief for the Time being. [Repealed by The Constitutional Act, 1791]

XIII. Provided always: That nothing in this Act contained shall extend to authorize or impower the said legislative Council to lay any Taxes or Duties within the said Province, such Rates and Taxes only excepted as the Inhabitants of any Town or District within the said Province may be authorized by the said Council to assess, levy, and apply, within the said Town or District, for the Purpose of making Roads, erecting and repairing publick Buildings, or for any other Purpose respecting the local Convenience and Oeconomy of such Town or District.

XIV. Provided also, and be it enacted by the Authority aforesaid: That every Ordinance so to be made, shall, within six Months, be transmitted by the Governor, or, in his Absence, by the Lieutenant-governor, or Commander in Chief for the Time being, and laid before his Majesty for his Royal Approbation; and if his Majesty shall think fit to disallow thereof, the same shall cease and be void from the Time that his Majesty's Order in Council thereupon shall be promulgated at Quebec.

XV. Provided also: That no Ordinance touching Religion, or by which any Punishment may be inflicted greater than Fine or Imprisonment for three Months, shall be of any Force or Effect, until the same shall have received his Majesty's Approbation.

Appendix 2

XVI. Provided also: That no Ordinance shall be passed at any Meeting of the Council where less than a Majority of the whole Council is present, or at any Time except between the first Day of January and the first Day of May, unless upon some urgent Occasion, in which Case every Member thereof resident at Quebec, or within fifty Miles thereof, shall be personally summoned by the Governor, or, in his absence, by the Lieutenant-governor, or Commander in Chief for the Time being, to attend the same.

XVII. And be it further enacted by the Authority aforesaid: That nothing herein contained shall extend, or be construed to extend, to prevent or hinder his Majesty, his Heirs and Successors, by his or their Letters Patent under the Great Seal of Great Britain, from erecting, constituting, and appointing, such Courts of Criminal, Civil, and Ecclesiastical Jurisdiction within and for the said Province of Quebec, and appointing, from Time to Time, the Judges and Officers thereof, as his Majesty, his Heirs and Successors, shall think necessary and proper for the Circumstances of the said Province.

XVIII. Provided always, and it is hereby enacted, That nothing in this act contained shall extend, or be construed to extend, to repeal or make void, within the said province of Quebec, any act or acts of the parliament of Great Britain heretofore made, for prohibiting, restraining, or regulating, the trade or commerce of his Majesty's colonies and plantations in America; but that all and every the said acts, and also all acts of parliament heretofore made concerning or respecting the said colonies and plantations, shall be, and are hereby declared to be, in force, within the said province of Quebec, and every part thereof.

Source: Avalon Project – Great Britain: Parliament – The Quebec Act: October 7, 1774

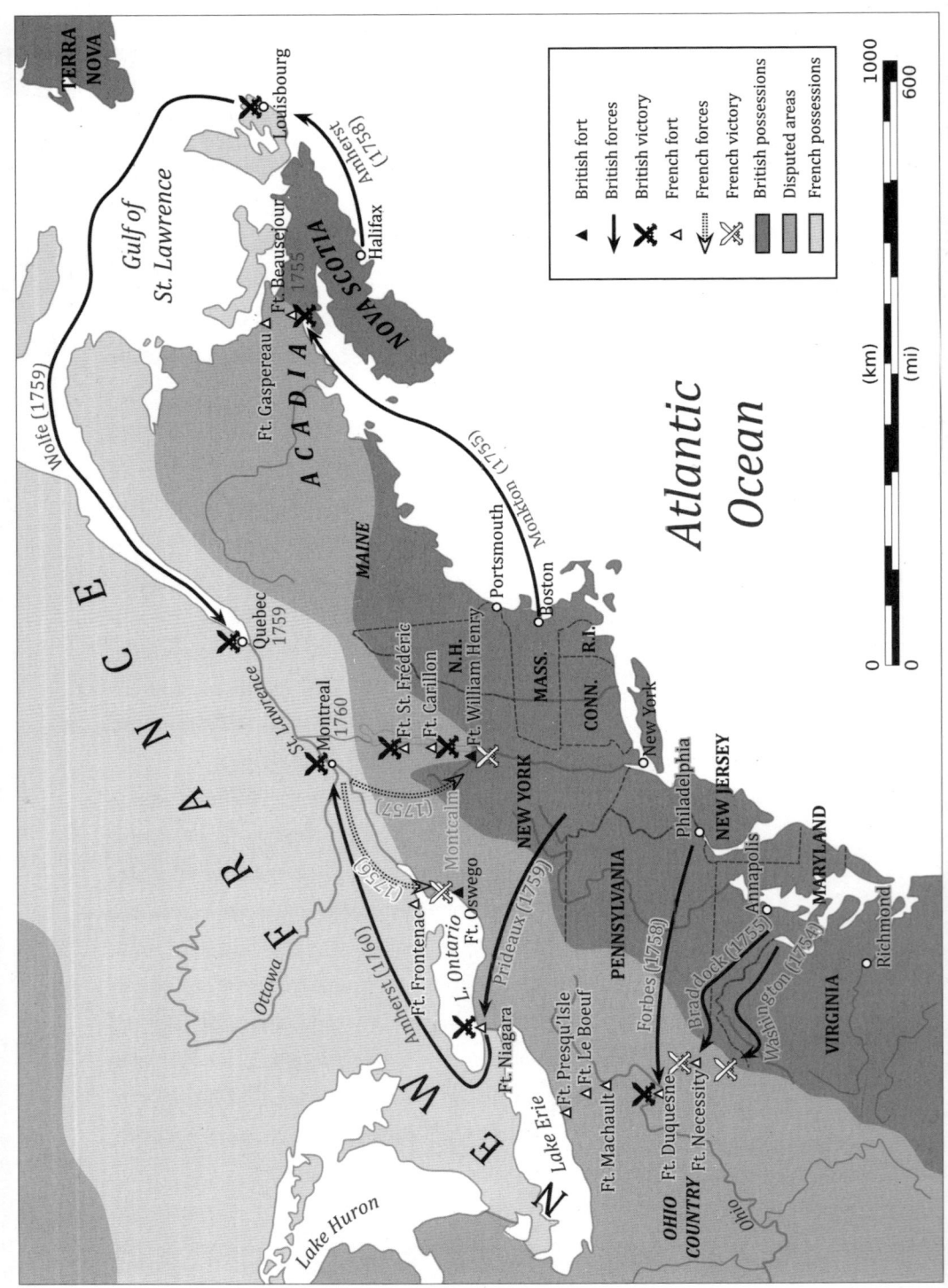

The French and Indian War of 1754–63. (Adapted from work by Hoodinski, Creative Commons licence CC BY-SA 3.0)

Braddock's failed expedition to Fort Duquesne, 1755. (Library of Congress)

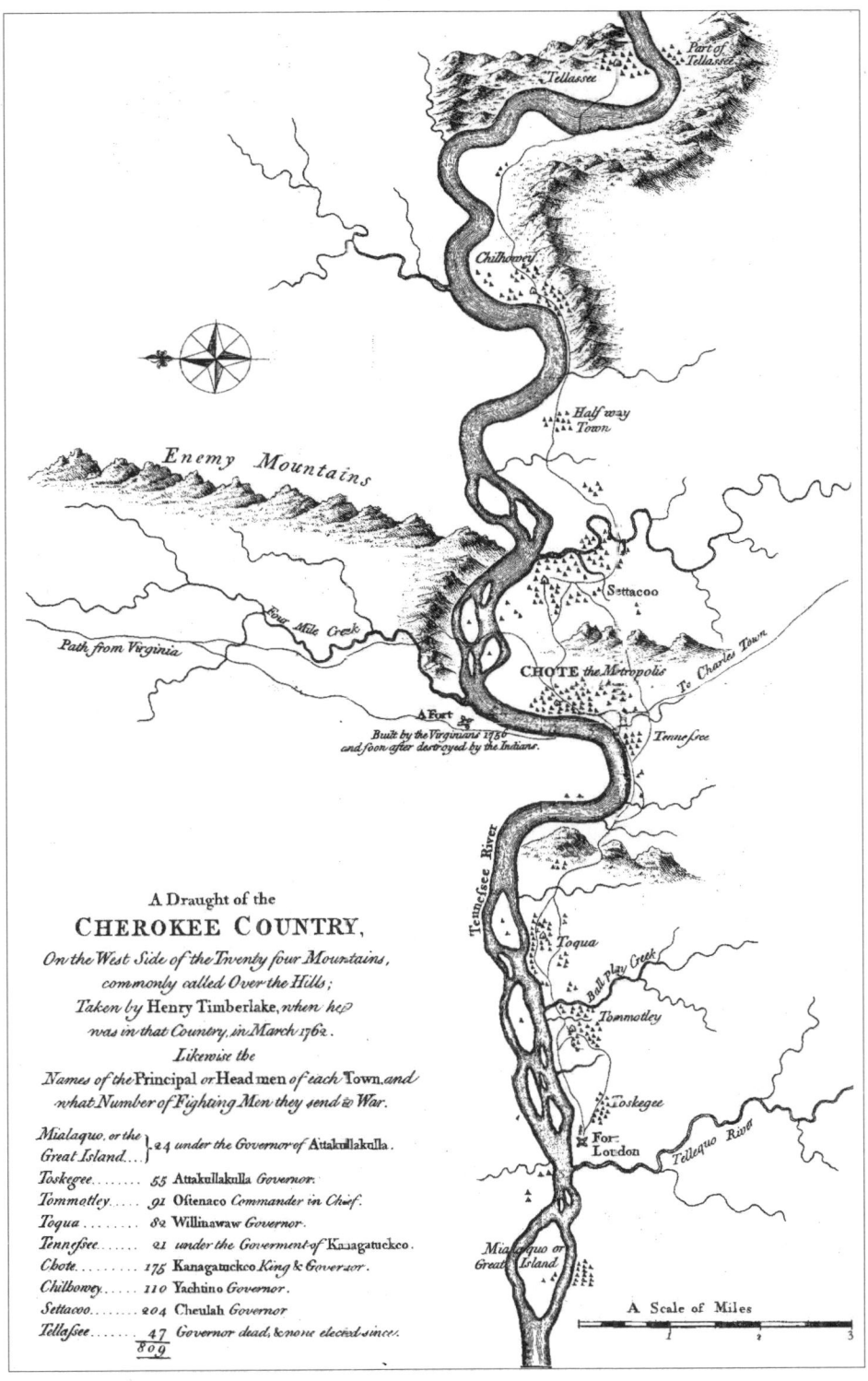

Above: A map of the Cherokee country made by Henry Timberlake in 1762. (Henry Timberlake, *Memoirs*, 1765)

Opposite: The French occupation of the Ohio Valley, 1755. (Library of Congress)

Previous spread: Mitchell map, 1755. British North American claims as Halifax wished his colleagues and the public to see them. (Library of Congress)

This spread: Carrington Bowles map, 1763. British North America as perceived after the Seven Years' War. (Library of Congress)

Forts and settlements of America in 1763, at the outbreak of Pontiac's War.

Previous spread: Forts and settlements of North America at the beginning of Pontiac's War in 1763.

This spread: Bennett and Sayer's map of North America after 1775. (Library of Congress)

NOTES

1 Borderlands

1. John Brewer, *The Pleasures of the Imagination: English Culture in the Eighteenth Century* (Harper Collins, London, 1997) 25–27.
2. R. C. Simmons, *The American Colonies: From Settlement to Independence* (Norton, New York and London, 1981) 174–186; Jeremy Gregory and John Stevenson, *The Routledge Companion to Britain in the Eighteenth Century* (Routledge, Abingdon) 244.
3. Frederick J. Turner, *The Significance of the Frontier in American History* ([1893] LM Publishers, reprint, n.d.)
4. Patrick Spero, *Frontier Country: The Politics of War in Early Pennsylvania* (University of Pennsylvania Press, Philadelphia, 2016) 6–9.
5. Matthew Ward, *Making the Frontier Man: Violence, White Manhood and Authority in the Early Western Backcountry* (University of Pittsburgh Press, Pittsburgh, 2023) 116–118.
6. R. Dean Snow, *The Iroquois* (Blackwell, Cambridge Massachusetts, 1996) 110.
7. Richard White, *The Middle Ground: Indians, Empires and Republics in the Great Lakes Region, 1650–1815* (University of Cambridge Press, Cambridge, 1991.
8. Colin G. Calloway, *The Western Abenakis of Vermont, 1600–1800: War, Migration, and the Survival of an Indian People* (University of Oklahoma Press, Norman, 1990) 160–164.

9. Anthony F. C. Wallace, *Teedyuscung: King of the Delawares, 1700–1763* (Syracuse University Press, 1990) 18–30; Spero, *Frontier Country* 95–96.
10. Brewer, *The Pleasures of the Imagination*, 27–29.

2 Lord Halifax Has a Vision

1. W. A. Speck, 'Dunk, George Montagu, Second Earl of Halifax (1716–1771), in *The Oxford Dictionary of National Biography* September 2012 https://doi-org.lonlib.idm.oclc.org/10.1093/ref:odnb/8266; Beaumont, *Colonial America and the Earl of Halifax*, 69–77.
2. T. R. Clayton, 'The Duke of Newcastle, the Earl of Halifax, and the American Origins of the Seven Years' War', *Historical Journal*, Vol. 24, No. 3 (Sep., 1981), pp. 573–603, esp. 573–577.
3. Beaumont, *Colonial America and the Earl of Halifax*, 77–79.
4. *ibid.*, 82–85.
5. *ibid.*, 45–48.
6. Wilbur R. Jacobs (ed.), *The Appalachian Indian Frontier: The Edmond Atkin and Plan of 1755* (University of Nebraska Press, Norman, 1967).
7. Desmond Clarke, *Arthur Dobbs Esquire: Surveyor Geneal of Ireland, Prospector and Governor of North Carolina* (The Bodley Head, London, 1958); Robert M. Calhoon, 'Dobbs, Arthur (1689–1765)', *Oxford Dictionary of National Biography* 3 January 2008, https://doi-org.londonlib.idm https://doi-org.lonlib.idm.oclc.org/10.1093/ref:odnb/7711
8. Matthew H. Edney, 'John Mitchell's Map of North America (1755): A Study of the Use and Publication of Official Maps in Eighteenth-Century Britain', *Imago Mundi*, Vol. 60, No. 1 (2008), pp. 63–85.
9. A very preceptive account of these inner Cabinet workings can be found in T. R. Clayton, 'The Duke of Newcastle, the Earl of Halifax, and the American Origins of the Seven Years' War', *Historical Journal*, Vol. 24, No. 3 (Sep., 1981), pp. 571–603.
10. Beaumont, *Colonial America and the Earl of Halifax*, 51–57.
11. Plank, *An Unsettled Conquest*, 122–139.
12. Jacob M. Price, 'Hanbury, John (1700–1758)', in *The Oxford Dictionary of National Biography* 2008 version, https://doi-org.lonlib.idm.oclc.org/10.1093/ref:odnb/53741.

13. A useful summary of this correspondence is in Alfred P. James, *The Ohio Company: Its inner History* (University of Pittsburgh Press, Pittsburgh, 1959) 11–15.

3 The Fall of a Half-King

1. Richard S. Grimes, *The Western Delaware Indian Nation: Warriors and Diplomats* (Lehigh University Press, Bethlehem, 2017) 39–46; Calloway, 'Red Power and Homeland security: Native Nations and the Limits of Empire in the Ohio Country', in Kate Fullagar and Michael A. McConnell /(eds.), *Facing Empire: Indigenous Experience in a Revolutionary Age* (Johns Hopkins University Press, Baltimore, 2018) 145–162.
2. Fred Anderson, *Crucible of War: The Seven Years' War and the Fate of Empire in British North America* (Faber, New York and London, 2000) 18.
3. *ibid.*, 25.
4. *ibid.*, 25–26.
5. 'A Copy of the Instrument of Writing', CO 5_1328_007, f. 321; Kenneth P. Bailey, *The Ohio Company of Virginia and the Westward Movement*, (Arthur H. Clark, Glendale, California, 1939) 35–36; Eric Hinderaker, *Elusive Empires: Constructing Colonialism in the Ohio Valley, 1673–1800* (Cambridge University Press, Cambridge, 1997) 40.
6. 'The Treaty with the Indians at Logstown', CO_5_1327_Part2_025, ff. 263–276; 'The Commissioner's Journal to the Six United Nations of Indians on the River Ohio, in May 1752', CO_5_1327_Part 2_39, ff. 310–321.
7. 'Instructions for George Washington, Esq.', Williamsburg, 30 October 1753, CO5_1328_007, ff. 47–48.
8. Edward G. Lengel, *First Entrepreneur: How George Washington Built His – and the Nation's – Prosperity* (Boston 2016) 22–27.
9. Warren F Hofstra, *The Planting of New Virginia: Settlement and Landscape in the Shenandoah* Valley (Johns Hopkins University Press, Baltimore and London, 204) 241–248.
10. Anderson, *Crucible of War*, 46–49.
11. *ibid.*, 50–52.
12. *ibid.*, 60–61.
13. *ibid.*, 61–62.
14. *ibid.*, 62–63.

4 The Breaking of the Covenant Chain

1. Timothy J. Shannon, *Indians and Colonists at the Crossroads of Empire: The Albany Conference of 1754* (Cornell University Press, Ithaca and London, 2000), 127–128.
2. Kevin Kenny, *Peaceable Kingdom Lost: The Paxton Boys and the Destruction of William Penn's Holy Experiment* (Oxford University Press, Oxford, 2009), 55–59
3. Kenny, *Peaceable Kingdom Lost*, 59–61.
4. Shannon, *Crossroads of Empire*, 169–171.

5 Cherokees

1. Adapted from James Mooney, *History, myths, and sacred formulas of the Cherokees* (Historical images, Asheville, North Carolina, 1992) 260.
2. Lewis to Dinwiddie, Chota, 23 July, and Halifax Smith's Creek, 11 October 1756, enclosing 'Talks from Old Hop, Ostenaco, Skiagusta, Standing Turkey, and the Warrior of Settico', CO 5/17, ff. 370–377.

6 Direct Intervention

1. Halifax, 'Methods of disappointing the French Encroachments in North America', 7 November 1754, Newcastle Papers, BL Add MSS 33,029, 138–142
2. Mattherw H. Edney, 'John Mitchell's Map of North America (1755): A Study of the Use and Publication of Official Maps in Eighteenth-Century Britain', *Imago Mundi*, Vol. 60, No. 1 (2008), pp. 63–85
3. N. A. M. Rodger, *The Command of the Ocean: A Naval History of Britain, 1649–1815* (Allen Lane, London, 2004) 263

7 Failed Offensive

1. Lee McCardell, *Ill-Starred General: Braddock of the Coldstream Guards* (University of Pittsburgh Press, 1958, reprinted 1986) 158.
2. Anderson, *Crucible of War*, 94–96; the accusation is repeated, in qualified terms, in Calloway, *The Indian World of George Washington*, 105–106.
3. McCardell, *Ill-Starred General*, 141, 186–188, 190–191, 194–196; Calloway, *The Indian World of George Washington*, 106–107.
4. Washington to Robert Orme, [Mount Vernon, 15 March 1755], The Papers of George Washington Digital Edition, Colonial Series (7 July 1748–15 June 1775), Volume 1 (7 July 1748–14 August 1755).

5. McCardell, *Ill-Starred General*, 160–161.
6. Ward, *Breaking the Backcountry*, 60–61
7. Anderson, *Crucible of War*, 110–112.

8 Wars in the Forest
1. Ward, *Breaking the Backcountry*, 106–107; Anderson, *Crucible of War*, 163–164
2. Anderson, *Crucible of War*, 162–163; Ward, *Breaking the Backcountry*, 51.
3. Campbell, *Speculators in Empire*, 58–59
4. Webb to Loudoun, German Flats past 12 at night, 17 August 1756; Loudoun to Webb, Albany, 19, 23 August 1756 CO_5/47 Part 2 ff 155–158, 195–196 (copies).
5. Anderson, *Crucible of War*, 150–157.
6. *ibid.*, 192–195.
7. *ibid.*, 195–196.
8. *ibid.*, 196–198.
9. *ibid.*, 198–199.

9 Pitt, Recovery and Conquest
1. 'Filius Gallicus' to Mirepoix, America 1 January 1756, 1 March 1756, CO 5_52_004 ff. 7–11, 12–25.
2. Jacobs (ed.), *Appalachian Indian Frontier*, passim.
3. Steven Brumwell, 'Campbell, John fourth earl of Loudoun (1705–1782
4. Rodger, *Command of the Ocean*,
5. Black, *Pitt the Elder*, 130–138, 172.173.
6. Anderson, *Crucible of War*, 303–306.
7. Jeremy Black, *George III: America's Last King* (Yale University Press, New Haven and London, 2006), 60; O'Gorman, *The Long Eighteenth Century*.

10 The Forbes Expedition and the Treaty of Easton
1. John Forbes to his brother Hugh Forbes, Manchester, 17 October 1754, quoted in Oliphant, *John Forbes*, 72.
2. Calloway, *The Indian World of George Washington*, 150–151; Oliphant, *John Forbes*,123–126; Forbes to Bouquet, [Carlisle, 9 August 1758], *Bouquet Papers*, Vol 2, 344; Washington to Halkett, Camp at Fort Cumberland, 2 August 1758, *The Papers of George Washington Digital Edition* (Rotunda, 2008).

11 Southern Crisis
1. Oliphant, *Peace and War*, 79–84
2. *ibid.*, 101–104.
3. *ibid.*, 105–

12 The Anglo-Cherokee War
1. Oliphant, *Peace and War*, 110–111. A shorter, and perhaps more readable, account of all three Cherokee War campaigns is John Oliphant, 'The Anglo-Cherokee War' in Mark H. Danley and Patrick J. Speelman (eds), *The Seven Years' War: Global Views* (Brill, Leiden and Boston, 2012) 325–357.
2. Oliphant, *Peace and War*, 111–112
3. For a detailed account of the Montgomery campaign and its aftermath see, Oliphant, *Peace and War*, 113–139. For Grant's campaign and the peace-making, see *Ibid.*, 140–190.
4. Grant to Amherst, 30 March 1761, WO 34/47, f. 58.
5. [Christopher Gadsden], *Some observations on the two campaigns against the Cherokee Indians, in 1760 and 1761. In a second letter from Philopatrios* (Peter Tomothy, Charleston, 1762).
6. Oliphant, 'The Anglo-Cherokee War', 354–356; Kate Fullagar, *The Warrior, the Voyager and the Artist: Three Lives in an Age of Empire* (Yale University Press, New Haven and London, 2020) 29–30, 42–43; Duane H. King (ed) *The Memoirs of Henry Timberlake: The Story of a Soldier, Adventurer, and Emissary to the Cherokees, 1756–1765* (Museum of the Cherokee Indian, Cherokee, North Carolina, 2007) 55–56.

13 Lord Egremont Draws a Line
1. Egremont to Amherst, Whitehall, 12 December 1761, CO 5/214, f. 244.
2. Rodger, *Command of the Ocean*, 284–287
3. Rhoades, 'Blood and boundaries', 3–5.
4. Ellis to Egremont, Gray's Inn, 15 December 1762, Egremont Papers, PRO 30/47//6, ff. 246–247; Egremont to the Board of Trade (unsigned copy), Whitehall, February 1763, PRO 30/47, ff. 37–42.
5. Egremont to the Board of Trade, Whitehall, 14 July 1763, CO 5/65. Part 2_002; Matthew L. Rhoades, 'Blood and Boundaries: Virginia Backcountry Violence and the Origins of the Quebec Act, 1758–1775', *West Virginia History*, New Series, Vol. 3, No. 2 (Fall 2009), 1–22, https://www.jstor.org/stable/43265120.

6. Oliphant, 'The Cherokee Embassy to London', 19.
7. Halifax to the Board of Trade, Whitehall, 19 September 1763, SP 44/138, ff. 106–108.
8. See Appendix A.
9. Sosin, *Whitehall and the Wilderness*, 63–64.

14 Wyoming Tragedy
1. Anderson, *Crucible of War*, 531–532.
2. *ibid.*, 532–533.
3. Hamilton to Amherst, Philadelphia, 15 July, 17 October 1762, WO33/33 ff. 174, 176–178.
4. Wallace, *Teedyuscung*, 257–258
5. Amherst to Hamilton, New York, 8 July 1762, WO 34/32, f. 103 (copy); Hamilton to Amherst, Philadelphia, !5 July, 8 September, 15 October 1762, WO 34/33 and enclosure, ff.174–178 (copies).
6. Wallace, *Teedyuscung*, 258–261.
7. Kenny, *Peaceable Kingdom Lost*, 123–170.

15 Pontiac's War of Independence
1. Francis Parkman, *History of the Conspiracy of Pontiac and the war of the North American Tribes against the English Colonies after the conquest of Canada* (Charles C. Little and James Brown, Boston, 1851) 161–162; Howard H. Peckham, *Pontiac and the Indian Uprising* (Princeton University Press, Princeton, 1947) 107–111; Richard White, *The Middle Ground: Indians, Empires and Republics in the Great Lakes Region, 1650–1815* (Cambridge University Press, Cambridge, 1991) 270–314; Micael McConnell, *A Country Between: The Upper Ohio Valley and its Peoples, 1724–1774* (University of Nebraska Press, Lincoln and London, 1992) 159–206; Gregory Evans Dowd, *War under Heaven: Pontiac, the Indian Nations, and the British Empire* (Johns Hopkins University Press, Baltimore and London, 2002) 5–11; Richard Middleton, 'Pontiac: Local Warrior or Pan-Indian Chief?' *Michigan Historical Review*, Fall, 2006, Vol. 32, No. 2 (fall, 2006), 1–32.
2. Dowd, *War under Heaven*, 94–97.
3. *ibid.*, 118–120.
4. Gladwin to Amherst, CO 5/68_028, ff. 213–216; Calloway, *The Scratch of a Pen*, 71.

5. 'Intelligence brought to Fort Pitt by Mr. Calhoun [on the] 1st June 1763', CO 5/63_13, ff. 74-77.
6. Bouquet to Amherst, Camp at Edgehill, 26 Miles from Fort Pitt, 5, 6 & 11 August 1763, CO 5/63_037, ff. 241-242, 242-248, 250-251.
7. Dowd, *War under Heaven*, 157-158.
8. McConnell, *A Country Between*, 202-205.
9. Dowd, *War under Heaven*.

16 Plans and Boundaries
1. Brumwell, *Washington*, 178.

17 John Stuart's Empire
1. Corkran, *Creek Frontier*, 172-173
2. Snapp, *John Stuart*, 54-67
3. Alden, *John Stuart*, 200-204.
4. Corkran, *Creek Frontier*, 240-252.
5. Alden, *John Stuart*, 230-232; Nelson, *James Grant*, 56-57.
6. Calloway, *The Scratch of a Pen*, 109-111.

18 Speculation, Fraud, Murder and Revolt
1. Mississippi Company Articles of Agreement, [3 June 1763] *George Washington Papers Digital Edition*, Colonial Series (7 July 1748-15 June 1775), Volume 7 (1 January 1761-15 June 1767) (University of Virginia Press, Rotunda, Charlottesville, 2008).
2. Anderson, *Crucible of War*, 737-741.
3. Down, *War under Heaven*
4. Campbell, *Speculators in Empire*, 97-98; Wainwright, *George Croghan*, 211-217; Ward, *Frontier Man*, 114; Dowd, *War Under Heaven*, 'Proclamation of the Augusta Boys', CO 5/11331, ff. 310-311, 312-313.
5. Wainwright, *George Croghan*, 248-249; Campbell, *Speculators in Empire*, 123-124.

19 The Road to Fort Stanwix
1. Campbell, *Speculators in Empire*, 135-137.
2. *ibid.*, 142.
3. Rhoades, 'Blood and Boundaries', 11.
4. McConnell, *A Country Between*, 249-250.
5. *ibid.*, 156-160.

6. Campbell, *Speculators in Empire*, 153–154.
7. ibid., 165, 173
8. ibid., 164–166

20 Lord Hillsborough Stands His Ground
1. Peter Marshall, 'Hill, Wills, first marquess of Downshire, 1718–1793', *ODNB*, https://doi-org.lonlib.idm.oclc/10.1093/ref:odnb/13317.
2. Sosin, *Whitehall and the Wilderness*, 180.
3. 'The Formation of the Grand Ohio Company, [June? 1769],' *Founders Online*, National Archives, https://founders.archives.gov/documents/Franklin/01-16-02-0083. [Original source: *The Papers of Benjamin Franklin*, vol. 16, *January 1 through December 31, 1769*, ed. William B. Willcox. New Haven and London: Yale University Press, 1972, pp. 163–169.]
4. Washington to Botetourt, Mount Vernon, 9 September, 5 October 1770, Washington to Croghan, [Stewart's Crossing, Pennsylvania] 24 November 1770, *GWP Digital Edition*, 378–380, 388, 403; Dunmore to Hillsborough, 12 November 177; Sosin, *Whitehall and the Wilderness*, 191–192
5. Sosin, *Whitehall and the Wilderness*, 193–195.
6. ibid., 199–205.
7. ibid., 204–207.
8. ibid., 207–210.

21 The Path to Lochaber
1. John Stuart to Hillsborough, Charleston, 28 November 1770, enclosing the journal of the congress, CO 5/ 71_ ff3–5; the text of the treaty, with links to appropriate maps, can be found at jessfersonwest.unl.edu/archive/view_ doc.php?id=jef.00091.
2. Narrett, *The Cherokees*, 320–321.

22 Dunmore's Little War
1. McConnell, *A Country Between*, 255–257.
2. Washington to Dunmore, 15 June, 30 July 1772; 13, 12, 24 September 1773; 11 February 1774. Dunmore to Washington, 3 July, 24 September 1773; 18 April 1775; John Connolly to Washinton, Pittsburgh, 29 August 1773, *The Papers of George Washington Digital Edition*, Rotunda, 2008.
3. McConnell, *A Country Between*, 274; Hinderaker, *Elusive Empires*, 189–191; Calloway, *The Indian World of George Washington*, 207–208.

4. McConnell, *A country Between*, 275–276; Rhoades, 'Blood and Boundaries', 18.
5. McConnell, *A Country Between*,
6. Williams, *Dunmore's War*, 19–20, 238; McConnell, *A Country Between*, 276–279.
7. Williams, *Dunmore's War*, 277–293.
8. *ibid.*, 295–296.
9. *ibid.*, 300.
10. Ensign James Newell, quoted in Williams, *Dunmore's War*, 299.
11. William Crawford to Washington, Stewarts Crossing [Pennsylvania], 14 November 1774, *GWP*, 184–185; Williams, *Dunmore's War*, 302.
12. Resolutions adopted at a Meeting of the Officers under the command of Lord Dunmore, convened at Fort Gower', Northern Illinois University Digital Library, https://digital.lib.niu.edu.

23 *Lord Dartmouth's Intolerable Act*

1. Peter Marshall, 'William Legge, Second Earl of Dartmouth 91731–1801), *Oxford Dictionary of National Biography* (Oxford University Press 2004) https://doi-org.lonlib.oclc.org/1093/ref:odnb/16360.
2. B.D. Bargar, *Lord Dartmouth and the American Revolution*, University of South Carolina Press, Columbia, 1965); Dartmouth to Stuart, Whitehall, 3 March 1773, CO 5/74, f. 63.
3. Vernon P. Creviston, "No King unless it be a Constitutional King': Rethinking the Place of the Quebec Act in the Coming of the American Revolution', *The Historian*, 1, Vol. 73, No. 3 Fall 2011, 463–479
4. Wainwright, *George Croghan*, 293–294; Sosin, *Whitehall and the Wilderness*, 248.
5. Boulware, *Deconstructing the Cherokee Nation*, 57.
6. Bargar, *Lord Dartmouth and the American Revolution*, 131–132.

24 *Collapse*

1. Bargar, *Lord Dartmouth and the American Revolution*, 132–133.
2. *ibid.*, 133–138.
3. *ibid.*, 138–141.
4. *ibid.*, 140–145.
5. Jeremy Gregory and John Stevenson, *Britain in the Eighteenth Century, 1688–1820* (Routledge, Abingdon, 2007) 229–230; O'Gorman, *The Long Eighteenth Century*, 201.

BIBLIOGRAPHY

Primary Sources
Manuscripts
The National Archives, London
Colonial Office Papers
Egremont Papers
State Papers
War Office Papers
William Pitt, 1st Earl of Chatham: Papers

The British Library
Newcastle Papers

Staffordshire County Record Office
Dartmouth Papers

Clements Library, University of Michigan
Shelburne Papers, Microfilm, digitised.

Published Documents
Bernard, Francis, and Colin Nicolson. *The Papers of Francis Bernard: Governor of Colonial Massachusetts, 1760–69*. Publications of the Colonial Society of Massachusetts, Boston: Colonial Society of Massachusetts, 2007.

Bibliography

Brock, R. A., ed. *The Official Records of Robert Dinwiddie, Lieutenant Governor of the Colony of Virginia.* Vol. I. Richmond: Virginia Historical Society, 1883.

Jacobs, Walter R., ed. *The Appalachian Indian Frontier: The Edmond Atkin Report and Plan of 1755.* Lincoln: University of Nebraska Press, 1967.

King, Duane H., ed. *The Memoirs of Lt. Henry Timberlake: The Story of a Soldier, Adventurer and Emissary to the Cherokees, 1756–1765.* Cherokee, North Carolina: The Museum of the Cherokee Indians, 2007.

Mulkearn, Lois, ed. *George Mercer Papers Relating to the Ohio Company of Virginia.* Pittsburgh: University of Pittsburgh Press, 1954.

Smith, William James, ed. *The Grenville Papers, Being the Correspondence of Richard Grenville Earl Temple K.G., And the Right Hon: George Grenville, Their Friends and Contemporaries.* Vol. 3. London: John Murray, 1853.

Stevens, S. K., Donald. H. Kent, and Autumn L. Leonard. *The Papers of Henry Bouquet: Vol II: The Forbes Expedition.* Harrisburg: Pennsylvania Historical and Museum Commission, 1951.

Webster, J. Clarence, ed. *The Journal of Jeffrey Amherst: Recording the Military Career of General Amherst in America from 1758 to 1763.* Toronto and Chicago: Ryerson Press and University of Chicago Press, 1931.

Online Collections

The Papers of George Washington Digital Edition. Charlottesville: University of Virginia Press, Rotunda, 2008.

The Papers of Sir William Johnson. University of the State of New York. Division of Archives and History; Sullivan, James, 1873–1931; Flick, Alexander Clarence, 1869–1942; Lauber, Almon W.; Hamilton, Milton W. (Milton Wheaton), 1901–; Corey, Albert B. (Albert Bickmore). Internet Archive https://archive.org.

Secondary Sources

Adair, James. *History of the American Indians.* Reprint. Pantios Classics, 1775.

Additional, n.d.

Agbe-Davies, Anna. *Tobacco, Pipes, and Race in Colonial Virginia: Little Tubes of Mighty Power*. Walnut Creek (CA): Left Coast Press, Inc., 2015.

Alden, John Richard. *John Stuart and the Southern Colonial Frontier: A Study of Indian Relations, War, Trade and Land Problems in the Southern Wilderness, 1754–1775*. Ann Arbor: University of Michigan Press, 1944.

Alessi, Joseph P. *Settling the Frontier: Urban Development in America's Borderlands, 1600–1830*. Yardley: Westholme, 2020.

Anderson, Chad (Chad L.). *The Storied Landscape of Iroquoia: History, Conquest, and Memory in the Native Northeast*. Lincoln (NE): University of Nebraska Press, 2020.

Anderson, Fred. *Crucible of War: The Seven Years' War and the Fate of Empire in British North America, 1754–1766*. London: Faber, 2000.

Aquila, Richard. 'Down the Warrior's Path: The Causes of the Southern Wars of the Iroquois'. *American Indian Quarterly* 4, no. 3 (1978): 211–21. https://doi.org/10.2307/1184621.

Aston, Nigel, and Clarissa Campbell Orr, eds. *An Enlightened Statesman in Whig Britain: Lord Shelburne in Context, 1737–1805*. Woodbridge: Boydell Press, 2011.

Bahar, Matthew R. *Storm of the Sea: Indians and Empires in the Atlantic's Age of Sail*. New York: Oxford University Press, 2019.

Bailey, Kenneth P. *The Ohio Company of Virginia and the Westward Movement, 1748–1792: A Chapter in the History of the Colonial Frontier*. Forgotten Books reprint. Glendale, California: Arthur H. Clark, 1939.

Balcom, B. A., and Andrew John Bayly Johnston. 'Missions to the Mi'kmaq: Malagawatch and Chapel Island in the 18th Century'. *Journal of the Royal Nova Scotia Historical Society* 9 (2006): 115–40.

Bankhurst, Benjamin. '"Scum of the Earth, and Refuse of Mankind": The Negative Reputation of Irish Presbyterians on the Colonial American Frontier'. In *Irish Studies in Britain: New Perspectives on History and Literature*, 47–59. Newcastle: Cambridge Scholars, 2010.

Bargar, B. D. *Lord Dartmouth and the American Revolution*. Columbia: University of South Carolina Press, 1965.

Barr, Daniel P. *A Colony Sprung from Hell: Pittsburgh and the Struggle for Authority on the Western Pennsylvania Frontier, 1744–1794*. Kent (OH): Kent State University Press, 2014.

Bibliography

Barr, Daniel P. '"This Land Is Ours and Not Yours": The Western Delawares and the Seven Years' War in the Upper Ohio Valley, 1755–1758'. In *The Boundaries between Us: Natives and Newcomers along the Frontiers of the Old Northwest Territory, 1750–1850*, 25–40. Kent, Ohio: Kent State University Press, 2006.

Bauer, Brooke M. *Becoming Catawba: Catawba Indian Women and Nation-Building, 1540–1840*. Indians and Southern History. Tuscaloosa (AL): University of Alabama Press, 2022.

Beaulieu, Alain. 'The Acquisition of Aboriginal Land in Canada: The Genealogy of an Ambivalent System (1600–1867)'. In *Empire by Treaty: Negotiating European Expansion, 1600–1900*, 101–31. Oxford; New York: Oxford University Press, 2015.

Beaumont, Andrew D. M. *Colonial America and the Earl of Halifax, 1748–1761*. Oxford Historical Monographs. Oxford: Oxford University Press, 2015.

Berlau, John. *George Washington, Entrepreneur: How Our Founding Father's Private Business Pursuits Changed America and the World*. New York: All Points Books, 2020.

Bickham, Troy O. 'American Indians in the British Imperial Imagination, 1707–1815'. In *British North America in the Seventeenth and Eighteenth Centuries*, 228–54. The Oxford History of the British Empire Companion. Oxford; New York: Oxford University Press, 2013.

Black, Jeremy. *Fighting for America: The Struggle for Mastery in North America 1519–1871*. Chesham: Combined Academic [distributor], 2011.

Black, Jeremy. *George III: America's Last King*. New Haven and London: Yale University Press, 2006.

Black, Jeremy. *Pitt the Elder*. Cambridge: Cambridge University Press, 1992.

Blasi, Anthony Phillip. *Colonial Rangers of New England: From King Philip's War to the American Revolution*. Kindle. Charleston: The History Press, 2025.

Borneman, Walter R. *The French and Indian War: Deciding the Fate of North America*. New York: HarperCollins, 2006.

Boulware, Tyler. *Deconstructing the Cherokee Nation: Town, Region and Nation among Eighteenth Century Cherokees*. Gainesville: University Press of Florida, 2011.

Bragdon, Kathleen Joan. *Native People of Southern New England, 1650–1775*. Norman (OK): University of Oklahoma Press, 2009.

Brooks, Justin. 'Imperial Structures, Indigenous Aims: Connecting Native Engagement in Scotland, North America and South Asia'. In *Facing Empire: Indigenous Experiences in a Revolutionary Age*. Baltimore and London: Johns Hopkins University Press, 2018.

Brückner, Martin. 'The Spectacle of Maps in British America, 1750–1800'. In *Early American Cartographies*, 389–441. Chapel Hill (NC): University of North Carolina Press, 2011.

Brumwell, Stephen. 'Band of Brothers'. *History Today* 58, no. 6 (2008): 25–31.

Brumwell, Stephen. *George Washington: Gentleman Warrior*. London: Quercus, 2012.

Brumwell, Stephen. *Redcoats: The British Soldier in the Americas, 1755–1763*. Cambridge: Cambridge University Press, 2002.

Brumwell, Stephen. *White Devil: An Epic Story of Revenge from the Savage War That Inspired The Last of the Mohicans*. London: Weidenfeld and Nicolson, 2004.

Brumwell, Stephen. 'Wolfe's Men'. *History Today* 59, no. 9 (2009): 48–54.

Burnard, Trevor Graeme. *The Atlantic in World History, 1490–1830*. London: Bloomsbury Academic, 2020.

Buse, Dieter K., and Graeme S. Mount. *Untold: Northeastern Ontario's Military Past, Volume 1: 1662–World War I*. Sudbury (ON): Latitude 46, 2018.

Calloway, Colin G. *Pen and Ink Witchcraft: Treaties and Treaty Making in American Indian History*. Oxford: Oxford University Press, 2013.

Calloway, Colin G. *The Indian World of George Washington: The First President, the First Americans, and the Birth of the Nation*. Oxford: Oxford University Press, 2018.

Calloway, Colin G. *The Scratch of a Pen: 1763 and the Transformation of North America*. New York: Oxford University Press, 2006.

Calloway, Colin G. *The Shawnees and the War for America*. Penguin Library of American Indian History. New York: Viking Penguin, 2007.

Calloway, Colin G. *The Western Abenakis of Vermont: War, Migration and the Survival of an Indian People*. Norman: University of Oklahoma Press, 1990.

Calloway, Colin G. 'Urban Encounters'. *History Today* 71, no. 7 (2021): 66–75.

Calloway, Colin G. 'Sir William Johnson, Highland Scots, and American Indians'. *New York History* 89, no. 2 (2008): 163–78.

Campbell, Alexander V. 'Atlantic Microcosm: The Royal American Regiment, 1755–1772'. In *English Atlantics Revisited: Essays Honouring Professor Ian K. Steele*, 284–309. Montréal (PQ); London: McGill-Queen's University Press, 2007.

Campbell, William J. 'Converging Interests: Johnson, Croghan, the Six Nations, and the 1768 Treaty of Fort Stanwix'. *New York History* 89, no. 2 (Spring 2008): 126–41.

Campbell, William J. *Speculators in Empire: Iroquoia and the 1768 Treaty of Fort Stanwix*. Norman: University of Oklahoma Press, 2012.

Carp, Benjamin L. 'Changing Our Habitation: Henry Laurens, Rattray Green, and the Revolutionary Movement in Charleston's Domestic Spaces'. In *Material Culture in Anglo-America: Regional Identity and Urbanity in the Tidewater, Lowcountry, and Caribbean*, 285–309. The Carolina Lowcountry and the Atlantic World. Columbia (SC): University of South Carolina Press, 2009.

Carpenter, Roger M. *'Times Are Altered with Us': American Indians from First Contact to the New Republic*. The American History Series. Hoboken (NJ): Wiley Blackwell, 2015.

Carroll, Brian D. '"Savages" in the Service of Empire: Native American Soldiers in Gorham's Rangers, 1744–1762'. *New England Quarterly* 85, no. 3 (2012): 383–429. https://doi.org/10.1162/TNEQ_a_00207.

Cash, Sherri Goldstein. 'Roots in the Valley'. *New York History* 99, no. 1 (Winter 2018): 7–37.

Cashin, Edward J. *Guardians of the Valley: Chickasaws in Colonial South Carolina and Georgia*. University of South Carolina Press, 2009.

Cashin, Edward J. *William Bartram and the American Revolution on the Southern Frontier*. Columbia (SC): University of South Carolina Press, 2006.

Cave, Alfred A. 'The Delaware Prophet Neolin: A Reappraisal'. *Ethnohistory* 46, no. 2 (Spring 1999): 265–90.

Chernow, Ron. *Washington: A Life*. London: Allen Lane, 2010.

Chet, Guy. 'Colonial Failures, Imperial Triumphs, and the Loss of the American Colonies: Warfare and Bureaucratic Expansion in British North America'. In *The American Experience of War*, 21–32. Krieg in Der Geschichte, 51. Paderborn: Schöningh, 2010.

Clary, David A. *George Washington's First War: His Early Military Adventures*. New York; London: Simon & Schuster, 2011.

Clayton, T. R. 'The Duke of Newcastle, the Earl of Halifax, and the American Origins of the Seven Years' War'. *The Historical Journal* 24, no. 3 (September 1981): 571–603.

Cobb, Charles R. *The Archaeology of Southeastern Native American Landscapes of the Colonial Era*. Gainesville (FL): University Press of Florida, 2019.

Cobb, Charles R., and Stephanie Sapp. 'Imperial Anxiety and the Dissolution of Colonial Space and Practice at Fort Moore, South Carolina'. In *Rethinking Colonial Pasts through Archaeology*, 212–31. Oxford: Oxford University Press, 2014.

Conley, Robert J. *The Cherokee Nation: A History*. Albuquerque: University of New Mexico Press, 2007.

Conrad, Margaret. *At the Ocean's Edge: A History of Nova Scotia to Confederation*. Studies in Atlantic Canada History. Toronto; Buffalo; London: University of Toronto Press, 2020.

Corkran, David H. *The Creek Frontier 1540–1783*. Norman: University of Oklahoma Press, 1967.

Cornish, Rory T. *The Grenvillites and the British Press: Colonial and British Politics, 1750–1770*. Newcastle upon Tyne: Cambridge Scholars, 2020.

Coupland, R. *The Quebec Act: A Study in Statesmanship*. Oxford: Oxford University Press, 1925.

Crawford, B. Scott. 'A Frontier of Fear: Terrorism and Social Tension along Virginia's Western Waters, 1742–1775'. *West Virginia History* ns 2, no. 2 (2008): 1–29.

Creviston, Vernon P. '"No King Unless It Be a Constitutional King": Rethinking the Place of the Quebec Act in "The Coming of the American Revolution"'. *The Historian* 73, no. 3 (Fall 2011): 463–79.

Crocker, Thomas E. *Braddock's March: How the Man Sent to Seize a Continent Changed American History*. Yardley (PA): Westholme, 2009.

Crosby, Alfred. *Ecological Imperialism: The Biological Expansion of Europe, 900–1900*. 2nd, Kindle ed. Cambridge: Cambridge University Press, 2004.

Crytzer, Brady. *Guyasuta and the Fall of Indian America*. Yardley (PA): Westholme, 2013.

Dahl, Adam. *Empire of the People: Settler Colonialism and the Foundations of Modern Democratic Thought*. American Political Thought. Lawrence (KA): University Press of Kansas, 2018.

Darlington, William M., ed. 'Christopher Gist's Journals: With Historical Geographical and Ethnological Notes and Biographies of His Contemporaries'. Pittsburgh: J. R. Wilden, 1893. https://archive.org/details/christophergists00gistuoft/page/n5/mode/2up?view=theater.

DasSarma, Anjali, and Linford D. Fisher. 'The Persistence of Indigenous Unfreedom in Early American Newspaper Advertisements, 1704–1804'. *Slavery & Abolition* 44, no. 2 (2023): 267–91. https://doi.org/10.1080/0144039X.2023.2189517.

David, James Corbett. *Dunmore's New World: The Extraordinary Life of a Royal Governor in Revolutionary America – with Jacobites, Counterfeiters, Land Schemes, Shipwrecks, Scalping, Indian Politics, Runaway Slaves, and Two Illegal Royal Weddings*. Early American Histories. Charlottesville (VA): University of Virginia Press, 2013.

DeCorse, Christopher R., and Zachary J. M. Beier. *British Forts and Their Communities: Archaeological and Historical Perspectives*. Gainesville; Tallahassee; Tampa: University Press of Florida, 2018.

Dennis, Jeff W. *Patriots & Indians: Shaping Identity in Eighteenth-Century South Carolina*. Columbia (SC): The University of South Carolina Press, 2017.

Dewar, David. 'Eighteenth-Century Land Speculation at the Margins of the Anglo-American World'. *History Compass* 5, no. 1 (2007).

Dewar, David. 'Eighteenth-Century Land Speculation at the Margins of the Anglo-American World'. *History Compass* 5, no. 1 (2007).

Dewar, Helen. 'Canada or Guadeloupe?: French and British Perceptions of Empire, 1760–1763'. *Canadian Historical Review* 91, no. 4 (2010): 637–60.

Dickerson, Oliver Morton. *American Colonial Government 1696–1765: A Study of the British Board of Trade in Its Relation to the American Colonies, Political, Industrial, Administrative*. Cleveland, Ohio: Arthur H. Clark, 1912.

Dixon, David. *Never Come to Peace Again: Pontiac's Uprising and the Fate of the British Empire in America*. Campaigns and Commanders 7. Norman: University of Nebraska Press, 2005.

Dixon, David. '"We Speak as One People": Native Unity and the Pontiac Indian Uprising'. In *The Boundaries between Us: Natives and Newcomers along the Frontiers of the Old Northwest Territory, 1750–1850*, 44–65. Kent, Ohio: Kent State University Press, 2006.

Dodds Pennock, Caroline. *On Savage Shores: How Indigenous Americans Discovered Europe*. London: Weidenfeld and Nicolson, 2023.

Dolin, Eric Jay. *Fur, Fortune, and Empire: The Epic History of the Fur Trade in America*. New York; London: W. W. Norton & Co, 2010.

Dowd, Gregory Evans. *A Spirited Resistance: The North American Indian Struggle For Unity, 1745–1815*. Baltimore and London: Johns Hopkins University Press, 1992.

Dowd, Gregory Evans. *Groundless: Rumors, Legends, and Hoaxes on the Early American Frontier*. Early America: History, Context, Culture. Baltimore (MD): Johns Hopkins University Press, 2015.

Dowd, Gregory Evans. 'Indigenous Self-Vanishing? Relating the North American 'Iroquois Wars' and the Southern African Mfecane'. *William and Mary Quarterly* 79, no. 3 (2022): 393–424.

Dowd, Gregory Evans. *War under Heaven: Pontiac, the Indian Nations, and the British Empire*. Baltimore and London: Johns Hopkins University Press, 2002.

Doyle, David Noel. "Savage' Irishman? William Johnson and the Variety of America'. *Irish Historical Studies* 35, no. 137 (2006): 117–22.

Dunn, Walter S. (Walter Scott). *Choosing Sides on the Frontier in the American Revolution*. Westport (CT): Praeger, 2007.

Edney, Matthew H. 'John Mitchell's Map of North America (1755): A Study of the Use and Publication of Official Maps in Eighteenth-Century Britain'. *Imago Mundi* 60, no. 1 (2008): 63–85.

Edney, Matthew Henry. 'Competition over Land, Competition over Empire: Pubic Discourses and Printed Maps of the Kennebec River, 1753–1755'. In *Early American Cartographies*, 276–305. Chapel Hill (NC): University of North Carolina Press, 2011.

Egnal, Marc. *A Mighty Empire: The Origins of the American Revolution*. Ithaca (NY): Cornell University Press, 2010.

Ethridge, Robbie. 'The Origins and Coalescence of the Creek (Muscogee) Confederacy: A New Synthesis'. *Studies in Eighteenth-Century Culture* 52 (2023): 113–31. https://doi.org/10.1353/sec.2023.0012.

Ferris, Neal. *The Archaeology of Native-Lived Colonialism: Challenging History in the Great Lakes*. Tucson (AZ): University of Arizona Press, 2009.

Finucane, Adrian. 'Utopian Dreams and Untenable Realities: The Georgia Trustees' Failure to Stabilize the Frontier through Foreign Migration'. *Early American Studies: An Interdisciplinary Journal* 21, no. 2 (2023): 272–302. https://doi.org/10.1353/eam.2023.0007.

Fisher, Linford D. *The Indian Great Awakening: Religion and the Shaping of Native Cultures in Early America*. New York; Oxford: Oxford University Press, 2012.

Fitts, Mary Elizabeth. *Fit for War: Sustenance and Order in the Mid-Eighteenth-Century Catawba Nation*. Florida Museum of Natural History: Ripley P. Bullen Series. Gainesville (FL): University of Florida Press, 2017.

Flynn, Matthew J. *Settle and Conquer: Militarism on the American Frontier, 1607–1890*. Jefferson (NC): McFarland & Co., 2016.

Ford, Lisa. 'Empire and Order on the Colonial Frontiers of Georgia and New South Wales'. *Itinerario* 30, no. 3 (2006): 95–113.

Ford, Lisa. *The King's Peace: Law and Order in the British Empire*. Cambridge: Harvard University Press, 2021.

Fowler, Jonathan, and Earle Lockerby. 'Operations at Fort Beauséjour and Grand-Pré in 1755: A Soldier's Diary'. *Journal of the Royal Nova Scotia Historical Society* 12 (2009): 145–209.

Frank, Andrew K., and A. Glenn Crothers. *Borderland Narratives: Negotiation and Accommodation in North America's Contested Spaces, 1500–1850*. Gainesville (FL): University Press of Florida, 2018.

Friend, Craig Thompson. *Kentucky's Frontiers*. Bloomington (IN): Indiana University Press, 2010.

Fruchtman, Jack. 'Unrespectable and Reluctant Radical: Benjamin Franklin as a Revolutionary'. In *Unrespectable Radicals?: Popular Politics in the Age of Reform*, 5–20. Aldershot: Ashgate, 2008.

Fullagar, Kate. 'Envoys of Interest: A Cherokee, a Ra'iatean, and the Eighteenth-Century British Empire'. In *Facing Empire: Indigenous Experiences in a Revolutionary Age*. Baltimore: Johns Hopkins University Press, 2018.

Fullagar, Kate. *The Warrior, the Voyager and the Artist: Three Lives in an Age of Empire*. New Haven and London: Yale University Press, 2020.

Fullagar, Kate, and Michael A. McDonnell, eds. *Facing Empire: Indigenous Experiences in a Revolutionary Age*. Baltimore: Johns Hopkins University Press, 2018.

Fur, Gunlög Maria. *A Nation of Women: Delaware Gender Relations and Colonial Encounters*. Early American Studies University of Pennsylvania Press, 2009.

Furstenberg, François. 'The Significance of the Trans-Appalachian Frontier in Atlantic History'. *American Historical Review* 113, no. 3 (2008): 647–77.

[Gadsden, Christopher], *Some observations on the two campaigns against the Cherokee Indians, in 1760 and 1761. In a second letter from Philopatrios*. Charleston: Peter Tomothy, 1762.

Gailmard, Sean. 'Imperial Governance and the Growth of Legislative Power in America'. *American Journal of Political Science* 65, no. 4 (2021): 912–25. https://doi.org/10.1111/ajps.12601.

Gallay, Alan. *Colonial Wars of North America, 1512–1763: An Encyclopedia*. London: Routledge, 2020.

Gallay, Alan. 'South Carolina's Entrance into the Indian Slave Trade'. In *Indian Slavery in Colonial America*, 109–46. Lincoln (NE): University of Nebraska Press, 2009.

Gallman, Nancy, and Alan Taylor. 'Covering Blood and Graves: Murder and Law on Imperial Margins'. In *Justice in a New World: Negotiating Legal Intelligibility in British, Iberian, and Indigenous America*, [s.p.]. New York: New York University Press, 2018. https://doi.org/10.18574/nyu/9781479850129.003.0007.

Greer, Allan. *Property and Dispossession: Natives, Empire and Land in Early Modern North America*. Cambridge: Cambridge University Press, 2018.

Grenier, John. *The Far Reaches of Empire: War in Nova Scotia, 1710–1760*. Campaigns and Commanders: University of Oklahoma Press, 2008.

Grenier, John. *The First Way of War: American Warmaking on the Frontier, 1607–1814*. New York: Cambridge University Press, 2005.

Grenier, John. 'Warfare during the Colonial Era, 1607–1765'. In *A Companion to American Military History*, 7–21. Blackwell Companions to American History. Chichester: Wiley-Blackwell, 2010.

Gregory, Jeremy and Stevenson, John, *Britain in the Eighteenth Century, 1688–1820*. Abingdon: Routledge, 2007.

Griffin, Patrick. *American Leviathan: Empire, Nation, and Revolutionary Frontier*. New York: Hill and Wang, 2007.

Griffin, Patrick. *Experiencing Empire: Power, People, and Revolution in Early America*. Early American Histories. Charlottesville (VA); London: University of Virginia Press, 2017.

Griffin, Patrick. 'The Irish, Scots and Scotch-Irish and Lessons from the Early American Frontier'. *Journal of Irish and Scottish Studies* 3, no. 1 (2009).

Bibliography

Griffith, Samuel B. *The War For American Independence: From 1760 to the Surrender at Yorktown in 1781*. 2nd ed. Urbana and Chicago: University of Illinois Press, 2002.

Grimes, Richard S. *The Western Delaware Indian Nation, 1730–1795: Warriors and Diplomats*. Studies in Eighteenth-Century America and the Atlantic World. Bethlehem: Lehigh University Press, 2017.

Guider, John. *Voyage of the Adventure: Retracing the Donelson Party's Journey to the Founding of Nashville*. Nashville: Vanderbilt University Press, 2020.

Hahn, Steven C. *The Life and Times of Mary Musgrove*. Gainesville (FL): University Press of Florida, 2012.

Hall, Leslie. *Land and Allegiance in Revolutionary Georgia*. Athens and London: University of Georgia Press, 2001.

Hämäläinen, Pekka. *Indigenous Continent: The Epic Contest for North America*. New York: Liveright Publishing Corporation, 2022.

Hamilton, Michelle A. 'In the King's Service: Provisioning and Quartering the British Army in the Old Northwest, 1760–1773'. In *English Atlantics Revisited: Essays Honouring Professor Ian K. Steele*, 310–41. Montréal (PQ); London: McGill-Queen's University Press, 2007.

Hannings, Bud. *Forts of the United States: An Historical Dictionary, 16th through 19th Centuries*. Jefferson (NC): McFarland & Co., 2020.

Harless, Richard G. *George Washington and Native Americans: 'Learn Our Arts and Ways of Life'*. Fairfax, Virginia: George Mason University Press, 2018.

Harper, Steven Craig. *Promised Land: Penn's Holy Experiment, the Walking Purchase, and the Dispossession of the Delawares, 1600–1763*. Bethlehem, Pennsylvania: Lehigh University Press, 2006.

Hart, William B. *'For the Good of Their Souls': Performing Christianity in Eighteenth-Century Mohawk Country*. Native Americans of the Northeast. Amherst: University of Massachusetts Press, 2020.

Hatfield, April Lee. 'Colonial Southeastern Indian History'. *Journal of Southern History* 73, no. 3 (2007): 567–78.

Hatton, Heather. 'Narrating Sovereignty: The Covenant Chain in Intercultural Diplomacy'. *Journal of Early American History* 9, no. 2–3 (2019): 118–44. https://doi.org/10.1163/18770703-00902015.

Healey, Robynne Rogers. *Quakerism in the Atlantic World, 1690–1830*. The New History of Quakerism, 3. University Park: Pennsylvania State University Press, 2021.

Henry, Aaron James. *Districts, Documentation, and Population in Rupert's Land (1740–1840)*. Cham: Palgrave Macmillan, 2020.

Hermes, Katherine A. 'The Law of Native Americans to 1815'. In *The Cambridge History of Law in America. Vol. 1, Early America (1580–1815)*, 32–62. Cambridge: Cambridge University Press, 2008.

Herrmann, Rachel B. '"No Useless Mouth": Iroquoian Food Diplomacy in the American Revolution'. *Diplomatic History* 41, no. 1 (2017): 20–49. https://doi.org/10.1093/dh/dhw015.

Hinderaker, Eric. 'Diplomacy between Britons and Native Americans, c. 1600–1830'. In *Britain's Oceanic Empire: Atlantic and Indian Ocean Worlds, c. 1550–1850*, 218–48. Cambridge: Cambridge University Press, 2012.

Hinderaker, Eric. *Elusive Empires: Constructing Colonialism in the Ohio Valley 1673–1800*. Paperback. Cambridge: Cambridge University Press, 1999.

Hinderaker, Eric, and Mancall, Peter C. *At the Edge of Empire: The Backcountry in British North America*. Baltimore and London: Johns Hopkins University Press, 2003.

Hoffstra, Warren F. *The Planting of New Virginia: Settlement and Landscape in the Shenandoah Valley*. Baltimore and London: Johns Hopkins University Press, 2004.

Holton, Woody. 'The Ohio Indians and the Coming of the American Revolution in Virginia'. *The Journal of Southern History* 60, no. 3 (August 1994): 453–78.

Hoock, Holger. *Empires of the Imagination: Politics, War and the Arts in the British World, 1750–1850*. London: Profile Books, 2010.

Horn, Bernd. 'Deadly Encounter at Wood Creek, 8 August 1758'. In *Fortune Favours the Brave: Tales of Courage and Tenacity in Canadian Military History*, 19–40. Toronto: Dundurn Press, 2009.

Hornor, Elizabeth. 'Intimate Enemies: Captivity and Colonial Fear of Indians in the Mid-Eighteenth Century Wars'. *Pennsylvania History: A Journal of Mid-Atlantic Studies* 82, no. 2 (Spring 2015): 162–85.

Hotblack, Kate. *Chatham's Colonial Policy: A Study in the Fiscal and Economic Implications of the Colonial Policy of the Elder Pitt*. Facsimile reprint. Routledge, 1917.

Houston, Alan Craig. *Benjamin Franklin and the Politics of Improvement*. The Lewis Walpole Series in Eighteenth-Century Culture and History. New Haven (CT); London: Yale University Press, 2008.

Hrastar, John. *Breaking the Appalachian Barrier: Maryland as the Gateway to Ohio and the West, 1750–1850*. Jefferson (NC): McFarland & Co., 2018.

Hubbard, Robert Ernest. *General Rufus Putnam: George Washington's Chief Military Engineer and the 'Father of Ohio'*. Jefferson (NC): McFarland & Co., 2020.

Huggins, Stephen (Stephen Richard). *America's Use of Terror: From Colonial Times to the A-Bomb*. Lawrence: University Press of Kansas, 2019.

Hume, David. *Eagle's Wings: The Journey of the Ulster Scots and Scotch-Irish*. Newtownards, Co. Down: Colourpoint, 2011.

Humes, Alexander M. 'Shaping the Altamaha: The British-Spanish Struggle for Saint Simons Island, 1700–1748'. *Georgia Historical Quarterly* 104, no. 1 (2020): 1–31.

Ingram, Daniel. 'Anxious Hospitality: Indian "Loitering" at Fort Allen, 1756–1761'. *Pennsylvania Magazine of History & Biography* 133, no. 3 (2009): 221–54.

Ingram, Daniel. *Indians and British Outposts in Eighteenth-Century America*. Paperback. Gainesville: University Press of Florida, 2014.

Ireland, Patrick R. 'Irish Protestant Migration and Politics in the USA, Canada, and Australia: A Debated Legacy'. *Irish Studies Review* 20, no. 3 (2012): 263–81. https://doi.org/10.1080/09670882.2012.695613.

Ives, Timothy H. 'Reconstructing the Wangunk Reservation Land System: A Case Study of Native and Colonial Likeness in Central Connecticut'. *Ethnohistory* 58, no. 1 (2011): 65–89. https://doi.org/10.1215/00141801-2010-064.

Jacobs, Wilbur R. *Dispossessing the American Indian: Indians and Whites on the Colonial Frontier*. New York: Scribner, 1972.

Jacobs, Wilbur R., ed. *The Appalachian Indian Frontier: The Edmond Atkin and Plan of 1755*. University of Nebraska Press, 1967.

James, Alfred P. *The Ohio Company: Its Inner History*. Philadelphia: University of Pittsburgh Press, 1959.

Jennings, Matthew. *New Worlds of Violence: Cultures and Conquests in the Early American Southeast*. Knoxville (TN): University of Tennessee Press, 2011.

Johnson, Laura E. '"Goods to Clothe Themselves": Native Consumers and Native Images on the Pennsylvania Trading Frontier, 1712–1760'. *Winterthur Portfolio* 43, no. 1 (2009): 115–40. https://doi.org/10.1086/597283.

Johnston, A. John B. 'The Acadian Deportation in a Comparative Context: An Introduction'. *Journal of the Royal Nova Scotia Historical Society* 10 (2007): 114–31.

Josephy, Alvin R. *500 Nations: An Illustrated History of North American Indians*. London: Hutchinson, 1995.

Juricek, John T. *Colonial Georgia and the Creeks: Anglo-Indian Diplomacy on the Southern Frontier, 1733–1763*. Gainesville (FL): University Press of Florida, 2010.

Juricek, John T. *Endgame for Empire: British-Creek Relations in Georgia and Vicinity, 1763–1776*. Gainesville: University Press of Florida, 2015.

Kehoe, S. Karly, and Michael Easton Vance. *Reappraisals of British Colonisation in Atlantic Canada, 1700–1930*. Histories of the Scottish Atlantic. Edinburgh: Edinburgh University Press, 2020.

Kelsay, Isabel Thompson. *Joseph Brant: Man of Two Worlds*. Syracuse, New York: Syracuse University Press, 1984.

Kelton, Paul. *Cherokee Medicine, Colonial Germs: An Indigenous Nation's Fight against Smallpox, 1518–1824*. New Directions in Native American Studies, 11. Norman (OK): University of Oklahoma Press, 2015.

Kennedy, Dane Keith. 'On the American Empire from a British Imperial Perspective'. *International History Review* 29, no. 1 (2007): 83–108.

Kenny, Kevin. *Peaceable Kingdom Lost: The Paxton Boys and the Destruction of William Penn's Holy Experiment*. New York: Oxford University Press, 2009.

King, Duane H., ed. *The Cherokee Indian Nation: A Troubled History*. Knoxville: University of Tennessee Press, 1979.

Kruer, Matthew. 'Bloody Minds and Peoples Undone: Emotion, Family, and Political Order in the Susquehannock-Virginia War'. *William and Mary Quarterly* 74, no. 3 (July 2017): 401–36. https://doi.org/10.5309/willmaryquar.74.3.0401.

Kumamoto, Robert D. *The Historical Origins of Terrorism in America: 1644–1880*. New York: Routledge, 2014.

La Vere, David. *The Tuscarora War: Indians, Settlers and the Fight for the Carolina Colonies*. Chapel Hill: University of North Carolina Press, 2013.

Landes, Jordan. 'Recent Scholarship in Quaker Studies'. *Quaker History* 110, no. 1 (2021): 96–105. https://doi.org/10.1353/qkh.2021.0000.

Landsman, Ned C. *Crossroads of Empire: The Middle Colonies in British North America*. Regional Perspectives on Early America. Baltimore (MD): Johns Hopkins University Press, 2010.

Lannen, Andrew C. 'James Oglethorpe and the Civil-Military Contest for Authority in Colonial Georgia, 1732–1749'. *Georgia Historical Quarterly* 95, no. 2 (2011): 203–31.

Laramie, Michael G. *The European Invasion of North America: Colonial Conflict along the Hudson-Champlain Corridor, 1609–1760*. Santa Barbara (CA): Praeger, 2012.

Laramie, Michael G. 'The French Lake Champlain Fleet and the Contest for the Control of the Lake, 1742–1760'. *Vermont History* 80, no. 1 (2012): 1–32.

Lauzon, Matthew. 'Welsh Indians and Savage Scots: History, Antiquarianism, and Indian Languages in 18th-Century Britain'. *History of European Ideas* 34, no. 3 (2008): 250–69.

Leach, Douglas Edward. *Flintlock and Tomahawk: New England in King Philip's War*. New York: Macmillan, 1958.

Lee, Jacob F. *Masters of the Middle Waters: Indian Nations and Colonial Ambitions along the Mississippi*. Cambridge (MA): Belknap Press of Harvard University Press, 2019.

Lee, Wayne E. *Barbarians and Brothers: Anglo-American Warfare, 1500–1865*. Oxford: Oxford University Press, 2011.

Lee, Wayne E. 'Peace Chiefs and Blood Revenge: Patterns of Restraint in Native American Warfare, 1500–1800'. *Journal of Military History* 71, no. 3 (2007): 701–41.

Lee, Wayne E. 'The Military Revolution of Native North America: Firearms, Forts, and Polities'. In *Empires and Indigenes: Intercultural Alliance, Imperial Expansion, and Warfare in the Early Modern World*, 49–80. Warfare and Culture. New York: New York University Press, 2011.

Lee, Wayne E. 'Using the Natives against the Natives: Indigenes as "Counterinsurgents" in the British Atlantic, 1500–1800'. *Defence Studies* 10, no. 1–2 (2010): 88–105. https://doi.org/10.1080/14702430903392877.

LeMaster, Michelle. *Brothers Born of One Mother: British–Native American Relations in the Colonial Southeast*. Charlottesville (VA); London: University of Virginia Press, 2012.

Lemay, J. A. Leo. *The Life of Benjamin Franklin*. Philadelphia (PA): University of Pennsylvania Press, 2008.

Lemire, Beverly. 'Shirts and Snowshoes: Imperial Agendas and Indigenous Agency in Globalizing North America, c. 1660–1800'. In *Dressing Global Bodies: The Political Power of Dress in World History*, 65–84. Abingdon: Routledge, 2019. https://doi.org/10.4324/9781351028745-4.

Lengel, Edward G. *First Entrepreneur: How George Washington Built His – and the Nation's – Prosperity*. Boston: Da Capo Press, 2016.

Lennox, Jeffers. 'An Empire on Paper: The Founding of Halifax and Conceptions of Imperial Space, 1744–55'. *Canadian Historical Review* 88, no. 3 (2007): 373–412.

Lennox, Jeffers. 'Nova Scotia Lost and Found: The Acadian Boundary Negotiation and Imperial Envisioning, 1750–1755'. *Acadiensis: Journal of the History of the Atlantic Region* 40, no. 2 (2011): 3–31.

Little, Ann M. 'Wabanaki and Ursuline Catholicism in Quebec and Acadia: A Comparative Perspective'. In *Under the Veil: Feminism and Spirituality in Post-Reformation England and Europe*, 43–66. Newcastle: Cambridge Scholars, 2012.

MacLeitch, Gail D. *Imperial Entanglements: Iroquois Change and Persistence on the Frontiers of Empire*. Early American Studies. Philadelphia (PA): University of Pennsylvania Press, 2011.

Maier, Pauline. 'Whigs against Whigs against Whigs: The Imperial Debates of 1765–76 Reconsidered'. *William and Mary Quarterly* 68, no. 4 (2011): 578–82. https://doi.org/10.5309/willmaryquar.68.4.0578.

Mair, Edward. 'Slaves and Indians'. *History Today* 70, no. 2 (2020): 58–69.

Mapp, Paul W. *The Elusive West and the Contest for Empire, 1713–1763*. Chapel Hill: University of North Carolina Press, 2011.

Marsh, Dawn. 'Penn's Peaceable Kingdom: Shangri-La Revisited'. *Ethnohistory* 56, no. 4 (2009): 651–67. https://doi.org/10.1215/00141801-2009-025.

Marsh, Dawn G. *A Lenape among the Quakers: The Life of Hannah Freeman*. Lincoln (NE) and London: University of Nebraska Press, 2014.

Marshall, Peter. 'Colonial Protest and Imperial Retrenchment: Indian Policy 1764–1768'. *Journal of American Studies* 5, no. 1 (April 1971): 1–17.

Martin, Nicola. 'Lord Loudoun, the Highlands and Imperial Subjecthood in North America'. *Scottish Historical Review* 100, no. 2 (2021): 249–76. https://doi.org/10.3366/shr.2021.0517.

Martino, Gina M. *Women at War in the Borderlands of the Early American Northeast*. The David J. Weber Series in the New Borderlands History. Chapel Hill: University of North Carolina Press, 2018.

Mcardell, Lee. *Ill-Starred General: Braddock of the Coldstream Guards*. Pittsburgh: University of Pittsburgh Press, 1958.

McDonnell, Michael A. *A Country Between: The Upper Ohio Valley and Its Peoples, 1724–1774*. Lincoln and London: University of Nebraska Press, 1997.

McDonnell, Michael A. *Masters of Empire: Great Lakes Indians and the Making of America*. New York: Hill and Wang, 2015.

McDonnell, Michael A. 'The Indigenous Architecture of Empire: The Anishinaabe Odawa in North America'. In *Facing Empire: Indigenous Experiences in a Evolutionary Age*, 48–71. Baltimore: Johns Hopkins University Press, 2018.

Merrell, James. *Into the American Woods: Negotiators on the Pennsylvanian Frontier*. New York: Norton, 1999.

Merrell, James Hart. '"Our Bond of Peace": Patterns of Intercultural Exchange in the Carolina Piedmont, 1650–1750'. In *Powhatan's Mantle: Indians in the Colonial Southeast*, 267–304. Chesham: Combined Academic [distributor], 2007.

Merritt, Janes T. *At the Crossroads: Indians and Empires on a Mid-Atlantic Frontier, 1700–1763*. Chapel Hill: University of North Carolina Press, 2003.

Middlekauf, Robert. *Washington's Revolution: The Making of America's First Leader*. New York: Knopf, 2015.

Middleton, Richard. 'Pontiac: Local Warrior or Pan-Indian Leader?' *Michigan Historical Review* 32, no. 2 (Fall 2006): 1–32.

Middleton, Richard. *Pontiac's War: Its Causes, Course and Consequences*. London: Routledge, 2007.

Middleton, Richard, and Anne S. Lombard. *Colonial America: A History to 1763*. Oxford: Wiley-Blackwell, 2011.

Midtrød, Tom Arne. 'Strange and Disturbing News: Rumor and Diplomacy in the Colonial Hudson Valley'. *Ethnohistory* 58, no. 1 (2011): 91–112. https://doi.org/10.1215/00141801-2010-065.

Midtrød, Tom Arne. *The Memory of All Ancient Customs: Native American Diplomacy in the Colonial Hudson Valley*. Ithaca (NY): Cornell University Press, 2012.

Miller, David W. *The Forced Removal of American Indians from the Northeast: A History of Territorial Cessions and Relocations, 1620–1854*. Jefferson (NC): McFarland & Co., 2011.

Miller, Ivor. 'The Genesis of African and Indian Cooperation in Colonial North America: An Interview with Helen Hornbeck Tanner'. *Ethnohistory* 56, no. 2 (2009): 285–302. https://doi.org/10.1215/00141801-2008-059.

Misencik, Paul R., and Sally E. Misencik. *American Indians of the Ohio Country in the 18th Century*. Jefferson (NC): McFarland & Co., 2020.

Mohl, Allan S. 'The Rise and Fall of the Iroquois Confederacy: Its Influence on Early American History'. *Journal of Psychohistory* 34, no. 4 (2007): 347–61.

Monks, Sarah. 'The Wolfe Man: Benjamin West's Anglo-American Accent'. *Art History* 34, no. 4 (2011): 652–73. https://doi.org/10.1111/j.1467-8365.2010.00840.x.

Morgan, Kenneth. 'Robert Dinwiddie's Reports on the British American Colonies'. *William and Mary Quarterly* 65, no. 2 (2008): 305–46.

Morgan, Kenneth. 'Robert Dinwiddie's Reports on the British American Colonies'. *William and Mary Quarterly* 65, no. 2 (2008): 305–46.

Morito, Bruce. *An Ethic of Mutual Respect: The Covenant Chain and Aboriginal-Crown Relations*. Vancouver: UBC Press, 2012.

Moyer, Paul Benjamin. *Wild Yankees: The Struggle for Independence along Pennsylvania's Revolutionary Frontier*. Kindle. Ithaca and London: Cornell University Press, n.d.

Mullins, J. Patrick. '"A Kind of War, Tho' Hitherto an Un-Bloody One": Jonathan Mayhew, Francis Bernard, and the Indian Affair'. *Massachusetts Historical Review* 11 (2009).

Narrett, David. *The Cherokees: In War and at Peace, 1670–1840*. Kindle. Cambridge, Massachusetts, and London: Belknap Press of Harvard University Press, 2025.

Nelson, Paul David. *General James Grant: Scottish Soldier and Royal Governor of East Florida*. Gainesville: University Press of Florida, 1993.

Nester, William R. *The Great Frontier War: Britain, France, and the Imperial Struggle for North America, 1607–1755*. Westport, Conn.; Praeger, 2000.

Newell, Margaret Ellen. 'Indian Slavery in Colonial New England'. In *Indian Slavery in Colonial America*, 33–66. Lincoln (NE): University of Nebraska Press, 2009.

Newman, Andrew. *Allegories of Encounter: Colonial Literacy and Indian Captivities*. Chapel Hill: University of North Carolina Press, 2019.

Newman, Andrew. *On Records: Delaware Indians, Colonists, and the Media of History and Memory*. Lincoln: University of Nebraska Press, 2012.

Newman, Paul Douglas. 'Red Journalism: The Allegheny Indians, Ben Franklin's Pennsylvania Gazette, and the Ethnic Cleansing of Pennsylvania, 1747–1764'. *Journalism History* 45, no. 3 (2019): 227–49. https://doi.org/10.1080/00947679.2019.1631081.

Newton, Michael Steven. 'The Macs Meet the "Micmacs": Scottish Gaelic First Encounter Narratives from Nova Scotia'. *Journal of Irish and Scottish Studies* 5, no. 1 (2011): 67–96.

Norton, David J. *Rebellious Younger Brother: Oneida Leadership and Diplomacy, 1750–1800*. DeKalb (IL): Northern Illinois University Press, 2009.

Oats, Lynne, and Pauline Sadler. 'Accounting for the Stamp Act Crisis'. *Accounting Historians Journal* 35, no. 2 (2008): 101–43.

Odle, Mairin. *Under the Skin: Tattoos, Scalps, and the Contested Language of Bodies in Early America*. Early American Studies. Philadelphia: University of Pennsylvania Press, 2022.

O'Gorman, Frank. 'Shelburne: A Chathamite in Opposition and in Government 1760–82?' In *An Enlightened Statesman in Whig Britain: Lord Shelburne in Context, 1737–1805*. Woodbridge, Suffolk, UK: The Boydell Press, 2011.

O'Gorman, Frank. *The Long Eighteenth Century: British Political and Social History 1688–1832*. 2nd ed. London: Bloomsbury Academic, 2016.

Oliphant, John. *John Forbes: Scotland, Flanders and the Seven Years War 1707–1759*. London: Bloomsbury, 2015.

Oliphant, John. *Peace and War on the Anglo-Cherokee Frontier' 1756–1763*. Basingstoke: Palgrave Macmillan, 2001.

Oliphant, John. 'The Cherokee Embassy to London, 1762'. *Journal of Imperial and Commonwealth History* 27, no. 1 (January 1999): 1–26.

Ostler, Jeffrey. 'Locating Settler Colonialism in Early American History'. *William and Mary Quarterly* 76, no. 3 (July 2019): 443–50. https://doi-org.lonlib.idm.oclc.org/10.5309/willmaryquar.76.3.0443.

Ostler, Jeffrey. '"To Extirpate the Indians": An Indigenous Consciousness of Genocide in the Ohio Valley and Lower Great Lakes, 1750s–1810'. *William and Mary Quarterly* 72, no. 4 (2015): 587–622. https://doi.org/10.5309/willmaryquar.72.4.0587.

Ostler, Jeffrey, and Nancy Shoemaker. 'Settler Colonialism in Early American History: Introduction'. *William and Mary Quarterly* 76, no. 3 (2019): 361–68. https://doi.org/10.5309/willmaryquar.76.3.0361.

O'Toole, Fintan. *White Savage: William Johnson and the Invention of America*. London: Faber, 2005.

Ouzts, Clay. *Samuel Elbert and the Age of Revolution in Georgia, 1740–1788*. Macon: Mercer University Press, 2022.

Parkman, Francis. *History of the Conspiracy of Pontiac and the War of the North American Tribes against the English Colonies after the Conquest of Canada*. Boston: Charles C. Little and James Brown, 1851.

Parmenter, Jon William. 'After the Mourning Wars: The Iroquois as Allies in Colonial North American Campaigns, 1676–1760'. *William and Mary Quarterly* 64, no. 1 (2007): 39–82.

Paulett, Robert. *An Empire of Small Places: Mapping the Southeastern Anglo-Indian Trade, 1732–1795*. Early American. Athens: The University of Georgia Press, 2012.

Paulett, Robert. '"An Exact Union of System": Bute's Cabinet Revolution and Imperial Reform, 1762–63'. *Journal of British Studies Issue 4* 63, no. 4 (October 2024): 792–809. https://doi.org/10.1017/jbr.2024.117.

Peace, Thomas, and Kathryn Magee Labelle. *From Huronia to Wendakes: Adversity, Migrations, and Resilience, 1650–1900*. New Directions in Native American Studies, 15. Norman (OK): University of Oklahoma Press, 2016.

Peacey, Jason. *Making the British Empire, 1660–1800*. Studies in Imperialism. Manchester: Manchester University Press, 2020.

Peckham, Howard H. *Pontiac and the Indian Uprising*. Princeton (NJ): Princeton University Press, 1947.

Pedley, Mary Sponberg. '"A New and Accurate Map of the English Empire in North America" by a Society of Anti-Gallicans (London, 1755)'. In *Mappae Antiquae: Liber Amicorum Gèunter Schilder: Vriendenboek Ter Gelegenheid van Zijn 65ste Verjaardag*, 449–58. Utrechtse Historisch-Kartografische Studies, 6. 't Goy-Houten: Hes & De Graaf, 2007.

Peters, Marie. *The Elder Pitt*. London and New York: Longman, n.d.

Phillips, Andrew, and J. C. (Jason Campbell) Sharman. *Outsourcing Empire: How Company-States Made the Modern World*. Princeton (NJ): Princeton University Press, 2020.

Piker, Joshua Aaron. 'The Empire, the Emperor, and the Empress: The Interesting Case of Mrs. Mary Bosomworth'. In *European Empires in the American South: Colonial and Environmental Encounters*, 149–68. Chancellor Porter L. Fortune Symposium in Southern History Series. Jackson: University Press of Mississippi, 2017.

Pincus, Steven C. A. 'Reconfiguring the British Empire'. *William and Mary Quarterly* 69, no. 1 (2012): 63–70. https://doi.org/10.5309/willmaryquar.69.1.0063.

Plank, Geoffrey. *An Unsettled Conquest: The British Campaign Against the Peoples of Acadia*. Philadelphia: University of Pennsylvania Press, 2004.

Plank, Geoffrey. 'Deploying Tribes and Clans: Mohawks in Nova Scotia and Scottish Highlanders in Georgia'. In *Empires and Indigenes: Intercultural Alliance, Imperial Expansion, and Warfare in the Early Modern World*, 221–49. Warfare and Culture. New York: New York University Press, 2011.

Pluymers, Keith. *No Wood, No Kingdom: Political Ecology in the English Atlantic*. The Early Modern Americas Philadelphia: University of Pennsylvania Press, 2021.

Pointer, Richard W. *Pacifist Prophet: Papunhank and the Quest for Peace in Early America*. Lincoln (NE): University of Nebraska Press, 2020.

Preston, David L. (David Lee). '"We Intend to Live Our Lifetime Together as Brothers": Palatine and Iroquois Communities in the Mohawk Valley'. *New York History* 89, no. 2 (2008): 179–90.

Price, Jacob M. 'Who Cared About the Colonies? The Impact of the Thirteen Colonies on British Society and Politics, circa 1714–1775'. In *The Atlantic Frontier of the Thirteen American Colonies and States: Essays in Eighteenth Century Commercial and Social History*. Aldershot and Burlington: Variorum, 1996.

Prior, Charles. 'Beyond Settler Colonialism: State Sovereignty in Early America'. *Journal of Early American History* 9, no. 2–3 (2019): 93–117. https://doi.org/10.1163/18770703-00902013.

Prior, Charles. *Settlers in Indian Country: Sovereignty and Indigenous Power in Early America*.

Proud, James. *William Penn's 'Holy Experiment': Quaker Truth in Pennsylvania, 1682–1781*. San Francisco (CA): Inner Light Books, 2019.

Ray, Kristofer. *Cherokee Power: Imperial and Indigenous Geopolitics in the Trans-Appalachian West, 1670–1774*. Vol. 22. New Directions in Native American Studies, Norman: University of Oklahoma Press, 2023.

Ray, Kristofer. 'Cherokees and Franco-British Confrontation in the Tennessee Corridor, 1730–1760'. *Native South* 7 (2014): 33–67. https://doi.org/10.1353/nso.2014.0004.

Ray, Kristofer. 'Interpreting Native Trans-Appalachia, 1670–1770'. *XVII-XVIII; Revue de La Société d'études Anglo-Américaines Des XVIIe et XVIIIe Siècles* 78 (2021): [unpaged]. https://doi.org/10.4000/1718.8090.

Recco, Ianna. 'In the Flesh at the Heart of Empire: Life-Likeness in Wax Representations of the 1762 Cherokee Delegation in London'. *British Art Studies*, no. 21 (30 November 2021). https://doi.org/10.17658/issn.2058-5462/issue-21/irecco.

'Red Power and Homeland Security: Native Nations and the Limits of Empire in the Ohio Country'. In Kate Fullagar and Michael A. McDonnell (Eds.) *Facing Empire: Indigenous Experience in a Revolutionary Age*, 145–62. Baltimore: Johns Hopkins University Press, 2018.

Reid, John G. 'Empire, Settler Colonialism, and the Role of Violence in Indigenous Dispossession in British North America, 1749–1830'. In *Violence, Order, and Unrest: A History of British North America, 1749–1876*, 117–34. Toronto (Ont): University of Toronto Press, 2019. https://doi.org/10.3138/9781487531607-009.

Reid, John G. 'Imperial-Aboriginal Friendship in Eighteenth-Century Mi'kma'ki/Wulstukwik'. In *The Loyal Atlantic: Remaking the British Atlantic in the Revolutionary Era*, 75–102. Toronto; Buffalo: University of Toronto Press, 2012.

'Report from the Board of Trade to Egremont, 5 August 1763', 5 August 1763. Egremont Papers, PRO 30/47, ff. 95–98. TNA.

Reséndez, Andrés. *The Other Slavery: The Uncovered Story of Indian Enslavement in America*. Boston (MA): Houghton Mifflin Harcourt, 2016.

Reynolds, William R. *The Cherokee Struggle to Maintain Identity in the 17th and 18th Centuries*. Jefferson (NC): McFarland, 2015.

Rhoades, Matthew L. 'Blood and Boundaries: Virginia Backcountry Violence and the Origins of the Quebec Act, 1758–1775'. *West Virginia History* ns 3, no. 2 (2009): 1–22. https://doi.org/10.1353/wvh.0.0062.

Rhodehamel, John H. *George Washington: The Wonder of the Age*. New Haven: Yale University Press, 2017.

Richardson, Robbie. 'The Site of the Struggle: Colonialism, Violence and the Captive Body'. In *Native Americans and Anglo-American Culture, 1750–1850: The Indian Atlantic*, 39–55. Cambridge: Cambridge University Press, 2009.

Richter, Daniel K. *Facing East From Indian Country: A Native History of Early America*. Cambridge, Massachusetts, and London: Harvard University Press, n.d.

Richter, Daniel K. 'Stratification and Class in Eastern Native America'. In *Class Matters: Early North America and the Atlantic World*, 35–48. Early American Studies. Philadelphia (PA): University of Pennsylvania Press, 2008.

Richter, Daniel K. *Trade, Land, Power: The Struggle for Eastern North America*. Philadelphia: University of Pennsylvania Press, 2013.

Richwine, Lindsay. 'Comity at the Crossroads: How Friendships between Moravian and Native Women Sustained the Moravian Mission at Shamokin, 1745–1755'. *Pennsylvania History* 89, no. 1 (2022): 74–101.

Ridner, Judith. *A Town In-between: Carlisle, Pennsylvania, and the Early Mid-Atlantic Interior*. Early American Studies. Philadelphia (PA): University of Pennsylvania Press, 2010.

Rindfleisch. 'My Land Is My Flesh: Silver Bluff, the Creek Indians, and the Transformation of Colonized Space in Early America'. *Early American Studies* 16, no. 3 (Summer 2018): 405–30.

Rindfleisch, Bryan C. *Brothers of Coweta: Kinship, Empire, and Revolution in the Eighteenth-Century Muscogee World*. Columbia: The University of South Carolina Press, 2021.

Rindfleisch, Bryan C. *George Galphin's Intimate Empire: The Creek Indians, Family, and Colonialism in Early America*. Indians and Southern History: University of Alabama Press, 2019.

Rindfleisch, Bryan C. 'Metawney of Coweta, Muscogee Women, and Historical Erasure in the Eighteenth-Century Past and Our Present'. *Studies in Eighteenth-Century Culture* 52 (2023): 149–61. https://doi.org/10.1353/sec.2023.0014.

Rindfleisch, Bryan C. 'The Indian Factors: Kinship, Trade, and Authority in the Creek Nation & American South, 1740–1800'. *Journal of Early American History* 8, no. 1 (2018): 1–29. https://doi.org/10.1163/18770703-00801005.

Robbins, Paula I. *The Travels of Peter Kalm, Finnish-Swedish Naturalist, through Colonial North America, 1748–1751*. Fleischmanns, N.Y.: Purple Mountain Press, 2007.

Roberts, Strother E. *Colonial Ecology, Atlantic Economy: Transforming Nature in Early New England*. Early American (PA): University of Philadelphia Press, 2019.

Robinson, Emily Moberg. 'The Covenanter Diaspora: Presbyterian Rebellion in the Atlantic World'. *Scotch-Irish Studies* 2, no. 4 (2008): 23–44.

Russell, Peter E. 'Redcoats in the Wilderness: British Officers and Irregular Warfare in Europe and America, 1740 to 1760'. *William and Mary Quarterly* 35, no. 4 (1978): 629–52. https://doi.org/doi:10.2307/1923208.

Sadosky, Leonard J. *Revolutionary Negotiations: Indians, Empires, and Diplomats in the Founding of America*. Jeffersonian America. Charlottesville (VA): University of Virginia Press, 2009.

Sahle, Esther. *Quakers in the British Atlantic World, c.1660–1800*. People, Markets, Goods: Economies and Societies in History, 18. Martlesham: The Boydell Press, 2021.

Saxine, Ian. *Properties of Empire: Indians, Colonists, and Land Speculators on the New England Frontier*. Early American Places. New York: New York University Press, 2019.

Sayre, Robert. *Modernity and Its Other: The Encounter with North American Indians in the Eighteenth Century*. Lincoln (NE); London: University of Nebraska Press, 2017.

Schmidt, Ethan A. 'Beyond the New England Frontier: Native American Historiography Since 1965'. *Historical Journal of Massachusetts* 41, no. 2 (2013): 82–111.

Schumann, Matt, and Karl W. Schweizer. *The Seven Years War: A Transatlantic History*. London: Routledge, 2008.

Schutt, Amy T. *Peoples of the River Valleys: The Odyssey of the Delaware Indians*. Philadelphia: University of Philadelphia Press, 2007.

Scott, H. M. 'Wyndham, Charles, Second Earl of Egremont (1710–1763)'. In *Oxford Dictionary of National Biography*, n.d. https://doi-org.lonlib.idm.oclc.org/10.1093/ref:odnb/30139.

Seeman, Erik R. *Death in the New World: Cross-Cultural Encounters, 1492–1800*. Early American Studies. Philadelphia (PA): University of Pennsylvania Press, 2010.

Seib, Rebecca, Helen C. Rountree, and Maryland Historical Society. *Indians of Southern Maryland*. Baltimore (MD): Maryland Historical Society, 2014.

Seymour, Joseph. *The Pennsylvania Associators, 1747–1777*. Yardley (PA): Westholme, 2012.

Shannon, Timothy J. *Indians and Colonists at the Crossroads of Empire: The Albany Congress of 1754*. Ithaca and London: Cornell University Press, 2000.

Shannon, Timothy J. *Iroquois Diplomacy of the Early American Frontier*. The Penguin Library of American Indian History. London: Penguin, 2008.

Shannon, Timothy J. *Indian Captive, Indian King: Peter Williamson in America and Britain*. Cambridge (MA): Harvard University Press, 2018.

Shannon, Timothy J. 'King of the Indians: The Hard Fate and Curious Career of Peter Williamson'. *William and Mary Quarterly* 66, no. 1 (2009): 3–44.

Shannon, Timothy J. 'The World That Made Johnson'. *New York History* 89, no. 2 (2008): 111–26.

Shannon, Timothy J. 'War, Diplomacy, and Culture: The Iroquois Experience in the Seven Years' War'. In *Cultures in Conflict: The Seven Years' War in North America*, 79–104. Lanham (MD); Plymouth: Rowman & Littlefield, 2007.

Shefveland, Kristalyn Marie. 'The Many Faces of Native Bonded Labor in Colonial Virginia'. *Native South* 7 (2014): 68–91. https://doi.org/10.1353/nso.2014.0006.

Shoemaker, Nancy. 'Settler Colonialism: Universal Theory or English Heritage?' *William and Mary Quarterly* 76, no. 3 (2019): 369–74. https://doi.org/10.5309/willmaryquar.76.3.0369.

Shoemaker, Nancy. 'Wonder and Repulsion: North American Indians in Eighteenth-Century Europe'. In *Europe Observed: Multiple Gazes in Early Modern Encounters*, 173–94. Lewisburg (PA): Bucknell University Press, 2008.

Siddique, Asheesh Kapur. 'Governance through Documents: The Board of Trade, Its Archive, and the Imperial Constitution of the

Eighteenth-Century British Atlantic World'. *Journal of British Studies* 59, no. 2 (2020): 264–90. https://doi.org/10.1017/jbr.2019.281.

Silver, Peter Rhoads. *Our Savage Neighbors: How Indian War Transformed Early America*. New York; London: W. W. Norton & Co, 2008.

Silverman, David J. 'Purgatory: Interpreting Christian Missions and North American Indians'. In *Converging Worlds: Communities and Cultures in Colonial America*, 320–43. London: Routledge, 2012.

Silverman, David J. 'The Curse of God: An Idea and Its Origins among the Indians of New York's Revolutionary Frontier'. *William and Mary Quarterly* 66, no. 3 (2009): 495–534.

Simmons, R. C. *The American Colonies From Settlement to Independence*. Paperback. New York and London: Norton, 1981.

Sleeper-Smith, Susan. *Indigenous Prosperity and American Conquest: Indian Women of the Ohio River Valley, 1690–1792*. Chapel Hill: University of North Carolina Press, 2018.

Smallwood, Stephanie E. 'Reflections on Settler Colonialism, the Hemispheric Americas, and Chattel Slavery'. *William and Mary Quarterly* 76, no. 3 (2019): 407–16. https://doi.org/10.5309/willmaryquar.76.3.0407.

Smallwood, Stephanie E., ed. *The Grenville Papers, Being the Correspondence of Richard Grenville Earl Temple K.G., Ahd the Right Hon: George Grenville, Their Friends and Contemporaries*. Vol. 4. 4 vols. London: John Murray, 1853.

Smithers, Gregory D. '"Our Hands and Hearts Are Joined Together": Friendship, Colonialism, and the Cherokee People in Early America'. *Journal of Social History* 50, no. 4 (2017): 609–29.

Snapp, J. Russell. *John Stuart and the Struggle for Empire on the Southern Frontier*. Baton Rouge and London: Louisiana State University Press, 1996.

Snead, James E. 'The "secret and Bloody War Path": Movement, Place and Conflict in the Archaeological Landscape of North America'. *World Archaeology* 43, no. 3 (2011): 478–92. https://doi.org/10.1080/00438243.2011.607704.

Snow, Dean R. *The Iroquois*. Paperback. The Peoples of America. Oxford UK and Cambridge USA: Blackwell, 1996.

Sosin, Jack M. *Whitehall and the Wilderness: The Middle West in British Colonial Policy, 1760–1775*. Lincoln: University of Nebraska Press, 1961.

Southern, Ron. 'Martyrs and Messengers: Benjamin Franklin and the American Frontier, Moravians and the Nature of Reason'. In *Colonial Frontiers: Indigenous-European Encounters in Settler Societies*, edited by Russell, Lynette, 82–97. Manchester: Manchester University Press, 2001.

Spear, Jennifer M. 'Race Matters in the Colonial South'. *Journal of Southern History* 73, no. 3 (2007): 579–88.

Specht, Neva Jean. '"Being a Peaceable Man, I Have Suffered Much Persecution": The American Revolution and Its Effects on Quaker Religious Identity'. *Quaker History* 99, no. 2 (Fall 2010): 37–48.

Spero, Patrick. *Frontier Country: The Politics of War in Early Pennsylvania*. Philadelphia: University of Pennsylvania Press, 2016.

Spero, Patrick. 'Pennsylvania's Variegated Frontier'. *Pennsylvania History* 88, no. 3 (2021): 402–10.

Starbuck, David R. *The Archaeology of Forts and Battlefields*. The American Experience in Archaeological Perspective. Gainesville (FL): University Press of Florida, 2011.

Stark, Peter. *Young Washington: How Wilderness and War Forged America's Founding Father*. New York: Ecco, 2018.

Starkey, Armstrong. *European and Native American Warfare, 1675–1815*. London: UCL Press, 1998.

Steele, Ian K. *Warpaths: Invasions of North America*. New York and Oxford: Oxford University Press, 1994.

Stern, Jessica R. 'Native American Taste: Re-Evaluating the Gift-Commodity Debate in the British Colonial Southeast'. *Native South* 5 (2012): 1–37. https://doi.org/10.1353/nso.2012.0003.

Strobel, Christoph. *Native Americans of New England*. Santa Barbara (CA): Praeger, 2020.

Strong, John A. *The Unkechaug Indians of Eastern Long Island: A History*. Civilization of the American Indian Series, 269. Norman (OK): University of Oklahoma Press, 2011.

Taylor, Alan. 'Sir William Johnson's Interest: Indian Land and Transatlantic Power'. In *Native Americans and Anglo-American Culture, 1750–1850: The Indian Atlantic*, 94–111. Cambridge: Cambridge University Press, 2009.

Taylor, Alan. *The Divided Ground: Indians, Settlers, and the Northern Borderland of The American Revolution*. New York: Alfred A. Knopf, 2006.

Thornton, Russell. *The Cherokees: A Population History*. Lincoln and London: University of Nebraska Press, 1992.
Thrush, Coll-Peter. *Indigenous London: Native Travelers at the Heart of Empire*. The Henry Roe Cloud Series on American Indians and Modernity. New Haven: Yale University Press, 2016.
Tortora, Daniel. *Carolina in Crisis: Cherokees, Colonists and Slaves in the American Southeast, 1756–1763*. Chapel hill: University of North Carolina Press, 2015.
Truettner, William H. *Painting Indians and Building Empires in North America, 1710–1840*. Berkeley (CA); London: University of California Press, 2010.
Tucker, Spencer, James R. Arnold, and Roberta Wiener. *The Encyclopedia of North American Indian Wars, 1607–1890: A Political, Social, and Military History*. Santa Barbara (CA): ABC-Clio, 2011.
Turner, Frederick J. *The Significance of the Frontier in American History*. No place: LM Publishers, No date.
Urban, Mark. *Fusiliers: Eight Years with the Redcoats in America*. London: Faber, 2007.
Wainwright, Nicholas B. *George Croghan: Wilderness Diplomat*. Chapel Hill: University of North Carolina Press, 1959.
Waldstreicher, David. *A Companion to Benjamin Franklin*. Oxford: Wiley-Blackwell, 2011.
Wallace, Anthony F. C. *King of the Delawares: Teedyuscung 1700–1763*. Syracuse, New York: Syracuse University Press, 1990.
Ward, Matthew C. *Making the Frontier Man: Violence, White Manhood & Authority in the Early Western Backcountry*. Pittsburgh: University of Pittsburgh Press, 2023.
Ward, Matthew C. *Breaking the Backcountry: The Seven Years' War in Virginia and Pennsylvania, 1754–1765*. Pittsburgh: University of Pittsburgh Press, 2003.
Welland, Heather. *Political Economy and Imperial Governance in Eighteenth-Century Britain*. Routledge Studies in Eighteenth-Century Cultures and Societies. London: Routledge, 2021.
Wheeler, Rachel M. *To Live upon Hope: Mohicans and Missionaries in the Eighteenth-Century Northeast*. Ithaca (NY): Cornell University Press, 2008.
White, Richard. *The Middle Ground: Indians, Empires and Republics in the Great Lakes Region, 1650–1815*. Cambridge: Cambridge University Press, 1991.

Whitworth, Rex. *William Augustus Duke of Cumberland: A Life*. London: Leo Cooper, 1992.

Widder, Keith R. 'After the Conquest: Michilimackinac, a Borderland in Transition, 1760–1763'. *Michigan Historical Review* 34, no. 1 (2008): 43–61.

Widder, Keith R. 'The 1767 Maps of Robert Rogers and Jonathan Carver: A Proposal for the Establishment of the Colony of Michilimackinac'. In *Mapping in Michigan & the Great Lakes Region*, 63–90. East Lansing (MI): Michigan State University Press, 2007.

Williams, Glenn F. *Dunmore's War: The Last Conflict of America's Colonial Era*. Yardley (PA): Westholme Publishing, 2018.

Wilson, Jon, and Andrew Dilley. 'The Incoherence of Empire. Or, the Pitfalls of Ignoring Sovereignty in the History of the British Empire'. *Transactions of the Royal Historical Society* 1 (10 July 2023). https://doi.org/10.1017/S0080440123000063.

Witgen, Michael J. 'Rethinking Colonial History as Continental History'. *William and Mary Quarterly* 69, no. 3 (2012): 527–30. https://doi.org/10.5309/willmaryquar.69.3.0527.

Wood, Douglas McClure. '"I Have Now Made a Path to Virginia": Outacite Ostenaco and the Cherokee–Virginia Alliance in the French and Indian War'. *West Virginia History* ns 2, no. 2 (2008): 31–60. https://doi.org/10.1353/wvh.0.0018.

INDEX

Aix-la-Chapelle, Peace of 9, 28
Albany 29, 43–50, 72–73, 88, 91, 94, 99, 131–132, 135, 145
Abenakis 16
Allegheny
#Mountains 11, 34, 145
#River 30–32, 35, 38, 77, 102
Amherst, Jeffrey 88–89, 101, 104, 106–107, 110–111, 113–115, 119, 122–123, 127, 132, 136–137, 212
Anderson, Fred 39
Arkansas Indians 160–161
Armstrong, John 77
Attakullakulla (Little Carpenter) 64, 58, 98, 100, 102–103, 105, 108–109, 111–116, 119–120, 125, 127, 157, 159, 186–187, 191, 205
Aughwick 41, 66, 78
Augusta Boys 170
Augusta 106, 156, 164
Augusta, 1763 Congress of 157–160

Austria (Hapsburg monarchy) 9, 63, 88
Austrian Succession, War of 9, 26, 45, 91

Barrington, William Wildman, Viscount 150, 152, 185
Black Boys 169–170, 173, 190
Bladen, Martin 23
Blake, William 124, 128
Board of Trade 18, 22–23, 27–29, 37, 47–48, 54, 84, 87, 111, 122, 124, 126–129, 147, 153, 172, 174, 180, 182, 184–185, 199–201, 217
Boone, Daniel 12, 206
Boone, Thomas 128, 158
Bouquet, Henry 92, 94, 96–98, 100, 124, 142–145, 168, 170, 171, 174, 193, 212
Braddock, Edward 62–64, 65–76, 88, 91–94, 109, 117, 138, 141
Bradstreet 78, 88–89, 143–144, 212

Index

Bull, Captain (Delaware warrior) 133
Bull, William 107, 111, 113–115, 118
Bushy Run, battle of 142
Bute, John Stuart, Earl of 90, 124, 127, 147
Byrd 93, 100, 102, 107, 113, 119

Canada 9, 13, 17–18, 22, 26–27, 31, 32, 35, 49, 57, 72, 75, 82, 88, 89, 92, 122, 124, 127, 128, 138, 147–148, 197, 200–205, 209, 210, 222–229
Cameron, Alexander 186–187, 205
Camp Charlotte, treaty of 196
Carleton, Guy 202
Catawbas 15, 17–18, 31, 33, 66, 84, 95, 98–100, 103, 116, 118, 126, 156, 158, 160
Catawba River 102, 156
Carrington, Nathan 125
Charleston 58, 59, 97, 102, 104, 107, 111, 113, 115–116, 118–120, 124, 128, 157, 158, 162, 163, 205
Cherokee 14–15, 17–18, 29, 38, 52–60, 66, 76, 84, 93, 95, 98–100, 106–120, 123–126, 128, 135, 153, 156–160, 164, 166, 174–179, 181, 187–191, 196, 205–206
Chickasaws 15, 84, 115, 116, 118, 126, 158, 160, 165, 191
Choctaws 17, 18, 84, 111, 116, 118, 126, 158, 160, 165, 191
Connecticut 13, 16, 47, 49–50,
131–132, 143, 151–152, 178, 222
Connolly, John 192–193
Continental Congress 197, 201, 203–206
Cornstalk (Hokoleskwa) 193–196
Crawford, William 33, 192, 207
Creeks 15, 17, 53, 55–56, 84, 93, 109, 111–112, 153, 155, 156, 159–165, 191
Croghan, George 31–33, 58, 67, 99, 145, 150, 152, 165, 168–173, 175–178, 181, 185–186, 204–206
Crown Point 29, 62–63, 72–74, 78, 80, 88–89, 153
Cumberland, William Augustus, Duke of 29, 61–65, 68
Cumming, Thomas 166–168

Dartmouth, William Legge, Earl of 182–185, 197–199, 201–202, 204, 208–211
Delawares 14, 17, 30–31, 33–34, 38, 40, 47, 49, 68, 75–77, 95–96, 99, 101, 130–134, 141–145, 170, 189–191, 193
Denny, William 95, 99
Detroit 122, 135–138, 140–145, 153, 168, 171, 191, 194
Dobbs, Arthur 24, 27, 58
Dowd, Gregory 169
Dunmore, John Murray, Earl of 183, 191–197, 205–207

Easton 96, 98, 99, 101, 124, 130, 167
Egremont, Charles Wyndham,

Earl of 90, 121–129, 147, 153, 157, 158, 163, 198, 211
Ellis, Henry 113, 122–123, 126, 129
Etchoe, battles of 109–110, 117–118, 142

Fairfax, Lord 27
Farmer, Major 161
Florida 13, 17–18, 122–124, 126–127, 129, 147–148, 158, 160–165
Forbes, John 88, 89, 91–101, 102, 141
Fort Bedford 140, 142
Fort Bull 72, 78, 80
Fort Carillon *see* Ticonderoga
Fort Chartres 168, 171
Fort Cumberland 65, 68, 69, 71, 77
Fort Edward Augustus 141
Fort Ligonier 98, 140, 142
Fort Loudoun (Pennsylvania) 104, 169–170
Fort Loudoun (Chota) 103–104, 106–107, 109, 111, 114, 157, 169, 170
Fort Miami 139
Fort Ontario 79, 145
Fort Oswego 43, 72, 78–80, 135, 145,
Fort Prince George 57, 104–105, 106–108, 110–112, 114–116, 118–119, 122
Fort St Frédéric *see* Crown Point
Fort Ontario 79, 145
Fort Frontenac 78, 88–89
Fort Ligonier 98, 140

Fort Stanwix 175, 177, 181, 183, 186–188, 164
Fort Toulouse 115, 126, 159, 161–162
Fox, Charles James 202
Fox, Henry 62, 84–85
Franklin, Benjamin 47, 50, 67, 151–153, 172, 181, 184, 199, 209
Franklin, William 172, 175, 181
Frontier, concept of 10–12
Frontier, settler mentalities 12–13, 101, 169–170, 173, 180

Gage, Thomas 70, 91, 109, 112, 117, 119, 142–144, 147, 149–150, 154, 160–161, 164, 168, 170–171, 185, 200–201, 212
Galphin, George 159
George II 9, 22, 58, 61, 71, 86–87, 89, 120, 122, 124–125, 127, 130
George III 90, 120–121, 124–125, 127, 150, 162, 166, 197–198, 203, 209
Georgia 11, 13, 18, 53–54, 113, 119, 122, 124, 126, 156, 158–160, 163–165
German Flats 78, 174, 191
Gist, Christopher 33–34, 36, 39–41
Glen, James 56–58, 66, 84, 93–94
Gladwin, Major 138–141
Gooch, Sir William 27–28
Grand Ohio Company 182
Great Island aka Long Island 113, 119, 124, 186–187
Greenbrier Company 176

Index

Grant, James 96–98, 107–109, 113–122, 142–143, 153, 163, 212
Gun Merchant, the 156, 159

Halifax, George Montagu Dunk, Earl of 18, 20–29, 42, 47, 49, 57–58, 62–63, 71, 83–85, 87–88, 90, 128–129, 153, 157, 163, 168, 180, 198
Halifax, Nova Scotia
Hanbury, John 24, 27–28
Handel, George Freidrich 10, 19, 20
Hanover 63, 83, 86–88, 199
Hard Labour, Treaty of 164, 176, 179, 186, 188, 19
Havana 123–124, 126, 162
Hendrick (Theyanoguin) 45–50, 73–74
Henry, Patrick 204
Hillsborough, Wills Hill, Earl of 127, 129, 152–154, 179, 180–185, 186, 199, 202, 208–209, 211
Holston River 113, 119, 112, 186–187
Hudson River 43, 44, 49, 73, 91
Hurons 14, 78

Illinois 13, 135, 136–137, 140, 145, 152–153, 160–168, 170–172, 190
Illinois Company 150, 172
Indiana Company 178
Ironcutter, John 173

Johnson, William 45–49, 65–66, 72–74, 83–84, 92, 94–96, 99, 122, 130, 132, 136, 143–145, 147, 149–150, 152, 157, 164–165, 168, 170, 172, 174–179, 181, 183, 184, 189, 191, 193, 211
Johnson Hall 45, 143, 175
Johnstone, William 158, 160–161

Kanawha River 30, 153, 164, 176, 181–182, 194
Kasaké, Charlot 145
Kelérec, Louis 137
Kennebec River 29
Kentucky land claims 33, 191, 193, 196, 205
Kentucky River 30, 188, 205
Keowee 57, 104–106, 108, 114–115
Kiashut 135–136
Kittanning 30, 77
Kuskusky 95, 101

Lake Champlain 16, 26, 43, 62, 72–74, 88
Lake George 73–74, 80, 83
Lake Erie 31, 32, 35, 135, 143
Lake Huron 123, 144
Lake Michigan 31, 122–123, 141
Lake Ontario 43, 72, 222
Lancaster 101, 130, 131, 133
Lancaster, Treaty of 31, 33
Lantagnac, Louis de 137
Lee family 166–204
Lee, Richard Henry 204
Lee, Thomas 32, 67
Lee, William 182
Lewis Andrew 59, 60, 98, 176, 194–196
Lochaber, treaty of 181, 186, 187

Logan, John (Tah-gah-jute) 192, 194, 196–197
Logstown 30, 32–33, 35, 36
Long Island, see Great Island
Louisiana 13, 17, 18, 25, 31, 34, 57, 72, 122, 126, 135, 137, 172
Loyal Company 33, 168, 183
Loyalhannon 96, 97–98, 100 (see also Fort Ligonier)
Lydius, John Henry 49–50
Lyman, Phineas 151–152

Mahicans 16
McGillivray, Lachlan 159
Malatchi 156
Maryland 13, 27, 31, 33, 47, 68, 75, 76, 77, 92, 141, 166
Massachusetts 13, 25, 29, 47, 72, 84, 198–199, 201, 207, 209
Miami Indians 30, 34
Miami River 30–32
Michilimackinac 140, 144, 154
Middle ground 15, 46, 136, 165
Mill Creek 131
Mississippi Company 151, 163, 166, 168, 182
Mississippi River 11, 13–14, 25, 53, 57, 64, 126, 151–153, 166, 168, 172
Mitchell, John 24–25, 63
Mingos 31, 33–34, 36, 38–40, 66, 68–69, 75, 101, 132, 135, 141–142, 189, 192, 197
Mobile 156, 160, 161, 162
Mobile River 29
Mohawk people 15–16, 44–49, 72–74, 78, 80, 116, 174, 178
Mohawk River 174–176, 43–45

Monongahela River 30, 39, 68–70, 73
Montcalm, Louis Joseph de 75, 79–82
Mortar, the 103, 156, 161–162
Muskingum River 30

Neolin 138
New England 13, 16, 25, 44, 48, 71–72, 75, 86, 124, 149 (see also individual colonies and Susquehanna Company)
New France, see Canada
New Hampshire 13, 47, 199
New Jersey 13, 143, 172
New Orleans 13, 26, 161
New York 13, 16–17, 26, 43–50, 62, 69, 72, 75, 80, 86, 91, 107, 111, 113, 124, 141–143, 168, 171, 175–177, 183, 192, 204
Niagara 63, 68, 72, 88, 122, 135, 140, 143–145, 190, 194
Ninety Six 56–57, 106, 113, 186
North Carolina 18, 24, 28, 53, 58, 103, 106, 158, 186
North, Lord Frederick 198–199
Nova Scotia (Acadia) 16, 18, 25–26, 29, 62, 71

Ohio Company of Virginia 24, 32–37, 68, 94, 129, 167, 182
Ohio country 14, 17, 26–27, 29, 30–37, 41–42, 51, 57, 62–63, 67, 99, 129, 137–138, 143–145, 151–153, 168, 171, 174, 177178, 182, 186, 191–192, 194–195, 197, 200, 202–205, 222

Index

Ohio nations 31, 34–37, 40–41, 44, 63, 65, 69, 75–76, 88, 94–95, 99, 101, 130, 134–135, 137, 141, 143–145, 168, 171, 175–178, 183, 185, 189, 193, 194–195 (see also Delawares, Mingos and Shawnees)
Ojibwes 138, 140
Ostenaco (aka Ostenaca, Judd's Friend) 59, 76, 113–115, 119–120, 124, 128, 159, 205
Ottawas 34, 135, 140,–141, 194
Ouiatenon 139, 171

Parkman, Francis 137–138
Paxton Boys 133, 190
Penn family 13, 130, 132–133, 178, 182
Pennsylvania 13, 17, 27, 29–34, 40, 41, 47–50, 56, 59, 66–68, 72, 75–77, 92–94, 96, 98–99, 107, 130, 134, 140–141, 143, 169, 173, 176–179, 191–193, 204, 222
Pensacola 156, Congress of 161–162
Philadelphia 72, 75, 78, 92, 95, 101, 132–133, 168–169, 171, 184, 201, 203
Picolata, Congress of 163–164
Pisquetomen 30, 95–95, 99, 101
Plan of 1764 147–154, 164
Point Pleasant, battle of 194–196
Pontiac (Obwaandi'eyaag) 137–141, 143–146, 171
Pontiac's War 135–156, 160, 167, 168, 169, 193
Potawatomi 135

Pownall, John 23, 84
Pownall, Thomas 84
Presque Isle 35, 135, 140, 142
Proclamation of 1763 129, 145–146, 150, 153, 167, 181, 204, 210–211, 213–220, 221–225
Prussia 9, 63, 83, 88, 90

Quebec, see Canada
Quebec Act 197, 201, 204, 206, 208–210, 213–221

Rhode Island 13, 47, 201
Robinson, Sir Thomas 25, 57
Royal fireworks 9–10, 19–20, 212

Saluda, Treaty of 58
Sandusky 136, 139, 144
St Augustine 163
St Clair, Sir John 67, 92–93
Sandusky 136, 139, 144
Sargent, John 181
Savannah River 54, 106, 156, 159
Scarouady, 31, 65, 66, 75
Scioto River 30, 172, 194–197
Scots-Irish settlers 24, 22, 44, 101, 133
Seroweh 109–111, 113–114, 116–117, 119, 159
Settico 54–55, 103
Sharpe, Horatio 66
Shelburne, William Petty, Earl of 109–111, 113–114, 116–117, 119, 159
Shingas 30, 34, 65–66, 75, 77, 95, 99, 101, 141–142
Shirley, William 21–22, 71–73, 77–79, 83–85, 88

Shorey, William 125, 126
Sidelong Hill 170
Small Tribes 160
South Carolina 10, 24, 53–55, 59, 66, 76, 84, 92–93, 103–105, 107, 113–116, 119, 122, 124, 128, 142, 157–158, 162–163, 186
Spring Gardens, Vauxhall, 10, 19, 128
Stamp Act 150, 180, 199
Stump, Frederick 173
Suffering Traders 152, 172, 174, 178–179, 181
Sugar (Plantation Duties) Act 149, 151
Sugar Town 108
Susquehanna Company 151, 132, 134, 142
Susqhehanna River 17, 32, 47, 49–50, 76, 95, 99, 131–134, 142, 145, 173–174, 177
Sycamore Shoals 206

Tahaiadoris 135
Tamaqua 30, 95, 101, 141
Tellico 54–55
Ticonderoga 74, 80, 88–89
Tistoe 108, 114
Timberlake, Henry 124–125, 128
Tennessee (Cherokee) River 53, 176
Togulki 156
Townshend, Charles 151–153
Transylvania Company 205–206
Turner, Frederick J. 10–11
Tyers, Jonathan 10, 19

Vandalia 176, 185, 192, 199, 202, 204, 206
Vauxhall, see Spring Gardens
Venango 35, 135, 140
Virginia 13, 24, 27–28, 31–34, 36–42, 50, 54, 57–60, 67–69, 75–77, 85, 92–94, 98, 100, 102–103, 107, 111, 113, 115–116, 119–120, 124, 128–129, 141–142, 151, 158, 166–167, 170, 176–178, 182–183, 185, 186–187, 191–197, 204–205

Wabash Confederacy 170–171, 190–191
Wabash River 166
Walker, Thomas 176
Walpole Associates (Company) 181–184
Walpole, Richard 181
Walpole, Thomas 181
Ward, Matthew 12
Weiser, Conrad 49
Western Confederacy 171
Wharton, Samuel 168, 172, 178, 181–185, 204–207 (*see also* Baynton, Morgan & Wharton, merchants)
White, Richard 12, 15
Wolf, the, of Keowee 108, 186–187
Wolf, the, of Mocolossus 161
Wolfe, James 88–89
Wood Creek 78, 80, 177
Wright, James 158, 159
Wyandots 33, 75, 140, 142
Wyoming 49–50, 95–99, 130–134